PIPE FITTINGS

NIPPLES   PIPE LENGTHS UP TO 22 FT.   STRAIGHT COUPLING   REDUCING COUPLING   COUPLING   NUT   CAP

STRAIGHT TEE   REDUCING TEE   STREET TEE   STRAIGHT CROSS   REDUCING CROSS

90° ELBOW   45° ELBOW   REDUCING ELBOW   90° STREET ELBOW   45° STREET ELBOW   45° Y-BEND

UNION (3 PARTS)   PLUG   BUSHING   CAP   RETURN BEND

90°   45°   STREET   UNION TEES
UNION ELBOWS

90° ELBOW   90° ELBOW

REDUCING TEE   REDUCER

PLUG   45° ELBOW   TEE

Here are the common steel pipe fittings. Nipples are simply short lengths of pipe threaded on both ends. Reducing fittings join two different sizes of pipe.

Compression fittings of the flared-tube type are the easiest for the novice to handle when working with copper tubing.

STANDARD STEEL PIPE
(All Dimensions in Inches)

Nominal Size	Outside Diameter	Inside Diameter	Nominal Size	Outside Diameter	Inside Diameter
1/8	0.405	0.269	1	1.315	1.049
1/4	0.540	0.364	1 1/4	1.660	1.380
3/8	0.675	0.493	1 1/2	1.900	1.610
1/2	0.840	0.622	2	2.375	2.067
3/4	1.050	0.824	2 1/2	2.875	2.469

SQUARE MEASURE
144 sq in = 1 sq ft
9 sq ft = 1 sq yd
272.25 sq ft = 1 sq rod
160 sq rods = 1 acre

VOLUME MEASURE
1728 cu in = 1 cu ft
27 cu ft = 1 cu yd

MEASURES OF CAPACITY
1 cup = 8 fl oz
2 cups = 1 pint
2 pints = 1 quart
4 quarts = 1 gallon
2 gallons = 1 peck
4 pecks = 1 bushel

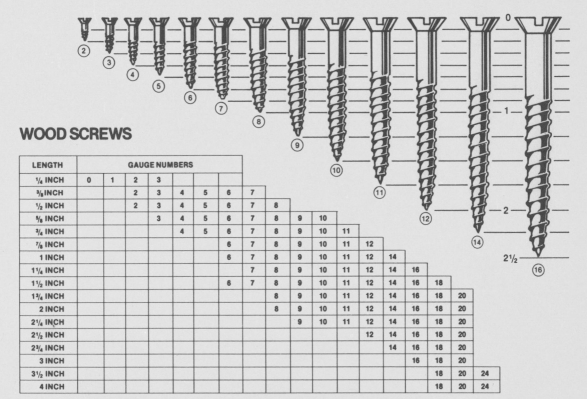

WOOD SCREWS

LENGTH	GAUGE NUMBERS														
1/4 INCH	0	1	2	3											
3/8 INCH			2	3	4	5	6	7							
1/2 INCH			2	3	4	5	6	7	8						
5/8 INCH				3	4	5	6	7	8	9	10				
3/4 INCH					4	5	6	7	8	9	10	11			
7/8 INCH							6	7	8	9	10	11	12		
1 INCH							6	7	8	9	10	11	12	14	
1 1/4 INCH								7	8	9	10	11	12	14	16
1 1/2 INCH							6	7	8	9	10	11	12	14	16	18
1 3/4 INCH									8	9	10	11	12	14	16	18	20
2 INCH									8	9	10	11	12	14	16	18	20
2 1/4 INCH										9	10	11	12	14	16	18	20
2 1/2 INCH													12	14	16	18	20
2 3/4 INCH														14	16	18	20
3 INCH															16	18	20
3 1/2 INCH																18	20	24
4 INCH																18	20	24

WHEN YOU BUY SCREWS, SPECIFY (1) LENGTH, (2) GAUGE NUMBER, (3) TYPE OF HEAD—FLAT, ROUND, OR OVAL, (4) MATERIAL—STEEL, BRASS, BRONZE, ETC., (5) FINISH—BRIGHT, STEEL BLUED, CADMIUM, NICKEL, OR CHROMIUM PLATED.

Popular Mechanics

do-it-yourself encyclopedia

The complete, illustrated home reference guide from the world's most authoritative source for today's how-to-do-it information.

YEARBOOK

1989

HEARST DIRECT BOOKS

NEW YORK

This book is published with the consent and cooperation of POPULAR MECHANICS Magazine.

POPULAR MECHANICS Staff:
Editor-in-Chief: Joe Oldham
Managing Editor: Bill Hartford
Graphics Director: Bryan Canniff
Automotive Editor: Tony Swan
Home and Shop Editor: Steven Willson
Electronics/Photography Editor: Stephen A. Booth
Boating/Outdoors Editor: Joe Skorupa
Science Editor: Timothy H. Cole
Editorial Production: John Bostonian Jr.

**POPULAR MECHANICS ENCYCLOPEDIA
1989 YEARBOOK**

Editor:
  C. Edward Cavert
Manufacturing:
  Ron Schoenfeld
Book Design and Production:
  The Bookmaker
  Fairfax, Virginia
Editorial Assistance:
  Wilma Cavert
  Nancy Coggins
  Barbara S. Hatheway

ISBN 0-87851-099-0
Library of Congress Catalog Card Number: 85-81760

10 9 8 7 6 5 4 3 2 1
Printed in the United States of America

Although every effort has been made to ensure the accuracy and completeness of the information in this book, Hearst Direct Books and Popular Mechanics Magazine make no guarantees, stated or implied, nor will they be liable in the event of misinterpretation or human error made by the reader or for any typographical errors that may appear. Plans for projects illustrated in this book may not meet all local zoning and building code requirements for construction. Before beginning any major project, consult with local authorities or see a structural architect. WORK SAFELY WITH HAND AND POWER TOOLS. WEAR EYE PROTECTION. READ MANUFACTURER'S INSTRUCTIONS AND WARNINGS FOR ALL PRODUCTS.

Credits and Acknowledgments

The following people have significant contributions to the *1989 Popular Mechanics Encyclopedia Yearbook.*

Craft Projects: *Craft Projects: Custom Designs* (page 4) by Thomas Klenck; photos: Brian Kosoff. *Fine Dining* (page 8) by Rosario Capotosto; photos: Rosario Capotosto, color photos: J.R. Rost; technical art: Eugene Thompson. *Secret Secretary* (page 13) by Ralph S. Wilkes; photos: Ralph S. Wilkes, color photo: J.R. Rost; technical art: Dyck Fledderus. *Baking Cart* (page 18) by Neal Barrett; photos: Neal Barrett, color photo: J.R. Rost; technical art: Eugene Thompson. *Stepstool and Chair* (page 23) by Clark Caswell; photos: Peggy Caswell, color photo: J.R. Rost; technical art: Eugene Thompson. *Book Stand* (page 27) by Rosario Capotosto; photos: Rosario Capotosto. *Heirloom Toboggan* (page 29) by August Capotosto; photos: August Capotosto, color photo: Alex Layman; technical art: Eugene Thompson.
Electrical Improvements: *Fluorescent Fixture Repair* (page 37) by Merle Henkenius; illustrations: George Retseck. *Aluminum House Wiring Hazards* (page 44) by Merle Henkenius; illustrations: George Retseck. *Bathroom Ventilator Installation* (page 46) by Paul Barrett; illustrations: George Retseck. *Testing Appliances with an Ohmmeter* (page 50) by Mort Schultz; illustrations: George Retseck. *Telephone Repairs* (page 52) by Mort Schultz; illustrations: George Retseck. *Doorbell Repairs* (page 56) by Merle Henkenius; illustrations: George Retseck. *Air Conditioner Basics* (page 59) by Lee Green; illustrations: George Retseck; map derived from Association of Home Appliance Manufacturers booklet, *Consumer Selection Guide for Room Air Conditioners.*
Plumbing Improvements: *Water Heater Replacement* (page 62) by Merle Henkenius; illustrations: George Retseck. *Bathtub Drain Repairs* (page 67) by Merle Henkenius; illustrations: George Retseck. *Guide to Toilet Repairs* (page 68) by Merle Henkenius; illustrations: George Retseck. *Common Bathroom Repairs* (page 75) by Merle Henkenius; photos: Merle Henkenius.
Home Repairs: *Overhead Garage Door Repair* (page 78) by Rosario Capotosto; illustrations: George Retseck. *Fix a Problem Door* (page 80) by Paul Barrett; illustrations: George Retseck. *Reglazing Windows* (Page 84) by Rosario Capotosto; illustrations: George Retseck.
Photography: *Fun With Film* (page 85) by George Schaub; color photos by George Schaub. *Inner Visions* (page 86) by Armand Ensanian; photos: Armand Ensanian. *Night Shots* (page 87) by George Schaub; photo: Carl J. Santoro. *One On One* (page 88) by Armand Ensanian; photo: Armand Ensanian. *Shoot The Moon* (page 89) by Armand Ensanian; Photo: Armand Ensanian. *Focus On Speed* (page 90) by John Lamm; photos: John Lamm. *Fading Memories* (page 91) by Stephen A. Booth; photos: Ferdinanda Lisa, restoration by Reiter/Dulberg Labs. *Developing Strategies* (page 92) by George Schaub; photos: George Schaub.
Home Additions: *Folding Stairway Installation* (page 93) by Paul Barrett; illustrations: George Retseck. *Floor Tile Installation* (page 98) by Paul Barrett; illustrations: George Retseck. *Slate Floor Tile Installation* (page 103) by Paul Barrett; illustrations: George Retseck. *Bow Window Installation* (page 107) by Joseph Truini; color photo: Carl Weese, photos: Joseph Truini. *Entry Door Installation* (page 110) by Joseph Truini; color photo: Carl Weese, photos: Joseph Truini.
Lawn and Garden: *Lawn Spreader Selection* (page 113) by Patricia and Richard L. Parish; illustrations: George Retseck. *Starter Pull-Rope Replacement* (page 115) by Mort Schultz; illustrations: George Retseck. *Small Engine Overhaul* (page 118) by Mort Schultz; illustrations: George Retseck.
Home Electronics: *Home Video Systems* (page 123) and *Digital Audio Tape* (page 127) by James B. Meigs and Frank Visard, photos: Brian Kosoff.
Shop Tools: *Band Saw Guide* (page 131) by Rosario Capotosto; photos: Rosario Capotosto. *Saber Saw Guide* (page 136) by Rosario Capotosto; photos: Rosario Capotosto.
Shop Projects: *Benchmark Worbench* (page 145) by Rosario Capotosto; color photo: J.R. Rost, black-and-white photos: Rosario Capotosto; technical art: Eugene Thompson. *Small Parts Cabinet* (page 150) by Rosario Capotosto; color photo: J.R. Rost, black-and-white photos: Rosario Capotosto; technical art: Eugene Thompson. *Power Tool Table* (page 153) by Rosario Capotosto; color photos: J.R. Rost, black-and-white photos: Rosario Capotosto; technical art: Eugene Thompson.
Shop Tips: *Using Dowel Pins, Making a Miterbox, Sharpening Cutlery, Preventative Protection, Respirators, Apply a Wax Finish* by Rosario Capotosto.

Contents

Craft Projects
Craft Projects: Custom Designs 4
Fine Dining 8
Secret Secretary 13
Baking Cart 18
Stepstool and Chair 23
Book Stand 27
Toboggan Heirloom 29

Electrical Improvements
Fluorescent Fixture Repair 37
Incandescent Lamp Repair 41
Aluminum House Wiring Hazards ...44
Bathroom Ventilator Installation 46
Testing Appliances With Ohmmeter .50
Telephone Repair 52
Doorbell Repairs 56
Air Conditioner Basics 59

Plumbing Improvements
Water Heater Replacement 62
Bathroom Drain Repairs 67
Guide to Toilet Repair 68
Common Bathroom Repairs 75

Home Repairs
Overhead Garage Door Repair 78
Fix a Problem Door 80
Deadbolt Lock Installation 82
Reglazing Windows 84

Photography
Fun with Film 85
Inner Visions 86
Night Shots 87
One on One 88
Shoot the Moon 89

Focus on Speed 90
Fading Memories 91
Developing Strategies 92

Home Additions
Folding Stairway Installation 93
Floor Tile Installation 98
Installing Slate Tile Floors 103
Bow Window Installation 107
Entry Door Installation 110

Lawn and Garden
Lawn Spreader Selection 113
Starter Pull-Rope Replacement 115
Small Engine Overhaul 118

Home Electronics
Home Video 123
Digital Audio Tape 127

Shop Tools
Band Saw Users Guide 131
Saber Saw Users Guide 136

Shop Projects
Benchmark Workbench 145
Small-Parts Cabinet 150
Portable Tool Table 153

Shop Tips
Using Dowel Pins 165
Making a Miterbox 167
Sharpening Cutlery 169
Preventative Protection 170
Respirators 172
Applying a Wax Finish 174

Index 175

Craft projects: custom designs

Projects in this Popular Mechanics Encyclopedia can be customized to your needs. By creating or modifying the design for a project you gain nearly total control over what it will look like. Not only do you experience the personal accomplishment that goes along with constructing a well-made piece, but you've also added something of yourself that will be there for years to come. There's little that compares with the satisfaction of watching your idea develop from a few sketches on paper to a tangible piece of fine workmanship for all to see.

The Importance of Drawing

Designing, like building, is a skill that can be learned. As with cutting and fitting wood, it takes practice with the tools of the trade. Design's most powerful tool is drawing. Drawing enables you to try out ideas without going to the time and expense of building them. By drawing, you can see what something will look like and how it will go together. You can also save ideas for future reference.

Many different types of drawings suit particular stages in the design process. Drafting, or mechanical drawing, provides accurate scale views of an object and is commonly used for shop drawings.

Two types of drafting are *orthographic* and *isometric* projection. In orthographic drawing, the 3-dimensional object is shown in a series of views, typically, the top, front and side. House plans refer to the front and side views as *elevations* and the top view is called the *plan*. Isometric drawing is more pictorial; it incorporates the three views in one image.

Freehand perspective sketching is a good way to play with ideas in a quick, fluid format. Here, accuracy is sacrificed to speed. You want to be able to record ideas as fast as you think of them. Freehand drawings are also a good way to show ideas to others. You can easily get an idea of how a corner cupboard would look, for example, if you photograph the room it is to be in, and trace the photograph with the cupboard drawn in place. Most texts on technical drawing can supply you with detailed information on both drafting and the elements of perspective drawing.

Begin at the Beginning

The first step in designing is to define the problem as completely as possible by listing what you want to achieve. Suppose your collection of tools is slowly overwhelming your existing storage space. This is a functional need and prompts a utilitarian solution. On the other hand, the new corner cupboard you're designing might be required to fit in with an existing set of furnishings, or be an example of some particular style you like. This nonutilitarian concern is of equal importance.

Begin by listing the functions of the piece. What must it do? What shouldn't it do? For example, a coffee table should provide a raised surface for supporting magazines and drinks, but it shouldn't be so large as to make part of the room inaccessible.

Next, list the aesthetic concerns. Note the particular way you want the piece to look. If this seems difficult, try instead to note the ways you *don't* want it to look. Either way you are defining an area that you feel comfortable with. For example, you may want dining room furniture to appear as a set and want the overall design to pay homage to tradition but not appear rustic. You may also want it to have some connection to contemporary style while still appearing elegant. These are aesthetic concerns.

The next step is to list all the constraints that will be placed on the design and building of the object. Do you have a limited budget with which to work? How much time can you allocate for

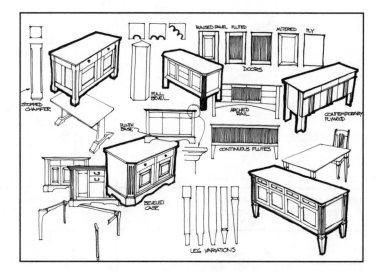

After defining the problem, begin investigating alternative solutions with freehand sketches. Allow each idea to stimulate the next. In these drawings of sideboard designs, various traditional elements are combined to experiment with new ideas. Designs of a more contemporary nature are noted as well. The final design evolved as a product of these sketches and the initial constraints.

the designing and building, and does it have to be completed by a certain date? Do you have the space, tools and skill necessary to complete the job? Can it be finished on site, if necessary, and can you get it through the door or out of the basement?

Investigating Possibilities

Once the problem has been defined and the constraints noted, you can turn your attention to the creative aspect of design. In this phase, your job is to generate a range of visual ideas from which you select your final design. The more ideas the better. Try, at this point, to forget about the constraints and requirements you have listed and be guided by the broadest possible definition of the problem. You will use these notes later to help you refine your ideas.

Start with a broad functional requirement of the object. A dining table must be a surface that supports food and drink, for example. Now, how many ways can you arrange that? Must the surface be flat? Can it be multileveled? Must it be solid or can it be a framework that contains dishes and glasses? Perhaps it can be expanded, or maybe assembled from smaller units. If it's a typical flat surface, how is it supported? Perhaps it hangs from the ceiling to be lowered when needed. Even if you think your ideas go beyond your specific goals, they may lead you to a solution that's appropriate. Furthermore, you may find that certain ideas, while not suitable for the immediate project, relate directly to some other problem that needs to be solved.

Now consider the aesthetic priorities in the same way. If you have a firm idea about the styling of the piece, become familiar with exist-

ing objects that are similar. Try to isolate the components that give the style its identity. Is it proportioning? A sense of lightness or delicacy? Perhaps it's the geometric nature of the style. Some styles are identified by an attention to detailed ornament while others are clean and simple. After reviewing the components of a style, start drawing alternative ways these elements can be put together. As with functional ideas, don't dismiss them too quickly. When trying to be creative, the worst thing is to be negative.

If you don't have a firm style in mind you can still proceed with this step, but the scope of possibilities will be much wider. Be prepared for ideas that are unfamiliar. Instead of researching existing styles, look to unrelated areas for inspiration. Investigate shapes found in nature and study other architectural and furniture forms. Try to interpret these shapes in your design. Solutions arrived at this way often take some getting used to. Don't be afraid to try anything new. Tradition connects us with our roots as well as providing a platform for exploration.

Harmony and Discord

Keep in mind that a finished design will be composed of elements that relate to each other visually. The shapes of the individual parts should be considered collectively. If, for example, you rout a ¼-in. round on the corners of all the pieces of a table, they will be visually connected in the finished piece. The object should convey a theme that is the product of the overall shape and the detailing of the parts. These relationships give the piece a sense of harmony.

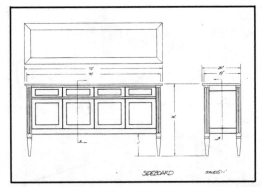

Drafting allows you to develop and refine actual construction details and proportioning.

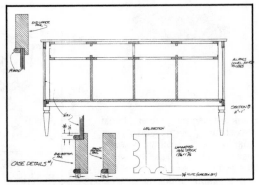

Constraints such as sizes and types of available material, contribute to the final design.

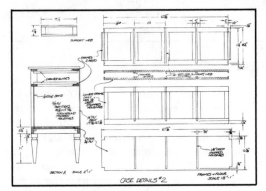

Cross sections help work on the inside and provide a clear description for you when you build.

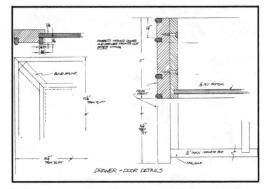

Detail views, such as those shown above, describe door and drawer construction and aid in building.

The predominant visual theme of a dining room set, for example, can be a simple rectangle. You can add stopped flutes to the legs for a unifying motif and half-round ¼-in. beading to define and highlight the frame edges. These ornamental details are complimentary because they are both linear elements with semicircular cross-sections. They are different because the flutes are recesses and appear framed in the legs while the beading can frame the drawers and doors and stand out proudly from the surface. The similarity between these design elements hold each piece together while the difference creates visual interest.

Selecting and Refining

Evaluate and synthesize ideas that solve your problem both functionally and aesthetically. Look over your drawings and begin combining ideas from each set to produce complete ideas. Weed out solutions that don't seem appropriate. Ideally you want to end up with one or two designs that satisfy your general requirements.

Return to your problem definition and list of constraints. You must evaluate your solutions using the initial set of priorities. Are there places where it falls short? Can it be made within your limitations?

Now is the time to decide on alterations necessary to make your idea suitable. You may have to use plywood instead of solid wood. Perhaps it must be collapsible or be transported. Occasionally you will find a very attractive idea that causes you to change your priorities. Further refinement of your design should occur on the drawing board where exact measurements, proportions and detailing of joints and ornaments takes place.

When drafting your design, choose a scale that allows the object to be drawn large enough to show all relevant details. If this isn't possible, draw large-scale detail views. Consult a reference guide for specifications on seat and table height or other necessary data. A good way to determine these specifications is to measure pieces that you use regularly and are familiar with. Determine any other dimensional constraints such as room size, ceiling height, dimensions of items to be stored, and available lumber sizes.

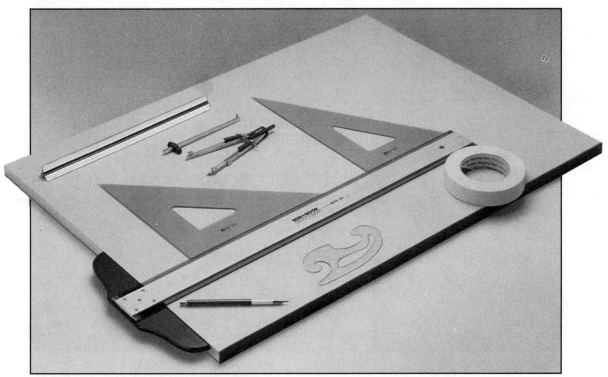

Drafting Equipment. Drawing boards are available in a range of sizes. A 23-in.×31-in. board should be large enough for most projects. To protect the board and provide a smooth surface for drawing, attach a vinyl board cover with double-faced tape. A T-square permits drawing parallel horizontal lines and an array of standard angles. Use an architect's scale to reduce your drawing to a manageable size. A bow compass with beam extension will handle arc and circle drawing chores. For curves that aren't circular, a French curve is useful. Mechanical pencils accept drawing leads or you can use individual pencils of the appropriate grades. Use a 4H pencil for construction and have a softer 2H or H pencil for object lines and lettering. Masking tape is best for holding the drawing paper because it reduces tearing when the drawing is removed. Most art supply stores stock all these items.

Drafting Your Design

Begin the drafting by drawing the elements that must conform to these standards and designing the variable dimensions to suit your sense of proportion. Don't expect to be satisfied the first time. Use tracing paper to draw overlays which allow you to adjust the finer points of design. When the form uses complex curves, or other elements where patterns would be useful, draw the object full size.

It's sometimes useful to make a model of the design. Scale models, or mockups, are made at the scale of the drawing or larger and can be constructed out of cardboard, paper or scraps of wood fastened together with hot glue or double-faced tape. These mockups are not intended to be finished products, but only to serve to make errors apparent before construction.

Once you are certain that your drawings are complete, you should create a cutting list. Itemize each piece, including the sizes it must be cut and dressed to. This greatly speeds up construction and helps eliminate cutting errors which mean wasted wood.

There is no one way to go about solving every design problem. Some problems require a great deal of creative exploration while others begin as refinements in a drafting. As both the designer and the builder, you have the unique opportunity to make changes to your design during the actual construction. Sketches, draftings and mockups all serve to prepare you for the construction *and* appearance of the finished piece. There is, however, no substitute for seeing and handling your ideas as they materialize.

Classic detailing is the main course in this exquisite mahogany dining room table. Delicately spiced with flutes, coves and bead molding, the table stands out as an example of refinement and good taste.

Fine dining

Few activities better illustrate our need to socialize than our dining rituals. Not only are these the times when families get together to discuss the day's events, but they are also the way we choose to accept friends and relatives into our homes. That makes the dining room of central importance to both domestic and social life. And perhaps because of this, it's the one room where most homeowners make a definite effort to assemble coordinated pieces of furniture. Whether it's Early American, French Provincial or contemporary, the overwhelming material of choice is wood.

In the following pages, you're shown not only how to build the pieces of a rich mahogany dining table, but also how to do the whole job with ordinary portable power tools. You don't need any expensive stationary shop equipment. The detailing, that may look complicated at first glance, is all designed to be done with the aid of several specialized jigs you can build yourself.

MATERIALS LIST
DINING TABLE

Key	No.	Size and description (use)
A	4	$2^{7}/_{16} \times 2^{7}/_{16} \times 28^{3}/_{16}$ mahogany (leg)
B	2	$1^{3}/_{16} \times 3 \times 64^{1}/_{2}$" mahogany (long apron)
C	2	$1^{3}/_{16} \times 3 \times 28^{1}/_{2}$" mahogany (short apron)
D	2	$1^{3}/_{16} \times 3 \times 30^{3}/_{8}$" mahogany (cross rail)
E	4	$1^{3}/_{16} \times 3 \times 4$" mahogany (cleat)
F	4	$1^{3}/_{16} \times 3 \times 7^{3}/_{4}$" mahogany (brace)
G	2	$1^{3}/_{16} \times 3 \times 36$" mahogany (end frame)
H	2	$1^{3}/_{16} \times 3 \times 72$" mahogany (side frame)
I	1	$^{3}/_{4} \times 30 \times 66$" mahogany (top panel)
J1	2	$^{1}/_{4} \times ^{7}/_{16} \times 64^{1}/_{2}$" mahogany (beading)
J2	2	$^{1}/_{4} \times ^{7}/_{16} \times 28^{1}/_{2}$" mahogany (beading)
K**		$^{1}/_{8} \times ^{7}/_{8}$" plywood (spline)
L	8	$1^{3}/_{16} \times 1^{3}/_{4} \times 3$" mahogany (glue block)
M	2	$^{1}/_{16} \times 1^{3}/_{16} \times 30$" mahogany (shim)
N	4	$^{5}/_{16} \times 3^{1}/_{2}$" lagscrew and washer
O	18	3" No. 10 fh screw
P	16	$1^{1}/_{4}$" No. 10 fh screw
Q	4	4d common nail
R	16	$^{3}/_{8}$"-dia. $\times 1^{1}/_{2}$" dowel

Misc.: Glue, 120- and 220-grit sandpaper, $^{1}/_{2}$" wire brads, red mahogany stain, and satin polyurethane varnish.
**18 linear ft. required.

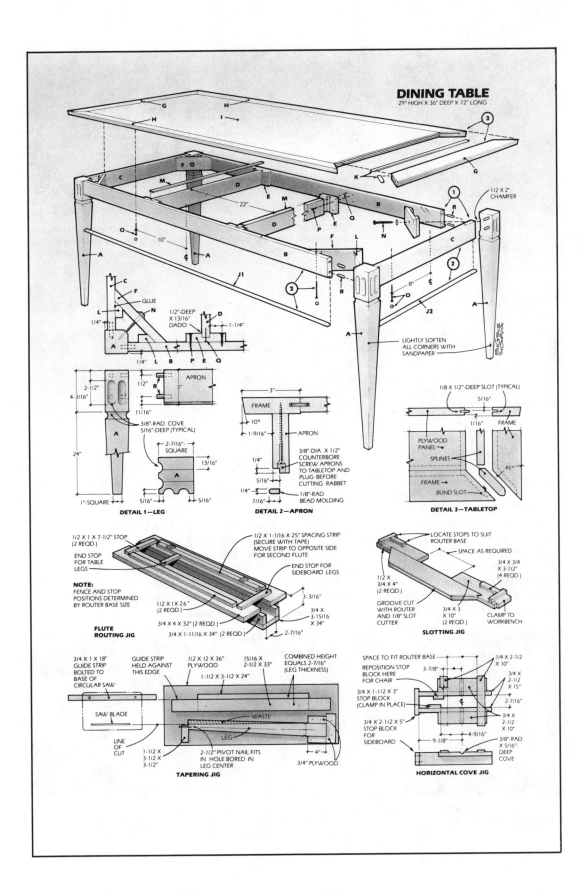

DINING TABLE
29" HIGH X 36" DEEP X 72" LONG

1/2 X 2" CHAMFER

22"

10"

8"

1/2"-DEEP X 13/16" DADO

1-1/4"

1/4"

GLUE

LIGHTLY SOFTEN ALL CORNERS WITH SANDPAPER

DETAIL 1—LEG
2-1/2"
4-3/16"
1/2"
11/16"
APRON
3"
3/8"-RAD. COVE 5/16"-DEEP (TYPICAL)
2-7/16"-SQUARE
13/16"
24"
1"-SQUARE
5/16"   5/16"

DETAIL 2—APRON
3"
FRAME
10°
1-9/16"
APRON
1/4"
3/8"-DIA. X 1/2" COUNTERBORE SCREW APRONS TO TABLETOP AND PLUG BEFORE CUTTING RABBET
5/16"
1/4"
7/16"
1/8"-RAD. BEAD MOLDING

DETAIL 3—TABLETOP
1/8 X 1/2"-DEEP SLOT (TYPICAL)
5/16"
1/16"
FRAME
PLYWOOD PANEL
SPLINES
45°
FRAME
BLIND SLOT

FLUTE ROUTING JIG
1/2 X 1 X 7-1/2" STOP (2 REQD.)
END STOP FOR TABLE LEGS
1/2 X 1-1/16 X 25" SPACING STRIP (SECURE WITH TAPE) MOVE STRIP TO OPPOSITE SIDE FOR SECOND FLUTE
END STOP FOR SIDEBOARD LEGS
NOTE: FENCE AND STOP POSITIONS DETERMINED BY ROUTER BASE SIZE
1/2 X 1 X 26" (2 REQD.)
3/4 X 4 X 32" (2 REQD.)
3/4 X 1-11/16 X 34" (2 REQD.)
3-3/16"
3/4 X 3-15/16 X 34"
2-7/16"

SLOTTING JIG
LOCATE STOPS TO SUIT ROUTER BASE
SPACE AS REQUIRED
3/4 X 3/4 X 3-1/2" (4 REQD.)
1/2 X 3/4 X 4" (2 REQD.)
GROOVE CUT WITH ROUTER AND 1/8" SLOT CUTTER
3/4 X 3 X 10" (2 REQD.)
CLAMP TO WORKBENCH

TAPERING JIG
3/4 X 1 X 18" GUIDE STRIP BOLTED TO BASE OF CIRCULAR SAW
GUIDE STRIP HELD AGAINST THIS EDGE
1/2 X 12 X 36" PLYWOOD
1-1/2 X 3-1/2 X 24"
15/16 X 2-1/2 X 33"
COMBINED HEIGHT EQUALS 2-7/16" (LEG THICKNESS)
SAW BLADE
WASTE
LINE OF CUT
LEG
1-1/2 X 3-1/2 X 3-1/2"
2-1/2" PIVOT NAIL FITS IN HOLE BORED IN LEG CENTER
4"
3/4" PLYWOOD

HORIZONTAL COVE JIG
SPACE TO FIT ROUTER BASE
REPOSITION STOP BLOCK HERE FOR CHAIR
3-7/8"
1/4 X 2-1/2 X 10"
3/4 X 2-1/2 X 15"
3/4 X 1-1/2 X 3" STOP BLOCK (CLAMP IN PLACE)
2-7/16"
3/4 X 2-1/2 X 5" STOP BLOCK FOR SIDEBOARD
3/4 X 2-1/2 X 10"
9-1/8"
4-9/16"
3/8"-RAD. X 5/16"-DEEP COVE

Select leg stock for color and grain orientation and insert headless brads to keep boards aligned during assembly.

Use a roller to spread the glue fast and evenly. Make sure the brads are placed in waste area of stock. Clamp until dry.

To rip legs, clamp the laminated leg stock to the worktable with a straightedge guide on top and scrap plywood underneath.

Starting the Table

The 2⁷⁄₁₆-in.-sq. stock for the table legs is made by gluing up three layers of commonly available ¹³⁄₁₆-in. lumber. If possible, use boards wide enough to get more than one leg from each lamination. Because you'll be hand planing the surfaces smooth, try to keep the grain orientation of each board the same before gluing. If you find it hard to judge the grain direction by looking at the board, make a trial pass with your plane. When selecting boards for each leg, keep in mind that mahogany can vary in color. Mark grain direction and stacking order on all pieces so you won't mix them up during assembly.

Ordinary white or yellow carpenter's glue is fine for making the leg laminations. Use a roller to apply glue fast and evenly. To keep the boards aligned during assembly, insert a pair of headless nails in the top and bottom boards of each lamination in an area that will become waste. Special double-pointed brads are available for this purpose or you can snip off the ends

of small brads and insert them with pliers. Clamp and let dry.

After the glue has set overnight, clamp the laminated stock to the worktable with a straightedge guide positioned on top for guiding the circular saw. Keep a scrap plywood panel underneath so you won't cut into your bench. Use a sharp blade for this cut—preferably one that's designed for ripping.

A detail that appears throughout the dining table is the horizontal cove on the legs. To cut this you'll need a ⅜-in.-rad. corebox bit mounted in a router. Build a jig to guide the router squarely across the leg faces at the appropriate distance from the end. Then cut the ⁵⁄₁₆-in.-deep cove on each face of every leg.

Construct the leg-tapering jig and secure a rip fence to the base of the circular saw with two bolts as shown in the drawing. The saw base rides on a rail that's the same height as the leg thickness. You can plane a piece of 1-in. stock to ¹⁵⁄₁₆ in. and nail it to a 2×4 (1½×3½-in.) to get

Horizontal coving jig guides the router squarely across each face of the leg. Use a ¾-in.-dia. corebox bit.

Construct a tapering jig to cut uniform tapers on all leg sides. Then, dress all rough-sawn surfaces with a hand plane.

Twin flutes cut with a router and a ⅜-in.-rad. corebox bit are positioned accurately with this guiding jig and spacer.

Slotting bit cuts spline grooves in plywood panel and frame. Use a stopping jig for blind grooves in miter joints.

C-clamps and wedges bring the end frame pieces into position. After glue has set, trim a 10° bevel on tabletop edges.

the correct height. Note the nail in the end stop block of the tapering jig. A corresponding hole centered in the bottom of each leg lets you pivot the leg so it's positioned correctly for cutting each face. When the leg tapers are completed, use a sharp smoothing plane to dress all rough-sawn surfaces.

The vertical fluting that appears on the two outward surfaces of each leg is also cut with the corebox bit. Construct the flute-routing jig and use a space that can be shifted from one side to the other for uniform flute spacing. Set the fences so the flutes are 5/16 in. from the leg corner. A plunge router is ideal for this stopped fluting. If yours is the regular fixed type, build your jig with higher sides and carefully lean the router into the wood at the start of each cut. Complete the legs by cutting a stopped chamfer on the inside corner of each leg with a router and chamfering bit. This simplifies boring the lagscrew hole for the corner block.

Making the Apron

Rip each apron piece to width, dress the sawn edges and cut to exact length. Joints that connect the rails to the legs are doweled. A completely adjustable doweling jig is better than the self-centering type because many of the joints require off-center holes. Use dowel centers to transfer the hole locations to the legs. The tabletop is fastened to the skirt by 3-in. No.10 fh screws. Counterbore 3/8-in.-dia. pilot holes

through the rails for the screws. The rails on all the pieces in the dining set are highlighted with a 1/4-in. bead set into a rabbet. Cut the rabbets with a straight bit mounted in the router and edge guide. Don't be tempted to use a piloted bit in lieu of the edge guide. The pilot will fall into the counterbores and ruin the cut.

You can make the bead molding with your router and two special cutters. A 1/8-in.-rad. half-round cutter produces the profile, and a slotting cutter with a pilot rips the trim to thickness. To make this molding, first install the half-round bit in the router so its cutting arc is flush with the router base. Then, working with the router base first against one face and then the opposite face, cut twin half-rounds on one edge of the 13/16-in.-thick stock. Install the slotting cutter in the router. Adjust so it's tangent to the bottom of the half-rounds already cut and rip slots along the bottom of each bead. Finally, use your circular saw guided by a straightedge to rip the two lengths of beading away from the stock. Use a wide board for making this trim. After each pair of beads is cut off, plane the rough sawn edge true and make another set.

Constructing the Top

Both the table and the sideboard feature tops assembled from a mahogany veneer plywood panel and surrounded by a solid wood frame. Begin by cutting the plywood for the tabletop panel square and to exact size. Use your circular

The table is delicately spiced with flutes, coves and bead molding. It stands out as an example of refinement and good taste.

saw with a sharp, fine-cutting blade guided by a straightedge. Because the circular saw tends to tear the top surface of the wood, first select the best side of the panel and then flip it over to make the cut.

Next, rip the tabletop frame pieces to width and plane the sawn edges smooth. Crosscut them slightly oversize in length and hold each piece up to the plywood panel to mark for the miters. The frame miter joints and the frame-to-panel joints are splined.

Use your router with a slot cutter to make the 1/8-in.-wide grooves. The spline joint at the miters doesn't extend through the corner. So, set up a stopping jig to cut these blind slots as shown in the drawing. When cutting the grooves, keep the base of the router on the top face of the frame pieces and panel for accurate registration.

Plywood, 1/8-in.-thick, was used for the splines shown but similar size hardboard could be used as well. They shouldn't fit too tightly. When the glue is applied they'll swell, making assembly difficult. If necessary, plane the spline surfaces for a slip fit.

Before gluing, dry assemble the top to ensure that all the pieces have been cut properly. First draw the long side pieces against the panel with bar clamps and then position the ends.

If you don't have bar clamps long enough to span the length of the top, use two C-clamps and wedges. Clamp the assembly tight and let the glue set overnight. After the glue has dried, plane the 10° bevel around the perimeter as shown in the drawing.

Assembling the Frame

Cut enough 3/8-in. dowels 1 1/2 in. long to assemble the entire skirt. Chamfer the ends with a file or sandpaper and groove each pin to let excess glue escape. You can also buy grooved dowel pins cut to length. Begin the assembly by applying slow-setting hide glue sparingly to the holes and dowel pins for the short end rails and legs. After these leg pairs have set, join them to the two long rails. Make sure the surface you're working on is flat; floors are not always as flat as they look. If necessary, place shims under the legs to keep the frame true.

After the glue has dried thoroughly, lay the tabletop upside down and position the leg and skirt assembly on it. Mark the hole positions for the top fastening screws and lightly mark with pencil the leg corner positions. Then, shift the frame aside to bore the screw pilot holes. Use a drill stop or masking tape wrapped around the bit to act as a depth guide.

Slide the frame back in place, align it with the pencil marks and secure the base to the top with 3-in. No.10 fh wood screws. To ensure extra rigidity to the tabletop panel, add two interior cross rails. Cut four cross-rail cleats each with a centered 13/16-in.-wide × 1/2-in.-deep dado as shown in the drawing. Then, rip the rails to size, crosscut them exactly to length and attach each cleat to a rail end with one 4d nail and glue. Screw the rail assemblies in place with 1 1/4-in. No.10 fh screws. Because the plywood panel is 1/16 in. thinner than the solid frame, you'll have to shim the cross rails on top for proper support. Next assemble the corner blocks and install them with 5/16 × 3 1/2-in. lagscrews and glue.

Finishing the Job

After the table has been assembled, trim the bead molding to fit the rabbets in the end and side apron pieces. Secure with glue and 1/2-in. brads. Let the glue dry and then scrape off squeeze-out with a sharp chisel. Using 120-grit sandpaper, ease the sharp corners on all table parts. Then, sand the entire table with 120-grit followed by 220-grit sandpaper and prepare for finishing by cleaning the table with a tack cloth.

Secret secretary

This unique piece of furniture is ideal for apartment dwellers, students and space-conscious homeowners. It combines the functions of a desk and chest of drawers in a compact package that will complement any traditional decor. Sometimes called a butler's desk, this chest has its roots in early American domestic life where the butler used it as a place to keep track of household operations. Although few of us today can afford such service to handle our domestic affairs, the butler's desk remains an attractive solution for household organizing. This version was designed specifically with the do-it-yourselfer in mind. Constructed of solid cherry and tastefully finished, this piece could very well become an heirloom in your family.

Fold up and close the top of this solid cherry butler's bureau and it transforms from efficient desk into an elegant dresser.

Starting Construction

The large side panels, fixed desktop and case top must be made by gluing together narrower stock. Depending on the widths available to you, you may also need to glue-up the drop-leaf desktop. Start by selecting the wood for each panel, paying particular attention to grain pattern and color. Check the growth rings that appear on the ends of the boards and try to arrange the wood so that the rings alternate—facing down on one board and up on the next. This tends to even out the cupping tendency of flat-sawn boards as the humidity changes. Mark the wood so it's not mixed up at assembly time. Crosscut the panel pieces and drawer fronts about 1 in. longer than their finished dimensions.

Prepare the panel pieces for assembly by first jointing one edge on each. Then rip each piece ¼ in. wider than necessary and joint the sawn edges. Hold each mating surface together and check for a good fit. Apply glue to the mating surfaces, lightly clamp the pieces together, and remove the excess glue. Use straight pieces of scrap stock lightly clamped across each end to keep the panel flat. These should be waxed to prevent them from being glued to the panel. Check that the panel has no twist, tighten the

BUTLER'S DESK

19-3/4″ DEEP x 39-1/8″ WIDE x 42-7/8″ HIGH

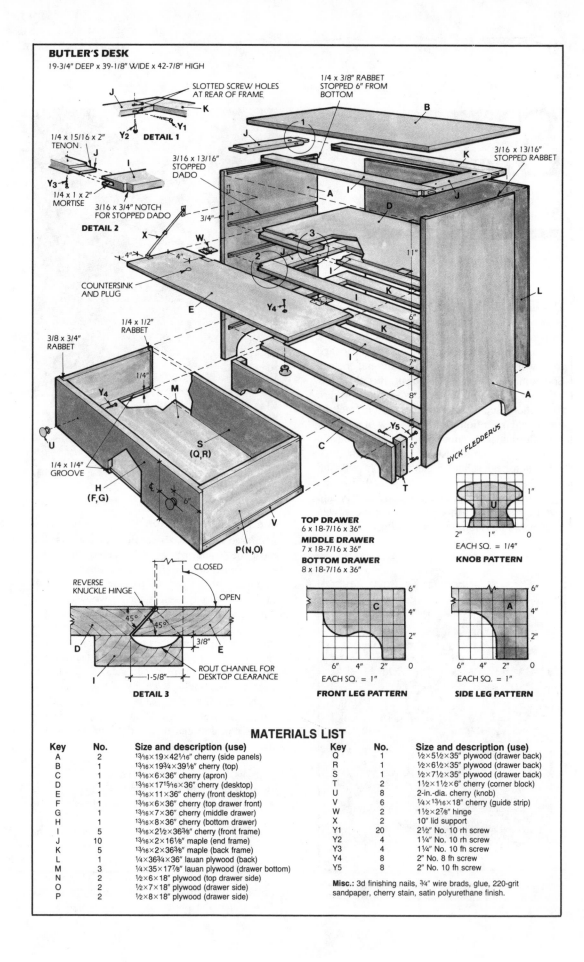

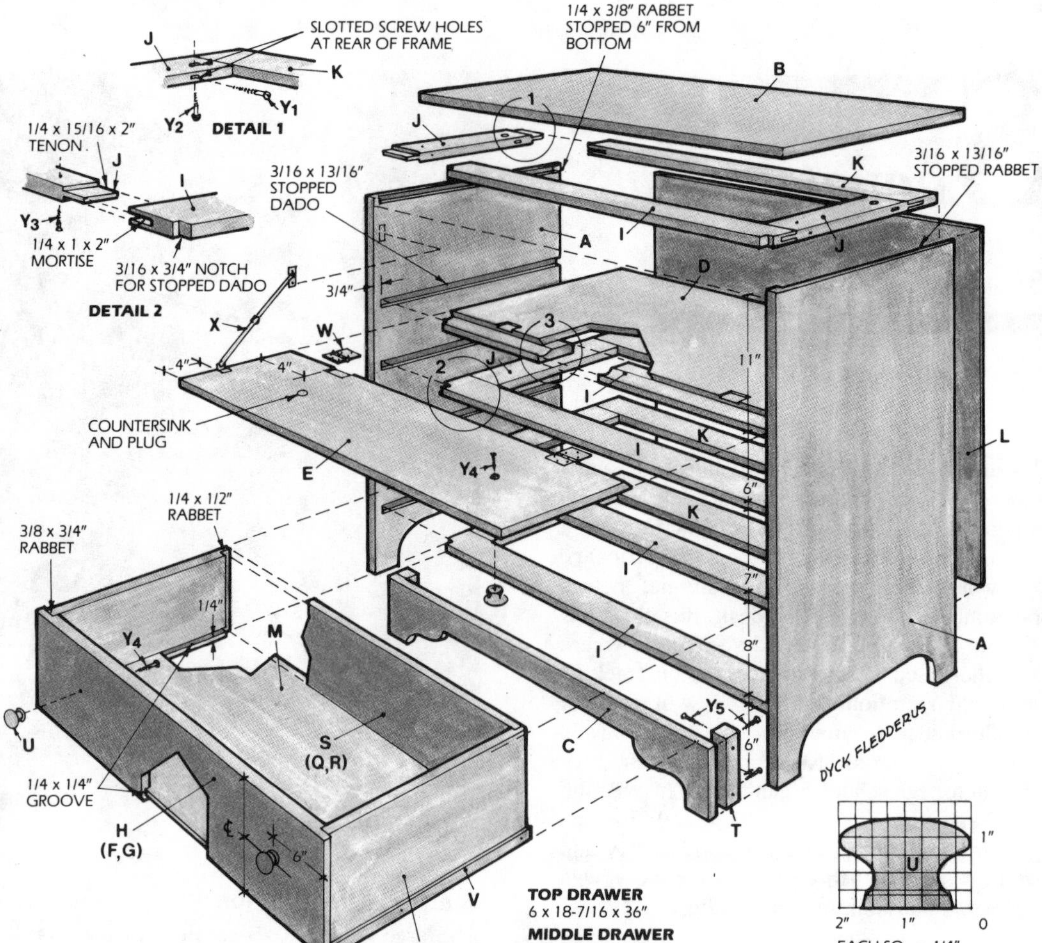
SLOTTED SCREW HOLES
AT REAR OF FRAME
J
K
Y1
Y2
DETAIL 1
1/4 x 15/16 x 2″
TENON
J
I
Y3
1/4 x 1 x 2″
MORTISE
3/16 x 3/4″ NOTCH
FOR STOPPED DADO
DETAIL 2
1/4 x 3/8″ RABBET
STOPPED 6″ FROM
BOTTOM
B
J
3/16 x 13/16″
STOPPED
DADO
K
3/16 x 13/16″
STOPPED RABBET
A
I
J
D
3/4″
X
W
4″
4″
COUNTERSINK
AND PLUG
E
Y4
11″
L
6″
7″
8″
6″
1/4 x 1/2″
RABBET
3/8 x 3/4″
RABBET
1/4″
Y4
M
S
(Q,R)
U
1/4 x 1/4″
GROOVE
H
(F,G)
6″
V
P(N,O)
C
Y5
T
DYCK FLEDDERUS
TOP DRAWER
6 x 18-7/16 x 36″
MIDDLE DRAWER
7 x 18-7/16 x 36″
BOTTOM DRAWER
8 x 18-7/16 x 36″
U
1″
2″
1″
0
EACH SQ. = 1/4″

KNOB PATTERN

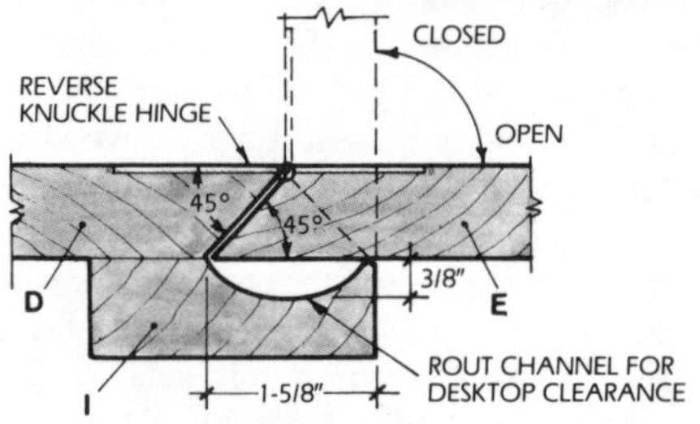
CLOSED
REVERSE
KNUCKLE HINGE
OPEN
45°
45°
D
E
3/8″
I
1-5/8″
ROUT CHANNEL FOR
DESKTOP CLEARANCE

DETAIL 3

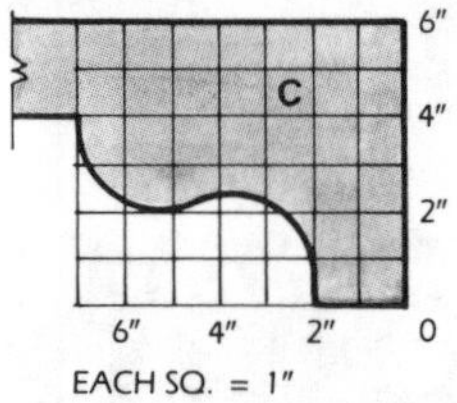
C
6″
4″
2″
6″
4″
2″
0
EACH SQ. = 1″

FRONT LEG PATTERN

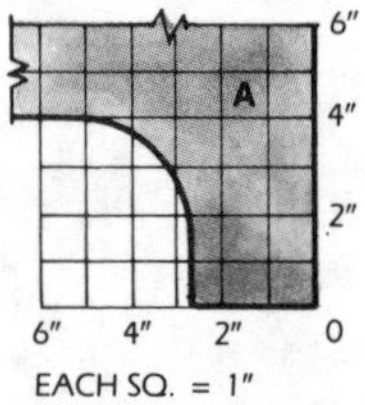
A
6″
4″
2″
6″
4″
2″
0
EACH SQ. = 1″

SIDE LEG PATTERN

MATERIALS LIST

Key	No.	Size and description (use)
A	2	13/16×19×42 1/16″ cherry (side panels)
B	1	13/16×19 3/4×39 1/8″ cherry (top)
C	1	13/16×6×36″ cherry (apron)
D	1	13/16×17 15/16×36″ cherry (desktop)
E	1	13/16×11×36″ cherry (front desktop)
F	1	13/16×6×36″ cherry (top drawer front)
G	1	13/16×7×36″ cherry (middle drawer)
H	1	13/16×8×36″ cherry (bottom drawer)
I	5	13/16×2 1/2×36 3/8″ cherry (front frame)
J	10	13/16×2×16 1/8″ maple (end frame)
K	5	13/16×2×36 3/8″ maple (back frame)
L	1	1/4×36 3/4×36″ lauan plywood (back)
M	3	1/4×35×17 7/8″ lauan plywood (drawer bottom)
N	2	1/2×6×18″ plywood (top drawer side)
O	2	1/2×7×18″ plywood (drawer side)
P	2	1/2×8×18″ plywood (drawer side)
Q	1	1/2×5 1/2×35″ plywood (drawer back)
R	1	1/2×6 1/2×35″ plywood (drawer back)
S	1	1/2×7 1/2×35″ plywood (drawer back)
T	2	1 1/2×1 1/2×6″ cherry (corner block)
U	8	2-in.-dia. cherry (knob)
V	6	1/4×13/16×18″ cherry (guide strip)
W	2	1 1/2×2 7/8″ hinge
X	2	10″ lid support
Y1	20	2 1/2″ No. 10 rh screw
Y2	4	1 1/4″ No. 10 rh screw
Y3	4	1 1/4″ No. 10 fh screw
Y4	8	2″ No. 8 fh screw
Y5	8	2″ No. 10 fh screw

Misc.: 3d finishing nails, 3/4″ wire brads, glue, 220-grit sandpaper, cherry stain, satin polyurethane finish.

1 Make the wide panels by jointing and gluing narrower stock. Clamp straight scrap stock across the panels to keep flat.

2 Lay out and cut a template for the leg profiles on the side panels. Saw to the line with a saber saw and sand the edge.

3 Dress the laminated panels with a hand plane or sander and finish with hand sanding. Be sure to keep the surface flat.

clamps, and let the glue dry overnight. Repeat this procedure for the desktop and cabinet top.

After the glue has dried, dress the surfaces with a hand plane or sander. Then, hand sand with a block and 220-grit paper. Rip the side panels about 1/16 in. oversize and remove this excess with the jointer or hand plane. Then cut to length. Next, make a template of the side panel leg cutout. Transfer the profile to the inside surface of each side panel. Cut to the line with a saber saw and clean up with a drum sander.

Lay out the 3/16-in.-deep dadoes and top-edge rabbet that house the five frames on the inside faces of the panels. To ensure that all the dadoes will be straight, square to the edge, and the correct size, construct a jig to guide the router and straight bit.

Lap join and nail 1×2 stock to make a rectangular frame that spans the width of the side panel. To determine the inside short dimension of the frame that will produce a 13/16-in. dado, subtract the router-bit size from the dado width and add the diameter of the router base. If you're using a 1/2-in. bit and your router base is 6 in. dia., the inside spacing will be 6 5/16 inches.

Test the jig on a scrap piece of wood to be sure the dado width is correct. Clamp the jig squarely on the side panel and attach a stop block at one end so the housings end 3/4 in. from the panel edge. After they're cut, square the stopped ends with a sharp chisel. Then, rout a 1/4-in.-deep × 1/2-in.-wide rabbet on the back inside edges of the panels for the 1/4-in. plywood back. Stop this rabbet 6 in. short of the panel bottom.

Making the Frames

Select the stock for the frames and joint, rip and crosscut each piece to exact dimensions. Next, set up the router table with a 1/4-in. straight bit to cut the mortises in the long frame members. Clamp a stop block to the router table fence so the cuts extend 2 in. from the end. Make several passes, increasing the depth of cut each time, to create the 1-in.-deep mortises. Use a sharp chisel to square the mortise ends. You can cut the tenons on a router table or table saw. Before cutting them in the final stock, make a test on scrap 13/16-in. stock, and check the fit with the mortises. Make sure shoulders are square and tenon length is 15/16 inch.

4 Cut the dadoes and top-edge rabbet with a router and straight bit. Guiding jig ensures straight and consistent width.

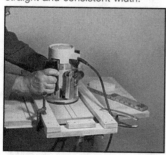

5 Cut the frame mortises with a 1/4-in. bit mounted in the router table. Make several passes to reach the desired depth.

6 The frame tenon cuts are guided by the miter gauge in the router table. Use 13/16-in. scrap to test cutter depth.

7 Test fit the mortise and tenon joints. The fit should be snug with a 1/16-in. gap at the mortise bottom for excess glue.

8 After the frames are assembled, seat them in the side panel dadoes and use a chisel to mark the front-edge notches.

9 Mark the profile for the clearance channel in the desktop frame. Make successive passes with a corebox bit to make the cut.

The frames are fastened to the case sides by screws. Bore 13/64-in. screw holes in the end frame pieces as shown in the drawing. The rear holes in each piece should be slotted to allow for movement in the side panels as the humidity changes. Bore two holes close together and clean away the waste with a chisel to make the slots. Glue and clamp the frames and check for square.

Fitting the Frames

The frames must be notched at the front to fit the stopped dadoes. Place each frame in its groove and use a chisel to mark the frame front-edge notch line. Cut this notch 3/4 in. back from the front edge. It's a good idea to number each frame so they're not mixed up. After the notches are cut, place each frame in its dado and mark the screw pilot-hole positions on the side panels. Then bore 5/32-in. pilot holes 1/2 in. deep. Wrap a piece of tape around the drill or use a drill stop to ensure that the hole doesn't break through the outside panel surface. Next, bore the holes in the top two frames for fastening the cabinet top and inside desktop, slotting the rear ones. The

front holes are countersunk for flathead screws and the rear ones are recessed so the roundhead screws won't interfere with drawer operation.

The front piece of the desktop frame must be channeled out to allow clearance for the fold-down top. Lay out the channel profile on the frame end as shown in the drawing, and use a corebox bit mounted in a router table to cut to the line. Make several passes to achieve the final profile.

Set the table saw to rip at a 45° angle and trim the edges of the fixed and drop-leaf desktops. Reset the saw to 90°, rip the panels to width, and then crosscut to length. Then, lay out the hinge mortises and cut with a sharp chisel. Bore screw pilot holes for the hinge screws and mount the hinges. Lay the desktop in position on the desktop frame and check to see that the leaf opens and closes properly and that its outside face is flush with the frame edge when closed.

Begin to assemble the case by first applying glue to the front 3 in. of each dado and the upper-edge rabbet. Screw each frame to the case sides with 2½-in. No.10 rh screws. Avoid overtightening the screws in the rear slotted holes.

10 Set the table saw for a 45° cut and rip one edge of the desktop fixed and pivoting panels. Guard retracted for clarity.

11 Lay out the reverse knuckle hinge positions on the desktop pieces and carefully cut the mortises with a chisel.

12 Temporarily assemble the pivoting desktop and desktop frame. Make sure front section clears the frame channel.

13 Assemble the frames to the cabinet sides with screws. Use glue at the frame fronts only.

14 Lay out front apron leg profile on ¼-in. stock. Use this template to mark apron ends and cut with a saber saw.

15 A drum sander mounted in a drill press smooths the apron leg profiles. Clean the inside corners by hand sanding.

Check that the cabinet is square and let the glue set.

Completing the Case

Cut two corner blocks for fastening the front apron and attach them to the case sides with 2-in. No.10 fh screws. Cut the apron to size and make a template for the apron leg profiles as shown in the drawing. Trace the outline on the apron and cut with a saber saw. A drum sander mounted in a drill press is useful for cleaning up the saw marks. Hand sand the inside corner of the profile where the drum can't reach. Then fasten the apron in place. Position the case top on the top frame flush with the back case edges and with equal overhang on the sides. Mark and bore screw pilot holes in the top and set it aside for finishing. Cut the ¼-in. plywood back panel and test fit it in the case. Set it aside to be finished before assembly.

Making the Drawers

Joint one edge of each drawer front. Set the table saw to rip the finished dimension of the first drawer and rip the front and sides. Then set the saw to rip ½ in. less and rip the drawer back. Repeat this with the two remaining drawer sizes. Cut the drawer bottoms to size. Using a router table or table saw with dado blade, cut the ⅜×¾-in. rabbets in the drawer fronts and ¼×½-in. rabbets in the sides. With a ¼-in. straight bit or dado blade, plow the ¼-in.-deep groove in the front and sides of each drawer. Fasten the drawer front, sides and back with glue and finishing nails and slide the drawer bottoms in place. Nail these to the drawer backs with 3d nails.

Before installing the guide rails, slide each drawer into the case and check the fit of the drawer front. Adjust where necessary and install the guide rails on the sides. Bore the screw holes for attaching the knobs and countersink for 2-in. No.8 fh screws.

The knobs are turned on a lathe from minimum 2-in. stock. Prepare two blanks about 8 in. long. Each blank will make four knobs. Center the stock on the lathe and turn the knobs to the profile shown in the drawing. Counterbore the knob screw holes in the pivoting desktop for ⅜-in.-dia. plugs and attach the two knobs.

16 Assemble the drawer components with glue and finishing nails and apply ¼-in.-thick hardwood guide strips to the sides.

17 Use a lathe and minimum 2-in.-thick stock to make the blanks for the knobs. Turn four knobs from each blank.

18 Thoroughly clean cabinet and wipe with a tack cloth. Then apply stain followed by three coats of urethane varnish.

Baking cart

Back in the days when baking was a daily chore for many households, it wasn't unusual for the kitchen to feature a specific area for preparing, kneading and rolling out the dough. Today, homemakers all over the country have rediscovered the art of baking as a way to produce high-quality breads and pastries for family and friends to enjoy.

The baking cart featured here not only complements this growing interest by providing the extra work and storage space that baking requires, but also is designed as an independent rollaway unit that fits neatly into any kitchen layout.

Making the Panels

The sides, back, bottom, shelf and partition are all made by gluing 1×4 stock edge to edge. Crosscut the stock for each panel slightly oversize. Apply glue and use pipe clamps above and below the panel to help distribute the pressure evenly. Make sure the panel is flat when clamped. After the glue has cured, scrape off any excess and glue the remaining panels the same way.

Use a belt sander to smooth the panel surfaces. Secure each piece to your workbench with clamps or between bench dogs for this operation. You can also toenail the panels to your worktable. Use small finishing nails placed at the panel ends and set below the surface.

MATERIALS LIST—BAKING CART

Key	No.	Size and description (use)	Key	No.	Size and description (use)
A	2	¾×21½×27¼" pine (side)	X	3	1¼×2½×17½" pine (blocking)
B	1	¾×27¼×29½" pine (back)	Y	2	¾×1¼×31" pine (long dentil)
C	1	¾×22¼×28½" pine (bottom)	Z	2	¾×1¼×24" pine (short dentil)
D	1	¾×22¼×20⅝" pine (partition)	AA	1	½×1½×17¾" pine (trim)
E	1	¾×19×22¼" pine (shelf)	BB	1	½×2¼×14½" pine (trim)
F	4	½×3×17½" pine (side cleat)	CC	1	¾×14½×34½" Corian (top)
G	2	½×3×24½" pine (back cleat)	DD	1	½×5¹⁄₁₆×24⅜" pine (drawer face)
H	6	¾×¾×22¼" pine (support strip)			
I	8	¾×3½×27¼" pine (leg)	EE	2	¾×3½×22¼" pine (drawer side)
J	2	¾×¾×30" pine (front strip)	FF	1	¾×3½×22⅞" pine (drawer front)
K	1	¾×¾×28½" pine (top back strip)	GG	1	¾×3×22⅞" pine (drawer back)
L	1	¾×¾×27" pine (back strip)	HH	1	¼×21¾×23⅜" plywood (bottom)
M	2	¾×¾×21½" pine (side strip)	II	4	2¼-in. resilient tread caster
N	1	¾×2×20¾" pine (spreader)	JJ	1	drawer pull
O	4	¾×1¼×4⅜" pine (block)	KK	20	2" No. 8 fh screw
P	2	¾×4⅜×22¼" pine (side guide)	LL	4	1" No. 10 fh screw
Q	1	¾×¾×24½" pine (drawer support)	MM	16	1¼" No. 8 fh screw
			NN	4	⅝" No. 3 rh screw
R	1	¾×¾×23" pine (drawer support)	OO		1" wire brad
S	2	¾×¾×21½" pine (drawer support)	PP		3d finishing nail
			QQ		4d finishing nail
T	2	¾×3½×24½" pine (short cap)	RR		6d finishing nail
U	2	¾×3½×31½" pine (long cap)			
V	1	¾×3½×17½" pine (cap filler)	**Misc.:** 120- and 220-grit sandpaper, glue, 4/0 steel wool, polyurethane varnish, mineral spirits.		
W	2	1¼×2½×29½" pine (blocking)			

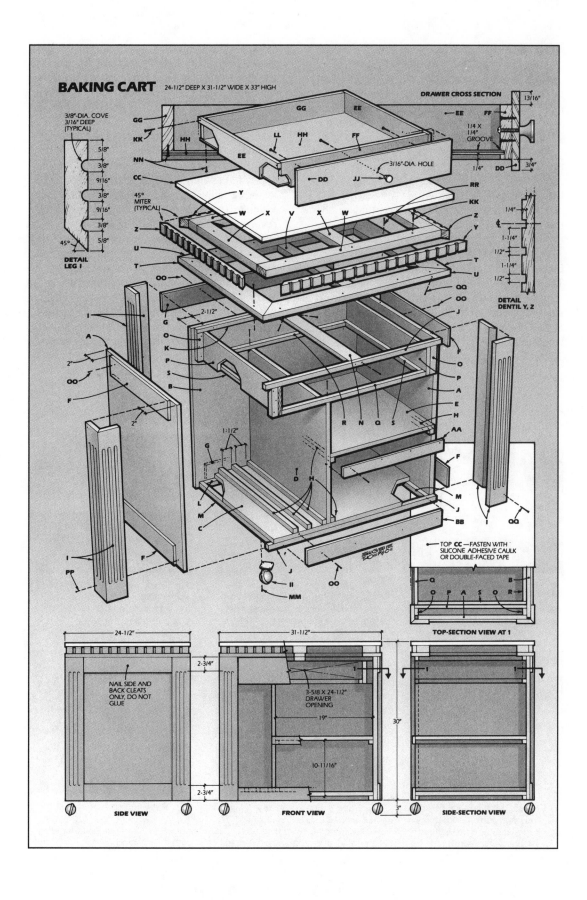

BAKING CART 24-1/2" DEEP X 31-1/2" WIDE X 33" HIGH

3/8"-DIA. COVE 3/16" DEEP (TYPICAL)

DETAIL LEG I

5/8"
3/8"
9/16"
3/8"
9/16"
3/8"
5/8"
45°

DRAWER CROSS SECTION
13/16"
1/4 X 1/4" GROOVE
1/4"
3/4"

45° MITER (TYPICAL)

3/16"-DIA. HOLE

DETAIL DENTIL Y, Z
1/4"
1-1/4"
1/2"
1-1/4"
1/2"

2"
2"

1-1/2"
2-1/2"

TOP CC — FASTEN WITH SILICONE ADHESIVE CAULK OR DOUBLE-FACED TAPE

TOP-SECTION VIEW AT 1

24-1/2"

NAIL SIDE AND BACK CLEATS ONLY, DO NOT GLUE

2-3/4"

2-3/4"

SIDE VIEW

31-1/2"

3-5/8 X 24-1/2" DRAWER OPENING

19"

10-11/16"

30"

3"

FRONT VIEW

SIDE-SECTION VIEW

Keep the sander moving at all times to avoid gouging the panel and use minimal pressure.

Mark the finished panel dimensions on each piece and lay out the cutting lines. Double check to be sure the layouts are square and to exact size. Clamp a straightedge to the panels for guiding your circular saw.

Rip 1×4 stock to ½ in. thick by 3 in. wide for the side and back cleats. Crosscut to length and secure to the panels with 3d finishing nails. Don't use glue because humidity changes will possibly crack or warp the panels if they're not free to move.

The Fluted Legs

Crosscut the 1×4 leg stock to exact length. Then, construct a jig to hold the pieces for routing the flutes. Cut a piece of ¾-in.-thick stock to 8 in. wide by 34 in. long for the jig base. Secure a piece of scrap stock cut to the same length as the legs to one side of the jig base. Then attach two end blocks to the base so the leg stock will be supported on three sides. Fasten stop blocks to the end pieces for limiting the travel of your router. These are positioned so the flutes begin 2¾ in. from each end. The spacing of the stop blocks is determined by the size of your router base.

Install a ⅜-in.-dia. corebox bit in your router and adjust the depth of cut to 3⁄16 inch. Adjust the router edge guide attachment to cut the center flute. After this flute has been cut on each leg piece, adjust the guide to cut an outer flute. When this cut is completed on all pieces, simply reverse the stock for a third flute.

Rip a 45° bevel along one edge of each leg piece. Assemble the legs by first placing one piece in your vise with the inner edge of the bevel in line with the bench top. Partially drive several 4d finishing nails in the beveled edge of the adjoining piece so their points poke through. Apply glue and press the second piece in place on the first. Drive the nails, set the leg aside to dry, and complete the remaining legs in the same manner.

1 Edge-glue 1×4 boards for panels. Alternate clamps above and below. Be sure panels lie flat when clamps are tightened.

2 Scrape off excess glue after it has cured and belt-sand panels smooth. Keep the sander moving with even pressure.

3 Mark panels to exact size for cutting. Clamp each panel to the worktable and use a straight board to guide the saw.

4 Select the best face of side and back panels and nail cleats in place. Don't use glue to avoid warping the panel.

5 Leg fluting jig holds leg pieces in place and limits router travel. Use a ⅜-in.-dia. corebox bit and router edge guide.

6 After ripping a 45° bevel on one edge of each leg piece, apply glue and nail pairs together with 4d finishing nails.

Assembling the Case

Attach two legs to the back with glue and 3d finishing nails. Attach the front legs to the sides the same way and then join the sides to the rear legs. Tie the cart front together by attaching the ¾-in.-sq. strips across the front at the top and bottom. Install the ledger strips around the inside bottom edges of the case for supporting the bottom and attach the strip at the top edge of the back. Toenail the spreader to the rear top strip and secure it at the front by nailing through the front strip.

Install the bottom to the bottom strips with glue and 3d finishing nails. Cut and install the corner blocks (**O**) and attach the drawer side guides to the blocks with glue and 4d finishing nails. Attach the drawer support strips to the drawer side guides. Then install the front and rear drawer supports (**Q** and **R**).

The ¾-in.-sq. strips on the cart bottom serve as dividers for tray storage and for holding the partition. After attaching these strips, slide the partition in place. Secure it by nailing through

the cart bottom and through the drawer support strips. Install the shelf cleats and the shelf.

Constructing the Top

Use a miter box to cut the 1×4 stock for the cap (**T** and **U**) to exact length and secure the pieces to the cart with 6d finishing nails. Use glue on the miter joints and nail through each joint to ensure a tight fit. Then, cut and install the cap spacer (**V**) over the center spreader as shown in the drawing.

Rip 2×3 stock to 1¼ in. thick by 2½ in. wide for the top blocking (**W** and **X**). Cut each piece to length and clamp in place on the cart. Secure the blocking with 2-in. No.8 fh screws.

To make the dentil molding, first crosscut a length of 1×12 stock to at least 36 in. long. Install an ½-in.-dia. straight bit in your router and route ¼-in.-deep dadoes across the face of the board leaving a 1¼-in.-space between each dado. Make sure that the workpiece is clamped firmly to the bench and use a straightedge clamped to the stock to guide your router. All

7 Secure the legs to back with glue and 4d finishing nails. Attach one leg to each side the glue and nail sides to rear legs.

8 After nailing ¾-in.-sq. strips across cart front, nail strips around bottom edge of sides and back to support bottom panel.

9 Glue and nail ¾-in.-sq. strip to upper back edge. Then secure the corner blocks with 3d finishing nails and glue.

10 Cut drawer guides to size and attach to the corner blocks. Then install the drawer supports to sides, front and back.

11 Use 3d finishing nails to attach strips to car bottom. These act as spacers for trays and the case partition.

12 Slide partition in and nail up through bottom. Secure top edge by nailing through front and rear drawer supports.

four lengths of dentil molding are ripped from this board. Cut at least 17 dadoes across the 1×12 stock to accommodate the long front and rear pieces.

Rip the dentil molding to 1¼ in. wide. Use a miter box to cut each piece to length and attach to the top blocking with 4d finishing nails and glue.

Cut and apply the trim strips (**AA** and **BB**) as shown in the drawing. Turn the cart upside down and mark and bore pilot holes for screwing the casters in place. Install the casters with 1¼-in. No.8 fh screws.

Making the Drawer

Cut all parts for the drawer to exact size. Use a dado blade mounted in the table saw to cut the grooves in the drawer sides and front that contain the drawer bottom. Join the sides, front and back with 2-in. No.8 fh screws. Slide the bottom in place, check that the drawer is square, then screw the bottom to the drawer back with ⅝-in. No.3 rh screws.

Cut the drawer face to size and attach to the drawer front with 1-in. No.10 fh screws. Bore the hole for the drawer pull and install.

Finishing the Cart

Set all nails and fill. Sand the entire cart with 120- then 220-grit sandpaper. For a durable natural finish, apply three coats of polyurethane varnish, thinning the first coat 30 percent with mineral spirits. Sand lightly and dust off between coats. After the final coat has dried, rub the cart with 4/0 steel wool for a satin finish.

You can cover the top with plastic laminate glued to a particleboard or plywood panel or you can use a slab of marble or granite for that authentic pastry-rolling surface.

13 After cutting 1×4 cap pieces to length, nail in place on cart. Use glue and nail through each joint.

14 Cut the 1¼-in.-thick spacer blocking to length and clamp in place. Secure to cap with 2-in. No.8 fh screws.

15 Begin the dentil molding by routing ½-in.-wide dadoes across 1×12 stock. Board clamped to work guides router.

16 Set table saw fence to rip 1¼-in.-wide strips of dentil molding. Miter pieces and install with finishing nails and glue.

17 After cutting drawer components to size, cut ¼×¼-in. groove in sides and front with dado blade.

18 Screw sides, front and back together and slide the bottom in. Secure bottom to back with ⅝-in. No.3 rh screws.

Starting Out

Begin construction by making patterns for the front and rear legs using ¼-in. plywood. Draw a 1-in.-sq. grid for each leg on the plywood. Then, transfer each point of intersection that the leg outline makes on the grid in the drawing to its corresponding position on your full-size grid on the plywood. To connect the points in a smooth curve, rip a 48-in.-long piece of scrap stock to ⅛ in. thick by ½ in. wide. Drive small brads at the intersection points on your grid, hold the flexible strip against the brads and trace the curve. Cut out both leg patterns, leaving ¼ in. extra on the bottom of the rear leg. Using these patterns, lay out a complete full-size side view of the chair as it is shown in the drawing. This layout will help you accurately dimension and position the remaining components.

MATERIALS LIST
STEPSTOOL/CHAIR

Key	No.	Size and description (use)
A	2	⅞×5¼×33¾″ oak (rear leg)
B	2	⅞×2×6½″ oak (side rail)
C	2	⅞×1¼×17¹¹⁄₁₆″ oak (rear support)
D	2	⅞×1½×3¼″ oak (wedge)
E	2	⅞×4½×16⁹⁄₁₆″ oak (front leg)
F	2	⅞×1¼×18⅜″ oak (front support)
G	3	⅝×2¼×13¼″ oak (slat)
H	1	¾×8⅞×15¾″ oak (rear seat)
I	1	¾×4½×15¾″ oak (front seat)
J	1	⅞×2×13¼″ oak (front rail)
K	1	⅞×4⅞×15¾″ oak (top step)
L	1	⅝×5¹³⁄₁₆×13¾″ oak (step)
M	1	⅝×6⁷⁄₁₆×13¾″ oak (step)
N	33	1½″ No. 6 drywall screw
O	4	2″ No. 6 drywall screw
P	6	2½″ No. 8 drywall screw
Q	2	3″ No. 8 drywall screw
R	45	⅜-in.-dia. plug
S	2	¾×1⅞″ hinge
T	1	latch

Misc.: 150-grit sandpaper, epoxy adhesive, paste wax, satin finish polyurethane varnish.

Stepstool and chair

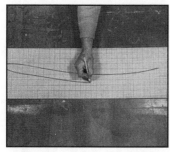

1 Begin leg templates by laying out 1-in.-sq. grid on ¼-in. plywood. Transfer front and rear leg profiles as shown in drawing.

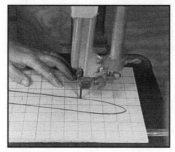

2 Cut out the front and rear leg patterns with a band saw or saber saw carefully following the pattern outline.

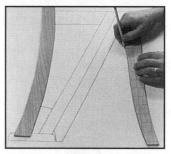

3 Draw a full-size layout of chair using the leg patterns. Specifications for the remaining pieces are taken from the drawing.

4 The trim angle for the middle support pieces is copied from the layout and transferred to the miter gauge for cutting.

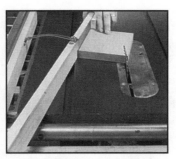

5 Use a tapering jig to cut bottom wedges at the required angle. Stop block behind stock keeps it in place during cut.

6 When all the side pieces are cut, place them on the full-size layout and check for fit. Trim components where necessary.

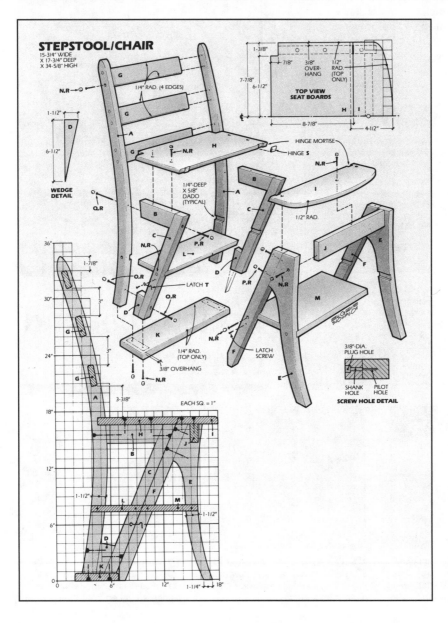

STEPSTOOL/CHAIR
15-3/4" WIDE
X 17-3/4" DEEP
X 34-5/8" HIGH

7 Clamp each side assembly to a corner of the worktable and mark and bore the plug, shank and pilot holes for screws.

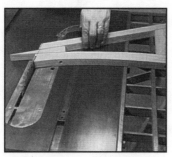

8 Trim the rear side bottom after assembly. Use your table saw with miter gauge set to the angle taken from the layout.

9 Mark the lines for the dadoes that house the steps. Using a straightedge guide, rout the 1/4-in.-deep by 5/8-in.-wide dadoes.

Keep in mind that the rear section pivots forward at the hinge position. The distance from the top of the rear leg to the seat should be equal to the height of the seat above the floor. This ensures that the rear leg tops will contact the floor when the unit is used as a stepstool.

Rip the 7/8-in.-thick rear leg stock to 6 in. wide and the front leg stock to 5 inches. Crosscut these pieces slightly longer than their leg patterns. Transfer the pattern profiles to the stock and use a bandsaw or saber saw to cut to the line.

Smooth the sawn edges with a drum sander or by hand with a spokeshave and sandpaper.

Rip the stock for the middle support pieces (**C** and **F** in the drawing) to 1 1/4 in. wide. Using your full-size layout as a guide for the support lengths, crosscut each piece slightly oversize. Use a sliding bevel gauge to copy the trimming angle. Then lay out and transfer this angle to the miter gauge on your table saw.

Trim the rear support 1/4 in. oversize in length at the appropriate angle and cut the front support to the exact length shown in your layout. The legs and supports of the rear side sections are connected by a rail (**H**) at the top and wedge (**D**) at the bottom. You can use a tapering jig (as shown in the photo) to cut the wedges. If you don't have a tapering jig, you can cut a piece of scrap 3/4-in. plywood to the required angle and guide this along the saw fence for cutting the wedges. You can also transfer the wedge shape from the layout and cut on your band saw.

Don't trim the points off the wedge bottoms as the entire rear section bottom will be trimmed after assembly. Cut the forward end of the upper side rails to the correct angle and transfer the line where they join the rear legs, using your layout as a guide. Band saw to the line. Lay the four parts that make up each rear side assembly

on the layout and check for proper fit and alignment. Repeat this alignment check for the front side components.

Side Assemblies

When you're sure all side components match your full-size layout you're ready for assembly. Clamp the pieces for one front side section in position on a corner of your worktable and mark the screw positions as shown in the drawing. When boring for the screws, keep in mind that you'll need to bore three holes for each screw. First bore the 3/8-in.-dia. hole for the oak plug. Then, bore the shank hole followed by the actual pilot hole. The shank hole must be just larger than the outside diameter of the screw thread. You can buy special drill bits designed for boring all three holes at once to speed the operation. After boring, screw fasten the two front side pieces together without epoxy. Repeat this procedure for the remaining front section and two rear sections. When all four sections are screwed together, position each on the layout to make sure the parts are properly aligned. If you're satisfied, remove the screws, apply epoxy to all joints and reassemble. Then, mark the bottom cut-off lines for the rear assemblies, set your miter gauge to the required angle as taken from the layout and saw to the line.

The Steps and Back

The steps (**L** and **M** on the drawing) are housed in dadoes cut in the side assemblies. Place each side section on the layout and transfer the step positions. Then lay a front and rear section—inside face up—on your worktable so the marks for the steps align. Clamp a straightedge guide over the sides to guide your router and 5/8-in.-dia. straight bit. After the dadoes are cut, plane the stock for the steps to 5/8 in. thick, joint one

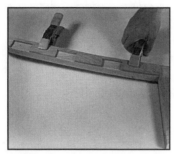

10 A ¼-in. plywood template of the upper rear leg has notches to help in positioning the slats before boring screw holes.

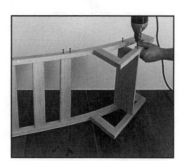

11 Dry assemble the units with drywall screws and check for fit. Remove screws, apply epoxy and reassemble.

12 Use a fine back saw and sharp chisel to cut the hinge mortises. Bore pilot holes and screw hinges in place.

edge on each and crosscut to the specified length. Obtain the exact width and bevel angle of each step from the full-size layout and trim the stock to width. Crosscut the back slat pieces and front rail to exact length and rip to width.

Before assembling the front and rear halves, construct a jig to hold the back slats in place. Temporarily tack two pieces of ¼-in. plywood together and trace the rear leg pattern on them. Mark notches at the slat positions as shown on the layout and saw out the notches with a saber saw. Separate the templates and clamp each to a rear section inside face.

Using bar clamps, dry assemble the rear side sections with the step. Place the slats in the template notches and temporarily clamp. Then mark the screw positions and bore the plug, shank and pilot holes for connecting the halves. Install the screws and check for proper alignment. Remove the screws from one side and apply epoxy to the mating surfaces. Fasten and repeat the procedure on the other side. After the rear section is completed, assemble the front halves, step and rail the same way.

Seat and Top Step

Prepare the seat pieces by trimming two boards slightly wider than necessary and planing to ¾ in. thick. Crosscut to exact length and cut to width following the dimensions and bevel angle shown in your layout. Notch the rear seat board to fit between the rear legs. Transfer the front edge shape of the forward seat piece from the drawing to scrap ¼-in. plywood and cut out. Trace this pattern on the seat stock, cut to the line and smooth the sawn edge with a drum sander or sandpaper and block. Mark the hinge positions and cut the hinge mortises with a dovetail saw and sharp chisel. Place each hinge in position on the rear seat piece and mark for

13 Turn chair upside down and position the ⅞-in.-thick top step. Mark and bore the hole for fastening with drywall screws.

the screw pilot holes. After boring, it's a good idea to tap the holes with a steel screw of the same size as the brass screws supplied with the hinges. This helps eliminate breaking the soft brass screws as they're driven into the hard oak. Lay the front piece on top and install the screws. Align the front and rear assemblies and clamp together. Stand the entire unit up in its chair position using ⅞-in.-thick piece of stock in place of the top step (**K**) to support the rear section. Position the seat and bore the screw holes. If the dry assembly of the seat is correct, remove the seat, apply epoxy and reinstall. Then, cut the top step to size, turn the chair upside down and install.

Completing the Piece

Use a plug cutter to make enough plugs for all the screws and glue the plugs in place. Trim the excess with a sharp chisel. Remove the hinges and hand sand the entire chair with 150-grit sandpaper. Clean up with a tack cloth and apply two coats of satin polyurethane varnish.

Keep the book open and your hands free with this easy-to-build solid oak book stand.

Book stand

This solid red oak book stand is designed to support any size volume, from recipe book to unabridged dictionary. This piece can hold the book while your hands are busy or keep an often used reference at your fingertips. It features a 3-position pivoting frame that ranges from 15° to 60° and folds flat for easy storage.

The design shown calls for ⅝-in.-thick stock. If you don't own a thickness planer, you may be able to get your supplier to plane down the more commonly available 13/16-in.-thick stock. Otherwise, buy the thicker oak and resaw it to a thickness slightly greater than ⅝ in. on your table saw or band saw. Before attempting to resaw the oak, however, rip it to 1½ in. wide, dress the sawn edges and crosscut each piece slightly longer than necessary. After resawing, sharpen your hand plane and smooth the sawn surface. Plane the full length of each piece in one continuous stroke and progress across the width evenly.

Next, cut each piece to exact length. Temporarily assemble the frames with clamps and mark the dowel hole positions as shown in the drawing. Remove the clamps and use a doweling jig to aid in boring the ¼-in.-dia. × 9/16-in.-deep holes.

If you own an extra long ¼-in. drill bit, you can bore the pivot pin holes through the two center short members and pivoting arm in one operation. If not, place these parts together, mark the hole centerline and use your doweling jig. Rebore the holes in the arm with a 17/64-in.-dia. bit to allow it to pivot easily.

Mark the notch positions on the lower frame center member. You can cut these with a dado blade, or use a regular blade and make several passes, shifting the stock after each cut. Note that the rear notch is slightly beveled to accept the arm in the 15° position. Use a sharp chisel to make this cut.

Assemble the two frames with ¼-in.-dia.× 1-in.-long dowels. If you're making up your own dowel pins from a long length, be sure to cut shallow grooves in them for excess glue to escape. Apply glue sparingly to dowels and holes, clamp each frame and check for square by measuring the frame diagonals.

Cut the pivot dowel to length and sand it for a slip fit in the frame. Attach the shelf to the upper frame with glue and four 3d finishing nails. To mark for the hinge screw holes, clamp the two frames together with a piece of thick cardboard in between. Then, hold each hinge in place and mark the centers with an awl.

Before installing the hinges and arm, sand the components and apply two coats of urethane varnish.

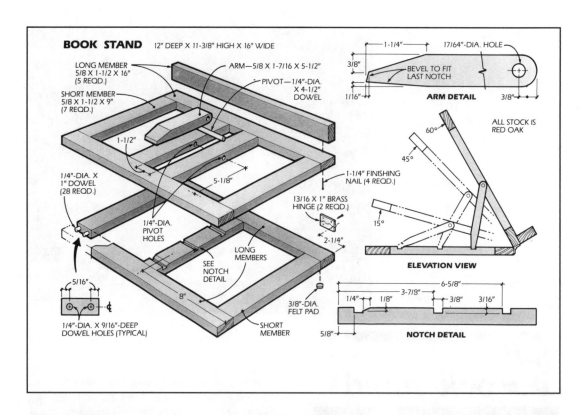

BOOK STAND 12" DEEP X 11-3/8" HIGH X 16" WIDE

LONG MEMBER
5/8 X 1-1/2 X 16"
(5 REQD.)

ARM—5/8 X 1-7/16 X 5-1/2"

PIVOT—1/4"-DIA.
X 4-1/2" DOWEL

SHORT MEMBER
5/8 X 1-1/2 X 9"
(7 REQD.)

1-1/2"

1/4"-DIA. X
1" DOWEL
(28 REQD.)

5-1/8"

1/4"-DIA.
PIVOT
HOLES

1-1/4" FINISHING
NAIL (4 REQD.)

13/16 X 1" BRASS
HINGE (2 REQD.)

2-1/4"

SEE
NOTCH
DETAIL

LONG
MEMBERS

5/16"

8"

3/8"-DIA.
FELT PAD

1/4"-DIA. X 9/16"-DEEP
DOWEL HOLES (TYPICAL)

SHORT
MEMBER

5/8"

1-1/4"

17/64"-DIA. HOLE

3/8"

BEVEL TO FIT
LAST NOTCH

1/16"

ARM DETAIL

3/8"

ALL STOCK IS
RED OAK

60°

45°

15°

ELEVATION VIEW

6-5/8"

3-7/9"

1/4"   1/8"   3/8"   3/16"

5/8"

NOTCH DETAIL

After trimming to width, resaw the stock to slightly greater than ⅝-inch. To safely rip thin stock, use a splitter and featherboard.

A sharp, finely-set hand plane makes quick work of dressing the rough-sawn edges. Be sure to follow the grain direction.

The joints are doweled with ¼-in.-dia.×1-in.-long dowels. A jig ensures accurate positioning and tape on bit indicates hole depth.

The three ⅜-in.-wide dadoes in the lower frame center cross-members are cut with a dado blade mounted in your table saw.

Apply glue sparingly to all dowels and holes in each frame and clamp until dry. Make sure the assemblies are square.

Slide a ¼-in.-dia.×3¾-in.-long dowel through the holes in the arm and crossmembers to act as a pilot pin.

Toboggan heirloom

Here's your chance to provide great winter memories for your family. This toboggan is designed to last for generations. Your children will be able to do more than reminisce; they can pass on the toboggan you make to their children as a family heirloom.

Begin Construction

This ash toboggan is constructed by laminating 1/16-in. ash veneer to create the J-shaped slats. While laminating curved shapes isn't difficult, it does require preparing a form on which the wood is bent and clamped. Begin by cutting the 20×96-in. form base. Nail five cleats underneath to allow space for the bolt heads used for fastening the forms. The toboggan shown here has fir plywood for the 3/4-in.-thick base, but particle board works just as well. The forms are made out of 2×4s.

Crosscut six lengths of 2×4 stock to 9¾ in. and rip them to 3¼ in. wide. Glue these together to create the 3×9¾-in.-sq. front form blank. Then lay out the 8¾-in.-dia. arc that represents the inside diameter of the bend and band saw to the line. Cut the inside profile for clamp access and the notch where the straight section joins. Choose the straightest piece of 2×4 available for the straight form and trim it to 3 in. wide and 75½ in. long. To make the form rigid, both sections are bolted to the base with 3/8-in.-dia.×3½-in.-long bolts. Counterbore the bolt holes so the washers and nuts will be recessed. Bore the bolt holes through the forms and panel, then install the bolts.

1 Glue up 2×4 stock to create the 3×9¾-in.-sq. front form blank. Lay out the profile and saw to the line.

2 After counterboring holes to recess the nuts, bore 3/8-in.-dia. holes through the forms and base for securing the bolts.

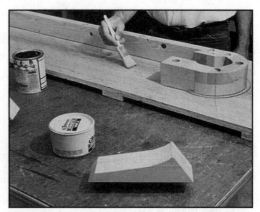

3 Keep lamination from being glued to form by applying a coat of varnish and two coats of paste wax to the components.

4 Tape each sheet of veneer to a straight piece of ³⁄₄-in. stock and true one edge. Jig clamped to fence holds the veneer.

5 Rip the veneer to 3 in. wide. Block clamped to fence keeps strip from lifting. Use sharp, fine-toothed blade for these cuts.

6 Prepare 1 lb. of plastic resin glue for each laminated slat. Apply a uniform coat to parts with a 3-in. paint roller.

7 After spreading glue, clamp the stack at the top front caul position. Bend laminations around the form, clamping as you go.

8 With the cauls in place, check that strips are even and fully tighten clamps starting at one end and working to the other.

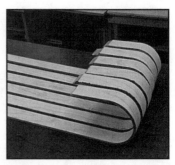

9 With the laminated sections completed, it only remains to trim to width and length before joining them together with cleats.

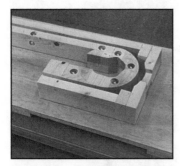

10 Attach the template support blocks to the base with 1¹⁄₂ No.10 fh screws. Notches in the end block ease the slat removal.

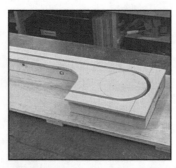

11 The four template pieces create a ⁷⁄₈-in. slot to guide the router when trimming the slat edges. Secure with finishing nails.

12 Use a straight bit and guide busing to dress the edges. After one edge on each piece is done, disassemble and flip over.

13 Clamp the slats together with a straightedge to guide the saber saw.

14 The straight ends of each lamination are cut individually on the table or radial-arm saw.

15 Clamp each cleat in place and bore pilot holes for the 1-in. No.12 brass screws.

Clamping blocks called *cauls* are used to hold the laminations against the form. To make the front cauls, cut six pieces of 2×4 to about 1 in. longer than the 9¾-in. finished length and rip them to 3¼ in. wide. Glue together in pairs to get the required 3-in.-thick pieces. Trim 52½° miters on each end to exact length. Then lay out the outside edge profile of the front of the toboggan on a piece of cardboard. Position the mitered cauls as shown in the drawing. Transfer the profile and cut each piece to the line. Trim a 2×4 for the long, straight caul to exact size. To keep the slats from being glued to the forms or cauls, apply a coat of varnish and two coats of paste wax to all the parts.

Preparing the Veneer

You'll need a total of 48 3-in.-wide strips of ⅟16-in. ash veneer for this project. Crosscut enough veneer for the job to 96 in. long. To true up one edge on each piece, tape a straight length of stock to the veneer and rip the outside edge of the veneer on your table saw. Rip each strip to 3 in. wide.

Apply plastic resin glue to the mating surfaces of eight strips, stacking them as you go. Position the stack end at the top front edge of the form and lightly clamp the first caul in place. Make sure the veneers are in contact with the base. Bend the laminations around the form, clamping each caul lightly. Then, starting at one end of the form, completely tighten all clamps.

Trimming the Slats

You can clean up the rough edges of the laminations with a router, straight bit and guide bushing that follows a ½-in.-thick plywood template positioned on the top of the form. Cut the 3-in.-high template supports and screw them to the form base from underneath. The notches in the end support are useful for freeing the slats from the form after an edge has been trimmed. Then, construct the template pieces and tack them in place with finishing nails. Rout one edge on each piece, taking shallow cuts to avoid splintering the ash. To rout the opposite edges, remove the template pieces and supports, flip them over and reassemble. Clamp the slats together, secure a guide to the top front section and trim the ends with a saber saw. Cut the straight ends with a table or radial-arm saw.

Putting it Together

Before assembling the toboggan, sand each slat first with 120- then 220-grit sandpaper. Cut six 1¼×15-in. cleats from ¹³⁄16-in. solid ash stock. The 1¼-in.-thick nose cleat must be made from heavier stock or you can laminate two pieces of ¹³⁄16-in. material. Install a ¼-in.-rad. rounding-over bit in your router and round the upper edges of the six slat cleats and the two forward edges of the nose cleat as shown in the drawing. Use a ½-in.-rad. rounding-over bit for the remaining nose cleat edges. A dado blade mounted in the table saw cuts the groove in the nose cleat.

Mark the rope and screw-hole positions as shown in the drawing. With the slats clamped together, slip the nose cleat in place and bore pilot holes for the 1¼ No.12 solid brass screws. Then, remove the cleat, bore and countersink the rope, screw shank holes and install. Remaining cleats are glued and screwed in from underneath. Countersink these screws ⅟16 in. below the surface.

Choose a varnish with high water resistance and additives to filter out the sun's ultraviolet rays which tend to turn the wood gray. Top off the varnish with two coats of paste wax. Finally, install the rope as shown in the drawing, pulling it tight and knotting it at the rear.

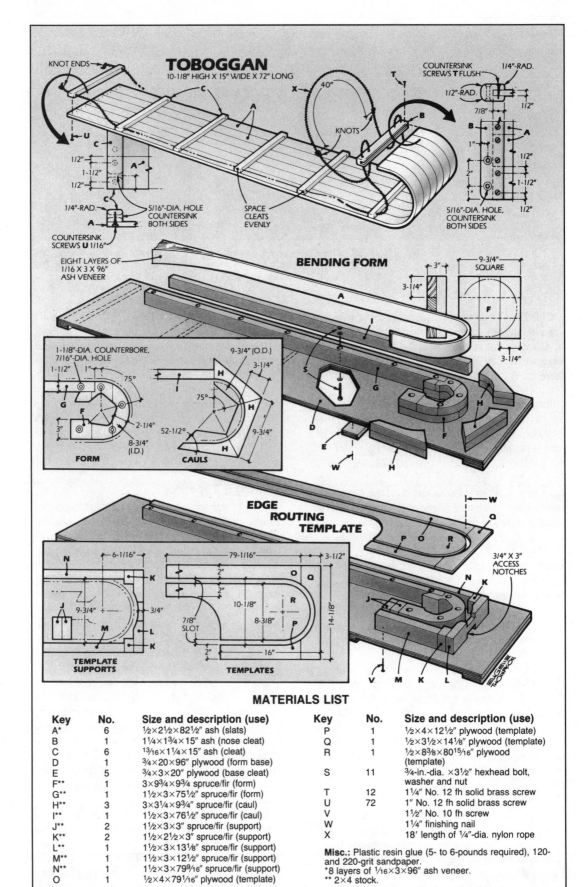

TOBOGGAN
10-1/8" HIGH X 15" WIDE X 72" LONG

KNOT ENDS

COUNTERSINK SCREWS **T** FLUSH

1/4"-RAD.

1/2"-RAD.

7/8"

1/2"

40°

KNOTS

C

A

X

B

U

C

1/2"
1-1/2"
1/2"

A

1"

1/2"

2"

1-1/2"

1/2"

B

A

1/4"-RAD.

C

A

5/16"-DIA. HOLE
COUNTERSINK
BOTH SIDES

SPACE
CLEATS
EVENLY

5/16"-DIA. HOLE,
COUNTERSINK
BOTH SIDES

COUNTERSINK
SCREWS **U** 1/16"

EIGHT LAYERS OF
1/16 X 3 X 96"
ASH VENEER

BENDING FORM

3"

3-1/4"

9-3/4"
SQUARE

A

I

3-1/4"

F

1-1/8"-DIA. COUNTERBORE,
7/16"-DIA. HOLE

1-1/2"   1"

75°

G   F

3"

2-1/4"

8-3/4"
(I.D.)

FORM

9-3/4" (O.D.)

3-1/4"

H

75°

H

52-1/2°

9-3/4"

H

CAULS

S

D

E

W

G

H

F

H

W

EDGE ROUTING TEMPLATE

W

Q

P   O   R

R

3/4" X 3"
ACCESS
NOTCHES

N

6-1/16"

K

O   Q

2"

2"

3/4"

79-1/16"

3-1/2"

J

9-3/4"

M

7/8"
SLOT

10-1/8"

R

8-3/8"

P

14-1/8"

L

K

2"

16"

**TEMPLATE
SUPPORTS**

TEMPLATES

N

K

L

J

A

V   M   K   L

MATERIALS LIST

Key	No.	Size and description (use)	Key	No.	Size and description (use)
A*	6	1/2×2 1/2×82 1/2" ash (slats)	P	1	1/2×4×12 1/2" plywood (template)
B	1	1 1/4×1 3/4×15" ash (nose cleat)	Q	1	1/2×3 1/2×14 1/8" plywood (template)
C	6	13/16×1 1/4×15" ash (cleat)	R	1	1/2×8 3/8×80 15/16" plywood (template)
D	1	3/4×20×96" plywood (form base)	S	11	3/4-in.-dia. ×3 1/2" hexhead bolt, washer and nut
E	5	3/4×3×20" plywood (base cleat)			
F**	1	3×9 3/4×9 3/4" spruce/fir (form)	T	12	1 1/4" No. 12 fh solid brass screw
G**	1	1 1/2×3×75 1/2" spruce/fir (form)	U	72	1" No. 12 fh solid brass screw
H**	3	3×3 1/4×9 3/4" spruce/fir (caul)	V	1	1 1/2" No. 10 fh screw
I**	1	1 1/2×3×76 1/2" spruce/fir (caul)	W		1 1/4" finishing nail
J**	2	1 1/2×3×3" spruce/fir (support)	X		18' length of 1/4"-dia. nylon rope
K**	2	1 1/2×2 1/2×3" spruce/fir (support)			
L**	1	1 1/2×3×13 1/8" spruce/fir (support)			
M**	1	1 1/2×3×12 1/2" spruce/fir (support)			
N**	1	1 1/2×3×79 9/16" spruce/fir (support)			
O	1	1/2×4×79 1/16" plywood (template)			

Misc.: Plastic resin glue (5- to 6-pounds required), 120- and 220-grit sandpaper.
*8 layers of 1/16×3×96" ash veneer.
** 2×4 stock.

Give the children some winter excitement with this toboggan. Construction details begin on page 29.

You can add the classic detailing to this mahogany dining room table from plans beginning on page 8.

This chest of drawers and desk combination is both beautiful and useful. Construction details for this Secret Secretary begin on page 13.

Plans begin on page 18 for this rollaway baking cart
with classic detailing that complements both traditional
and contemporary kitchens.

This oak duet features a stepstool and folding bookstand for your kitchen and study. Stepstool plans begin on page 23; bookstand on page 27.

Fluorescent fixture repair

Dismantling a fluorescent light fixture can be intimidating, because once you get past the tube, repair goes from the mechanical to the electrical in a hurry. Instead of the simple ON/OFF switch and familiar wire terminals characteristic of incandescent fixtures, what you'll find is an almost empty channel, a few meandering wires and the quintessential little black box. Somehow you expect more.

The fact is, fluorescent lamps are not much like incandescent lamps. To achieve the high efficiency and long life they've become noted for, they're more complex.

Even so, completely diagnosing and repairing a troublesome fluorescent fixture is well within the skills of the average do-it-yourselfer.

How Fluorescent Fixtures Work

Most of us have a fairly good idea of how an ordinary incandescent light bulb works. When you flip the switch to turn on the lamp you are closing an electrical circuit which sends current through a metal filament contained inside a glass bulb. The filament burns white-hot and becomes luminescent much in the same way that an electric range burner glows red when it's on. In short, the filament is the source of light. When something goes wrong, it's usually a break in the

circuit—a burned out filament or faulty switch. Fluorescent fixtures, on the other hand, rarely just quit working completely but show their ill health by flickering, producing less than normal light or hard starting.

A fluorescent tube glows because a mixture of mercury and argon gas, sealed inside, is charged with electricity. The charge is generated by a cathode filament at each end of the tube. When enough electrons are generated, the gas conducts an electrical arc through the tube. The charged mercury vapors radiate invisible ultraviolet light and a narrow band of the spectrum that is visible as a blue-green glow. This radiation falls on a fluorescent chemical coating on the inside surface of the glass tube which absorbs it and radiates light at a useful level and color.

The amount of electricity needed to keep the gas glowing is a lot less than to get it started. When you turn on a fluorescent fixture an initial voltage surge is sent across the filaments which charges the gas. Once current is established through the gas, the power is reduced to a normal operating level. Because the cathode filaments glow at full force only at startup,

The cathode filament charges the mercury gas. Fluorescent coating inside the tube changes the radiation to useful light.

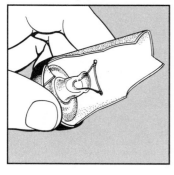

Blackened ends indicate tube should be replaced. Be sure the new tube matches the specs printed on the old tube's side.

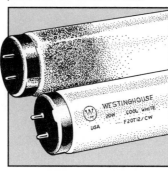

Round fluorescent tubes are only different in shape. The four pins correspond to the two found at ends of a straight tube.

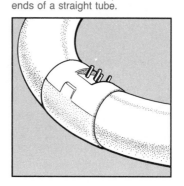

repeated switching on and off can actually be less efficient and cause the tubes to fail sooner than simply leaving the light on. In general, fluorescent lamps last years and burn five to six times more efficiently than incandescent bulbs of the same wattage.

Starters

Some fluorescent fixtures require a separate component to control the initial voltage surge to the filaments to begin current flow through the gas. This component is called a *starter*. If your fixture uses starters, you'll find one of these small cylindrical objects protruding from the lamp housing near each tube. When the filaments are hot enough to charge the gas, the starter switches off the high-voltage current. The charged gas then maintains the current flow at a reduced level. This two-step ignition explains the familiar hesitation of older lamps when they're first turned on.

Ballasts

The heart of every fluorescent fixture, old or new, is its *ballast* (that black box you were wondering about). A ballast is a kind of current-limiting transformer that serves two essential functions. When a fixture is turned on, its ballast provides a high flow of current to preheat the cathodes. Once gas conduction has taken place, the ballast reduces the current to a stable operating level.

Modern fixtures have ballasts designed to charge the tubes instantly without the need for starters. These are called *rapid-start* fixtures. While there are many different fluorescent fixture types in commercial use, virtually all fixtures used in residential lighting are of the pre-heat type with starters or rapid-start design. Both have tubes with 2-pin ends.

Where to Begin

If your fluorescent fixture is acting up, start by checking the tube. Most problems begin and end there. A tube will seldom go out abruptly, but will flutter and hesitate long before it fails completely. First, check the tube ends. A little gray discoloration is normal, but if the ends are black, the tube needs to be replaced.

To remove a defective tube, rotate it one-quarter turn and gently pull it down out of its holders. In the unlikely event your tubes have a single-pin configuration, push the tube in one direction against its spring-loaded holder and drop down the other end.

If the ends are not black, the tube may simply need to be reseated in its sockets or the pins may need to be cleaned. The constant vibration a house endures can cause a tube to slip, interrupting its contact with the socket. With the lamp switched on and the tube in place, try turning the tube slightly. If this doesn't work, remove the tube and inspect the ends. If you find dirt or corrosion on the pins, clean them and reinstall the tube. With fluorescent tubes you should look for little things. They can be temperamental. In some cases, you can get extra life out of a tube by simply removing it, turning it

Some units use starter switches. These have two contact pegs which lock into place when your press in and turn right.

Sockets mount on the channel with screws or by snapping in place. This design slides into a slot in channel cover.

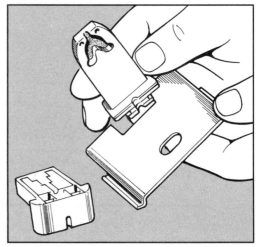

end for end, and putting it back. If nothing works, buy new tubes. As some fixtures are wired in series, you may have to replace both tubes, or two of four tubes within a fixture to correct the problem. If you'd like to ensure yourself several years of trouble-free operation, replace them all.

Starter Problems

Because starters fail about as often as tubes, many electricians replace them each time they replace a tube. Problems that signify starter trouble are continuous flickering and tubes that only glow at their ends. If you have a tube that's flickering all the time, try reseating the starter. Remove the tube, press in on the starter and turn it to the right to seat it properly.

If only the ends of a fluorescent tube light up, don't bother reseating the starter. Replace it. To remove a defective starter, press in and turn it to the left.

Defective Sockets and Ballasts

There is a limit to the amount of money you should invest in a fluorescent fixture. This limit becomes a factor when the lamp sockets and ballast appear defective. If you shop around, you'll find a new fixture can cost less than replacing the parts of an older fixture. Older fixtures, however, *can* be completely rebuilt. A classic old desk lamp, for example, can continue to offer years of service with an electrical overhaul.

Before you begin working with the wiring in the fixture, be sure the electricity is turned off at the master power panel in your home.

If you find that a lamp socket is broken or will no longer hold a tube against its contact, go ahead and replace it. When doing so, make sure the components you buy match the design and voltage rating of the originals. When in doubt, take the part with you for comparison.

To remove a defective socket, shut off the power and look for two mounting screws at the base of the socket. These screws are visible on some models but are concealed by a cover plate on others. Remove these screws to reveal the wire terminals on the socket. Disconnect the wires, fasten them to the replacement socket, and reinstall.

Some models have push-in wire connections. In this case, the wires will likely enter the front or back of the socket. To release each wire, slide a small screwdriver into the release slot next to the wire. Then, slide the stripped ends of the loose wires into the new socket connectors.

Replacing a Ballast

A defective ballast is signaled by a buzzing sound, sharp asphalt odor, tubes that glow only at their ends, or a black oily substance dripping from the fixture. When shopping for a new ballast, make sure you buy one with the same voltage rating and design characteristics as the original. Each fixture brand will have its own specific wiring diagram and installation procedures. Follow them carefully.

Many sockets have push-in terminals. To release a wire, push a small screwdriver into the release slot next to the wire.

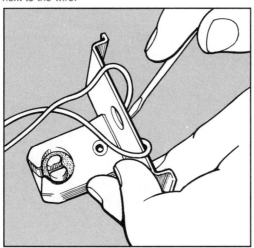

When installing a socket mounted to a snap-in plate, slip one tab into its slot and spread the channel for the other tab.

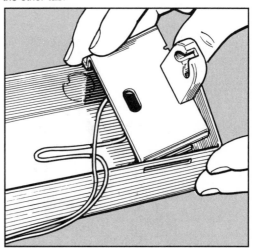

In general, the ballast is fastened to the channel by two or more sheetmetal screws. You'll find up to eight color-coded wires disappearing under the ballast cover. Two of these, the black and white wires, should be attached to the corresponding black and white wires of the house circuit with wire nuts. The ground wire from the house circuit is generally screwed directly to the metal channel with a sheetmetal screw. The remaining wires attach to the lamp sockets.

Start by undoing these wires from their sockets, taking care to note the position of each wire. It's a good idea to make a color-coded map of the wire connections so you have a reference when you're reassembling the unit. Then, undo the mounting screws and remove the ballast. Screw the new ballast in place and connect the new wires, keeping in mind the original wire connections and paying close attention to the wiring diagram supplied with the replacement ballast.

The socket shown here contains the seat for starter. When replacing this type, make sure you get an exact matching part.

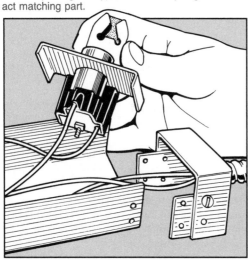

Ballast is held in place by two mounting screws and nuts. It's a good idea to make a wiring diagram before removing ballast.

Attach black and white wires from ballast to the corresponding house circuit wires. Ground wire is screwed to channel.

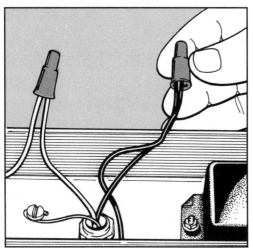

This desk lamp is a preheat model, but it has no starter. It's turned on by holding the switch down until the light pops on.

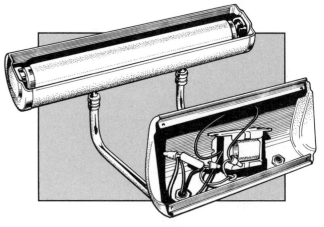

Incandescent lamp repair

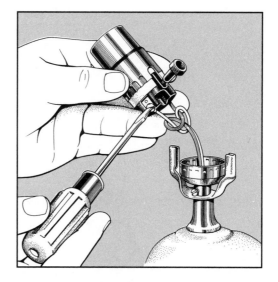

Incandescent lamps are basically all alike. Aside from stylistic differences, every lamp incudes the same electrical components—a plug, cord, socket and switch. These are the only components that can wear out in a lamp and each is a quick fix. If you have a lamp that has kept you in the dark too long, take heart in knowing that you can replace every part in it for around $10.

Troubleshooting a Lamp

When trying to locate a defective component, don't overlook the obvious. Always check the light bulb first. If you are satisfied that the bulb is not the problem, then go on to the plug.

If the plug is a screw-terminal type with a cardboard face plate, pry the face off and look for loose wires. Also check for frayed insulation or any apparent break or split in the cord.

If the plug and cord seem undamaged, look to the socket and switch. Sockets and switches either work or don't work. There isn't much in between. If your lamp has a line switch attached to the cord, you can replace it without touching the socket. Most lamp switches, however, are contained in sockets. Short of using a voltage tester to investigate further, you should probably just replace the socket and switch and be done with it.

The harp supports the lamp shade and is joined to socket cap with two small ferrules. To free the harp, lift up the ferrules.

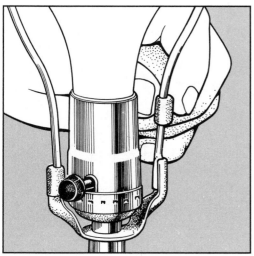

To remove the harp, squeeze the sides together and lift off the base. If harp is stuck, pliers may be required to free it.

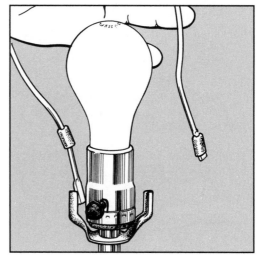

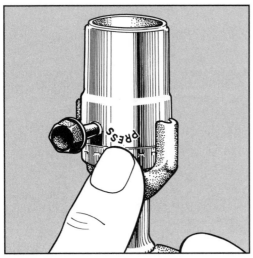

To remove socket, press and pull up where you see the word **PRESS** on socket shell. If stuck, pry up with small screwdriver.

Dismantling a Lamp for Repair

Taking a lamp apart is not difficult. It's a simple progression from shade to plug. The amount of dismantling you do will depend on how much repair your lamp needs.

Be sure the lamp is unplugged from the wall before starting any repair work. Start by undoing the lamp shade. Simply loosen the threaded cap, called a *finial*, and lift the shade up and off. Next, remove the bridged wire support, called a *harp*, by sliding upward the two metal ferrules on the harp bracket. Squeeze and lift the two halves of the harp until they come free. You will then be able to remove the socket.

Each socket has four elements—an outer shell, insulating sleeve, socket and socket cap. To separate the outer shell from the cap, press in and pry up where you see PRESS stamped into the metal shell. If you can't free the shell with your fingers, use a small screwdriver to pry it off. By removing the outer shell, you expose the insulating sleeve, socket and electrical terminals.

With the shell and sleeve removed, pull an inch or two of cable through the socket cap. Loosen the terminal screws on the socket and pull off the wires. Then use a small screwdriver to loosen the setscrew on the socket cap. Undo the Underwriter's knot in the cord and slide the cap off the wire. At this point, you will be ready to rebuild your lamp.

Replacing Plugs and Cords

Older cords with fabric covers should be replaced as a matter of course. Their rubber insulation and silk inner sleeves become hazardous with age. Zip cord is now the only cord approved for lamps by the NEC (National Electrical Code). Zip cord is stranded copper wire molded into a flexible plastic insulation that offers long-term protection. The plastic insulation may be colored or clear and is ribbed on one wire and smooth on the other. The wire on the ribbed side is the neutral wire—the other is the hot wire.

To expose the terminal screws, slide up the socket shell and insulating sleeve. Loosen terminal screws and pull off wires.

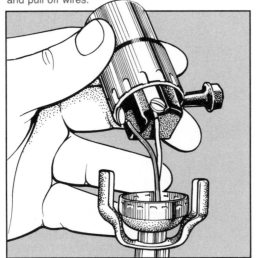

To remove socket cap, loosen setscrew and turn cap off threaded tube. Harp bracket and spacer will come off too.

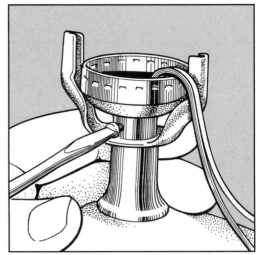

If your lamp cord was previously too short, now is the time to make it longer—simply buy the length you prefer. To avoid having to negotiate your new cord through the base and the threaded tube, tape your new cord to the old cord at the top of the lamp and pull them both through the lamp base. Once through, tie an Underwriter's knot in the socket end of the cord (see drawing) and install a plug on the other end.

The self-piercing plugs made for zip cord are literally a snap to use. They come in two pieces: a plastic body and a pronged insert. All you do is slide one end of the zip cord through the body and insert the unstripped cord into the prong slot. Make sure the wire by the smooth insulation (hot wire) goes to the smaller prong, and squeeze the prongs together. Then push the prongs into the plug body until they snap into place. A small spike on each prong pierces the insulation and makes contact with the stranded wire. Be sure you buy a plug for the size wire you using it with; a plug for 18 gauge wire will not work with the larger, heavy-duty 14-gauge zip cord.

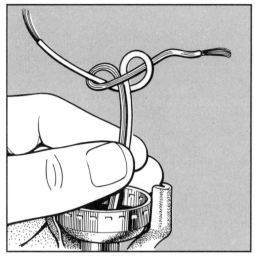

To prevent wire from coming off screws if cord is pulled, tie Underwriter's knot in end before attaching to terminal screws.

Replacing a Lamp Socket

To replace a lamp socket, start by pulling apart the two wires in the cord. You will need about 2 in. of separated wire. Strip ⅝ in. of insulation from each wire. Slide the old harp bracket and new socket cap over the cord and tie the wires in an Underwriter's knot. Then fasten the socket cap to the threaded tube with the setscrew.

Next, tighten the hot wire around the brass screw and the neutral around the silver screw. Slide the insulating sleeve and outer shell over the socket and snap the outer shell in place. Finally, replace the harp, shade, finial and bulb.

To install in-line switch, cut the positive wire on the smooth side and press it into place. Then screw switch sides together.

To install new plug, feed wire into plug body and slide end into pronged section. Squeeze prongs and snap into body.

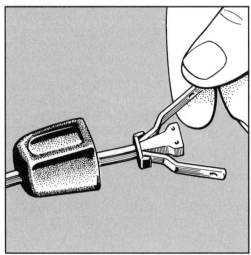

Newer switches and receptacles bear rating stamps indicating types of wire they accept. Switch shown is rated for copper and copper-clad aluminum, not solid aluminum.

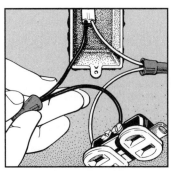

To adapt an ungrounded, end-of-circuit receptacle, splice new copper pigtails between terminal screws and aluminum wires. Use paste-filled wire nuts on wire ends.

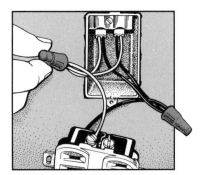

To adapt an ungrounded, middle-of-circuit receptacle, splice the new copper pigtails between each pair of like-colored wires and their proper terminal screws.

Aluminum house wiring hazards

If your home is between 15 and 40 years old, you may be living with a fire hazard buried in your walls: aluminum wiring. It was used widely after World War II because it was inexpensive and copper supplies were inadequate. The shortcomings of aluminum weren't fully realized until the mid-1970s, after hundreds of thousands of homes were already wired improperly.

The trouble with aluminum is that it's not as good a conductor as copper. As a result, it expands more than copper when carrying a charge and contracts more than copper when not carrying a charge. This doesn't harm the wire itself, but eventually it can loosen terminal screws on receptacles, switches and some light fixtures. These loose connections cause increased resistance which in turn creates heat and sometimes sparks which can start fires.

Another problem with aluminum wire is oxidation. When dissimilar metals are joined—for example, when aluminum touches brass screws or copper wires—electrolysis results. This corrodes the connection, further increasing resist-

ance. To correct the oxidation problem, electrical manufacturers started making copper-clad aluminum wire. This improvement, however, did little for the expansion-contraction problem. Finally, the industry responded by making switches and receptacles rated to accept aluminum and copper-clad wire as well as the traditional copper wire.

Because these newer devices are readily available, you can upgrade your aluminum wiring by simply replacing your old ones with new ones. Unfortunately, this is a relatively expensive undertaking. Your better choice is to splice new insulated copper pigtails between your aluminum or copper-clad wiring and the switch, receptacle or light fixture terminal screws. To avoid corrosion where the copper and aluminum meet, just pack each wire nut with anti-oxidation paste.

Identifying Dangerous Connections

The first thing to do is to investigate your present situation. Shut off the power to a specific circuit at your fuse box or breaker panel. Then remove the cover plate from a receptacle and inspect the metal yoke that is screwed to the wall box. This yoke should have a wire rating stamped into its surface. If you see the letters CU-AL (copper-aluminum), this means the receptacle is designed for both copper and aluminum wire so it doesn't make any difference what type of wire was used in your home. If you see CU and CU-CLAD, this means the unit is rated only for copper or copper-clad wire.

If, however, no designation appears, then the receptacle is appropriate only for solid copper wire. To find out what wire you have, pull out

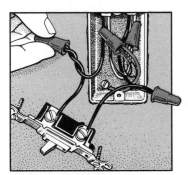

Because only the black (hot) wires are attached to a normal switch, add the pigtails only to the black wires. The other connections in the box remain the same.

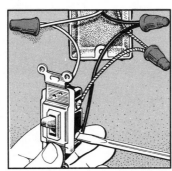

Three-way switches have three different colored wires. To avoid error, adapt only one wire at a time, making sure in each case that the pigtail goes to the original screw.

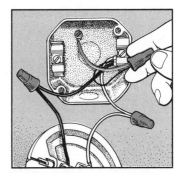

Most light fixtures have copper pigtails in place; simple porcelain ones don't. Add pigtails to the terminal screws and between the bare ground wire and metal box.

the receptacle and inspect the wire ends. If you see aluminum-colored wire or aluminum-colored wire encased in a copper jacket, the receptacle must be upgraded with copper pigtails.

The way you install the pigtails depends on what type of electrical cable is coming into the metal fixture boxes inside your walls. The drawings here show two different cables you're likely to encounter. The first is 2-wire cable without ground, which means just a black (hot) wire and a white (neutral) wire. The second type is 2-wire with ground which has the same black and white wires but also has a bare ground wire.

Making Conversions

To make the conversion, begin by shutting off the power to one circuit at the main service panel. Remove the cover plate and receptacle from the outlet box and disconnect the wires. Be sure to note which side of the receptacle was attached to the black wire and which was attached to the white wire. Then cut 6-in. lengths of insulated cable that are the same gauge as the wiring used in your house. Usually this will be 12 gauge, though some circuits are still wired with 14-gauge cable.

Strip about ⅝ in. of insulation off both ends of the black and white pigtails. Then attach these pigtails to the terminal screws on the receptacle, making sure you follow the same color code the receptacle had before. When in doubt, remember that the black (hot) wire should always go to the brass-colored terminal screws.

With the receptacle ends attached, pack appropriately-sized wire nuts with anti-oxidation paste and join the new copper pigtails to the ends of the existing aluminum wires, keeping the colors consistent: black-to-black and white-to-white. Make sure the wire nuts are turned down firmly on both wires. If there is a bare aluminum ground wire inside the box, just join a copper pigtail to this wire and then attach the other end of the pigtail to the back of the box.

If there are two cables coming into the box, two white and two black wires, the retrofit is the same idea, except you'll have to use larger wire nuts that can accommodate two aluminum wires and the pigtail at the same time.

When upgrading switches, remember that the switch unit is wired only between the black (hot) wires. The white wires should already be joined together in the box. Leave the white wires undisturbed and simply add the pigtails between the ends of the black wires and the terminal screws on the switch.

If you are adapting 3- or 4-way switches, you may find a red wire or a white wire with black tape on it inside the box. This coding is a matter of expedience to electricians, but it looks like a can of worms to just about everyone else. To keep from making a mistake, adapt only one wire at a time.

All but the simplest light fixtures—the inexpensive porcelain utility lights—come with copper-stranded leads that are attached to the circuit wire with wire nuts.

All that's required to adapt these fixtures is to simply remove the existing wire nuts, fill the nuts with anti-oxidation paste and reinstall them.

One last note: Not all circuit breaker or fuse connections are a problem with aluminum wire. It depends on how the individual service panel was designed and outfitted.

Bathroom ventilator installation

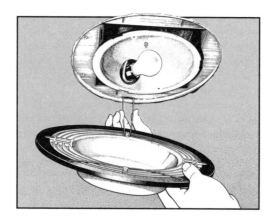

An effective way to end moisture problems in any bathroom—with or without a window—is to install a ventilator unit. A ventilator is simply a ceiling-mounted exhaust fan that draws out moist, stale room air and vents it through a duct to the outdoors. If your bathroom is located on the top floor, it is easiest to vent the unit through the roof. For bathrooms situated below another floor, you'll need to vent through the house wall. Both types of installations are shown here.

Ventilators are available in a wide variety of styles and sizes to suit your needs and decor. They're sold at home centers and kitchen and bath showrooms. Some units have a light with the exhaust fan.

What Kind of Unit?

Ventilators are rated according to the cubic feet of air they exhaust per minute (cfm) and by their operating nose level, which is measured in *sones*.

To determine the volume of your bathroom, multiply: length×width×height. An 8×10-ft. room with an 8-ft.-high ceiling contains 640 cubic feet. Therefore, a 100-cfm ventilator will exchange the room air in about 6½ minutes and more than nine times an hour. When selecting your ventilator, keep in mind that the minimum recommendation air exchange rate for bathrooms is eight exchanges per hour. Also, some ventilators can be placed directly over a tub or shower stall. For this type of installation, though, you *must* use a ground-fault circuit-interrupter (GFCI) as an added safety precaution against electrical shock.

In addition to the ventilator, you'll also need a length of round duct, either flexible or metal, a vent cap for mounting to the roof or sidewall, and, if any rewiring is necessary, some nonmetallic sheathed electrical cable.

Installation Procedures

The installation shown is the most common and the easiest: replacing an existing ceiling-mounted light fixture with a fan-light ventilator. For other installations, you'll have to tap into a nearby circuit and run an electrical cable to the ventilator's location.

Begin by shutting off the power to the fixture at the fuse box or circuit breaker panel. Remove the light fixture to expose the electrical box. Next, use an electrical circuit tester to check that power to the circuit is indeed off. Place one

1 Hold probe of tester on hot lead (black wire) and touch other probe to metal box. Power is off if tester light doesn't light up.

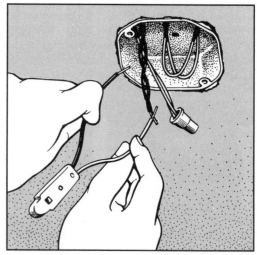

probe of the tester on the hot lead (black wires) and hold the other probe to the metal box. Just to be safe, check the other lead too.

When the tester verifies that the power is off, then it's safe to proceed. The box will be wired either at the end of the electrical run or, more likely, in the middle of a circuit. In either case, remove the existing electrical box. All the electrical connections will be made later in the junction box on the ventilator unit itself.

Notice that the box on the ventilator is usually positioned off to one side—it isn't mounted in the center of the unit. Therefore, it's important to position the ventilator so that its box is closest to the wires in the ceiling. Otherwise, the wires may not reach into the box and it would be impossible to make the necessary connections.

Next, hold the ventilator upside down against the ceiling and trace around its housing with a pencil. Using the pencil line as a guide, cut out the ceiling with a compass saw or utility knife.

Notice in the drawing that the hole from the old electrical box is located off-center, near the edge of the cutout. This will position the electrical box on the ventilator nearest to the existing wires.

Nail or screw wood blocks to the joists to provide solid support for mounting the ventilator. You may need to double-up the blocks in order to center the ventilator in the ceiling cutout. Test-fit the ventilator in the cutout to be sure that it sits flush with the finished ceiling.

Roof-Mounted Vent

From inside the attic, mark the desired vent-cap location on the roof between two rafters. Choose a spot near the ventilator to avoid a long duct-run with lots of bends. The straighter the duct-run is, the more efficiently the ventilator will work. Bore a ⅜-in.-dia. hole through the roof to establish the center of the vent cap. Push a brightly colored wire through the hole to make it easy to spot from outside.

Working now from the outside, use the ⅜-in.-dia. center hole as a reference point to lay out and cut the vent-cap hole. Make the cutout in the roof with a saber saw or compass saw.

Carefully pull out the nails from the shingles directly above the cutout. Then, slide the vent cap into place so that its flashing is *under* the upper course of shingles and *over* the lower course. Trim the shingles, if necessary, to cover the maximum amount of flashing. Remove the vent cap and spread roofing cement on the underside of the flashing.

Wall-Mounted Vent

When it isn't possible to vent through the roof, you'll have to run the duct above the ceiling and vent it out the side of the house.

Start by peeking up into the ceiling cutout to determine which direction the joists run. The duct will run between the joists and out the wall. It's easiest to vent out the nearest wall.

In the best of situations, you'll be able to reach the header from the ventilator cutout in the ceiling. But more likely, the wall will be too far away to reach. In this case, it's necessary to cut an access hole in the ceiling where it meets the wall to expose the header. Measure about 12 in. from the wall and cut out a section of the ceiling from the *center* of one joist to the *center* of the next. If you remove the ceiling section carefully, it can be replaced and patched later.

With the access hole cut, bore a ⅜-in.-dia. pilot hole through the header, sheathing and

2 Hold ventilator housing upside down against the ceiling and trace around its flange with a pencil to mark the cutout.

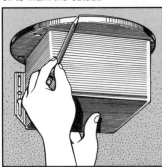

3 Cut away ceiling with a utility knife. Off-center cutout positions electrical box on ventilator nearest to the power cable.

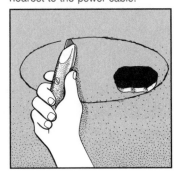

4 Nail wood-block supports to joists for mounting the ventilator. If possible, work from above in the attic or crawl space.

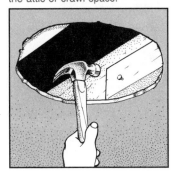

siding. Then, move outside and, using the pilot hole as a guide, lay out the wall vent-cap hole.

Cut the vent-cap hole with a saber saw. Slide the vent cap into the hole and hold it against the siding. Scribe a pencil line around the cap's flange onto the siding.

Pull the vent cap away, apply caulk inside the lines, and slide the cap back in place. Secure the vent cap by screwing through its flange with aluminum or stainless-steel panhead wood screws.

From the inside, slip the stabilizer ring over the vent-cap pipe and nail it to the header joist with 1-in. roofing nails. Attach the duct end to the vent-cap pipe with duct tape. Then, feed the duct between the joists until the free end has reached the ceiling cutout for the ventilator.

Wiring Procedures

The easiest way to make the electrical connections is from above in an attic. You can also fish the wires through the ventilator's box and make the connections from below if you are working on the first floor.

Attach a cable connector to the electrical cable. Be sure that the threaded, male portion of the connector is facing toward the end of the cable. Secure a 12-in. length of scrap wire to the cable end. This scrap-wire leader makes it easy to fish the cable into the box from below. Next, remove a circular knock-out plug from the side of the box. While holding the ventilator near the ceiling, make the final connections to attach the duct to the housing. Secure the joint with duct tape. Fish the scrap-wire leader through the knock-out hole. Pull the leader and cable into the box from below as you push the ventilator up into the ceiling. Fasten the ventilator to the ceiling with 1-in. No.6 panhead screws. Slip the locknut of the cable connector over the end of the leader wire and cable and thread it onto the connector. Tighten the nut to secure the connec-

5 Bore a ⅜-in.-dia. pilot hole through the roof, between two rafters, to establish the center of the roof-mounted vent cap.

6 After sawing the vent-cap hole, apply roof cement to cap's bottom surface and slide it under the upper shingles.

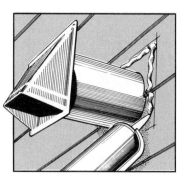

7 Fasten vent cap with roofing nails fitted with rubber washers. Nail through flashing and apply roof cement to nailheads.

8 To install a wall-mounted vent cap, first cut away the ceiling and bore a pilot hole through the header to the outside.

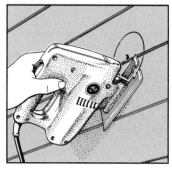

9 Using the pilot hole as a guide, cut out the vent-cap hole with a saber saw. Most vent caps accept 3-in. or 4-in.-dia. duct.

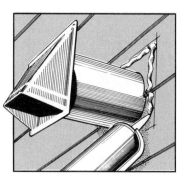

10 Hold vent cap against siding and mark its outline. Then, apply caulk inside the lines around the vent-cap cutout.

tor and cable to the box. Cable connectors are required by code. Check your local electrical code for other requirements. Now remove the scrap-wire leader from the cable end.

The ventilator is wired with two separate sets of leads so that the light and exhaust fan can be controlled by separate switches.

To operate them individually, you'll need to run a separate switch leg to the ventilator to handle the second switch. To operate the light and fan with one switch, simply connect the black wires in the housing to the black, hot lead of the cable. Then connect the white wires to the white, neutral cable lead. Secure the connections with wire nuts. Fasten the ground lead to the grounding screw in the box.

Installing the Fixture

With the wiring completed and the housing secured to the ceiling, the next step is to install the light fixture and the fan assembly. The

housing's two receptacles provide easy, plug-in installation.

Install the fan by inserting its two tabs into the housing and securing it with a single sheetmetal screw. Plug the fan into the receptacle. Next, plug the light fixture into the remaining receptacle and fasten it to the fan assembly with a wingnut. Although this is a typical installation, be sure to read the detailed instructions that come with your particular ventilator before starting the installation.

Install the grille and lens assembly. The assembly attaches to the housing with two spring-wire clips. Squeeze the clips together and insert them into slots cut in the housing. This system makes it easy to lower the lens to change the light bulb.

Install a light bulb and push the grille up to the ceiling to be sure that the clips hold it securely. Finally, turn on the power and flip the wall switch.

11 Push the vent cap tight against siding and fasten with panhead wood screws. Cut off any caulking that squeezes out.

12 Slip the stabilizer ring over the vent-cap pipe from the inside. Attach the ring to the header with 1-in. roofing nails.

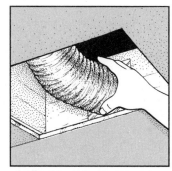

13 Attach the duct to vent-cap pipe with duct tape or use a nylon cable tie. Use flexible duct or round metal duct.

14 After making electrical and duct connections, fasten the ventilator's housing to the wood-block supports with screws.

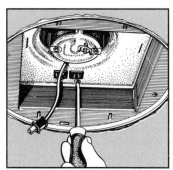

15 Install the exhaust fan in the housing and secure it with a sheetmetal screw. Plug the fan into the receptacle.

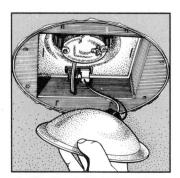

16 Plug the light fixture into the remaining receptacle and fasten it to the fan assembly with the wingnut provided.

Testing appliances with an ohmmeter

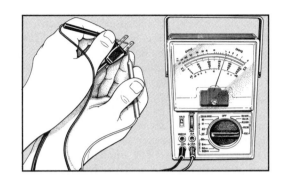

Here's how you can test and troubleshoot electrical appliances like a pro—safely and easily—using an ohmmeter. An ohmmeter can test virtually every electrical component in any appliance—small and major. This includes all power cords, switches, solenoids, relays, timers, thermostats and heating elements, to name just a few. By simply placing the meter's probes on the component's wires or terminals, you can determine quickly and safely if the part is defective.

Some of the typical tests that you can do include checking the water-level switch on a clothes washer, testing the thermostat of a refrigerator or freezer, and checking the heating element of a clothes dryer, electric range or oven. The owner's manual that comes with each meter provides more specific examples and instructions. If you're concerned about receiving an electrical shock, don't be. When using an ohmmeter, you *must* unplug the appliance from the electrical outlet during testing.

An ohmmeter can perform three vital electrical tests. One is for continuity to determine if a continuous, unbroken circuit exists. Another test measures the resistance to the flow of current. Every electrical component has a specified amount of resistance that is measured in ohms. Testing tells you if the component meets the requirements set for it. Ohmmeters can also test for short circuits.

What Kind of Meter?

The instrument shown in the drawing is a multitester known as a volt-ohm-milliammeter (VOM). Most people prefer a VOM over a straight ohmmeter because it expands their testing capabilities. A VOM can test for continuity and measure resistance (ohms), current (milliamps) and voltage. Regardless of whether you use a straight ohmmeter or a VOM, the continuity and resistance tests described here are performed the same way. Note, however, that the ohm scale on a VOM reads from right to left. At the highest end of the scale is the symbol for infinity (∞).

When the needle points to infinity, the meter isn't capable of measuring the resistance of the tested part. The circuit has infinite resistance to the flow of electricity. Therefore, an open circuit (lack of continuity) exists and you need a new part. When testing for continuity, you aren't seeking an exact numerical value. A circuit is either open or it isn't. If it's open, the needle will point to infinity. If the circuit isn't open, the needle will point to some value.

A VOM is powered by one or more batteries. Keep the batteries fresh to ensure accurate readings.

Meter Adjustments

The two holes, or jacks, in the face of the meter accept the test leads. Be sure to insert the red lead in the positive (+) jack and the black lead in the negative (−) jack. The ends of the leads have either metal probes, as shown, or alligator clips.

Before using a VOM or ohmmeter, you must adjust it to get accurate readings. First, *remove* the leads from the jacks and stand the meter upright on a flat, level surface. Insert a small-bladed screwdriver or knife into the pivot point of the needle and turn it slowly until the needle rests exactly on the infinity mark.

Insert the leads into the jacks and tie together the probes using a rubber band. Use the ohms adjustment control knob to set the needle to zero. Turn the knob until the needle rests on zero. If you can't get on zero exactly, the batteries may be weak—replace them.

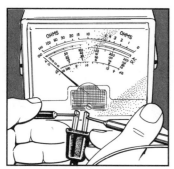

When needle points to infinity symbol, there may be a lack of continuity. Note the ohm scale reads right to left.

With the test leads removed from the jacks, use a small-bladed screwdriver or knife to set needle exactly on the infinity symbol.

Insert leads and tie together the probes with a rubber band. Adjust the needle exactly to zero with OHMS ADJ knob.

Checking Circuits

Most meters have a range-selector switch with three RX positions—RX1, RX10 and RX100. Some meters also have RX1000 (often designated RX1k) and RX10,000 (RX10k) settings for reading greater resistance values.

To determine the resistance of a circuit or component, simply multiply the RX value by the number that the needle points to. For example, if the range-selector is set on RX1 and the needle points to 50, the circuit has a resistance of 50 ohms. If the range-selector was set at RX10, the circuit has a resistance of 500 ohms.

When testing for continuity, start with the range-selector set at RX1. If the needle points to infinity, switch the selector to RX10 and then RX100. If the needle doesn't move off the infinity mark, an open circuit exists.

Often when checking the resistance value (ohms) with the meter set at RX1, you'll get a reading on the high end of the scale. Since the high end isn't calibrated very precisely, switch the selector to RX10 and bring the needle into the lower, more precisely calibrated end of the scale.

Exact Resistance

The exact resistance values of the parts of an appliance are printed on a wiring diagram that is glued to the appliance. Appliance manufacturers can also provide resistance values of specific parts. Another alternative is to check the resistance values listed in appliance repair books. The reading that you get doesn't have to equal exactly what's listed in the book. For example, a repair book lists the resistance value of an electric range cooking element at 50 ohms. If you get a reading of 45 ohms that's close enough. A much lower reading of 10 ohms would indicate that a short exists in the element. When a short exists, the meter will display a low value—the short is giving the electrical current a path around the resistance of the element.

When testing a circuit, don't hold the probes by the metal ends. There is some resistance through your body that will show up on the meter, giving you a false reading. When testing for continuity or resistance, it's important that the appliance's switch be turned on (even though the appliance is *not* plugged into an electrical outlet).

To test resistance value (ohms) of an electric range cooking element, place one probe on each prong of plug-in element.

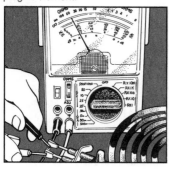

With both switches off, the meter shown here points to infinity indicating an open circuit: an erroneous diagnosis.

For a correct reading, the switches must be on. If an open circuit still is shown, then test the internal components.

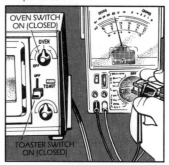

Telephone repair

In these days of planned obsolescence, it's nice to know that some things are built to last. Long before the introduction of the now-popular electronic telephone, the telephone company had installed millions of model 500 (rotary dial) and model 2500 (Touch-Tone) desktop phones. Both phone models have an estimated life span of 25 years, but most have lasted years beyond that. The best thing about these old, reliable telephones is that you can often fix them yourself —something that's almost impossible with an electronic phone.

The repairs for a rotary-dial or push-button phone are basically the same. Just don't be intimidated by the tangle of wires inside the phone. Besides, the wires are seldom the problem in a faulty phone.

Preliminary Checks

Before you start to fix a phone, be sure that it's the *phone* that needs fixing. The problem could also be caused by the phone wiring inside the house walls, in the wall jacks, the wiring outside the house, or the equipment that's located at the telephone company's central office.

Caution: Disconnect the phone's line cord from the wall jack before starting any repairs. If the cord is plugged in and the phone rings as you're working on it, you can get a severe electrical shock. The voltage developed when a telephone rings is approximately 60 to 90 volts.

How's That?

One of the most common problems with older phones is reception quality. Voices may sound muffled or distant. First, unscrew the earpiece cover from the handset and lift out the receiver. The receiver is attached to the handset with two wires. Tighten the screws that hold the wires to the receiver. Loose wires will cause bad reception. If that doesn't help, then loosen the screws to free the two wires from the receiver. Use a piece of very fine emery cloth or sandpaper to clean the Y-shaped wire terminals and the contacts on the back of the receiver. Now tap the receiver gently on a hard surface to loosen the carbon granules that are inside.

Carbon was used as a medium through which receiving is accomplished. Over the years, the carbon granules may have become compacted. For good reception, the granules must be loose. Hold the receiver near your ear and shake it. You should hear the granules rattling around. Newer electronic phones don't use carbon granule receivers.

Replace the wires to the receiver, place the receiver back in the handset and replace the earpiece cover. Now call someone and test the phone. If reception isn't improved, there are two more steps to take: servicing switch-hook contacts and replacing faulty parts.

Checking Contacts

The switch-hook contact assembly consists of a series of make-and-break points. The contacts are located inside the phone and are protected by a transparent plastic dust cover.

To expose these components inside the phone, turn it upside down and loosen the two screws holding the metal base to the plastic phone housing. The screws may be captive, meaning that they can be loosened but not removed (and possibly lost). The switch-hook contacts are located behind the dial, in front of the switch-hook (see drawing). To work on the contacts, remove the dial by loosening the screw on each side and pull it to one side. Then remove the clear plastic dust cover that protects the switch-hook contacts.

Using a screwdriver, press the tab on top of the cover while squeezing its sides. Lift up to free the cover. Then, use an ear syringe or compressed air to blow out dust and dirt from between the contacts.

Press down the switch-hook and release it slowly to open and close the contacts. If the contacts stick together, then further cleaning is necessary.

Replacement Part Remedies

Bad reception can also be caused by faulty cords. Modular cords—the kind you can unplug—are easy to test. Simply unplug the cords from the handset, phone and wall jack and connect them to another phone.

If that phone's reception is clear, then the cords are okay. Buy a new receiver for the problem phone, replace the cords and test the phone.

Telephone replacement parts are available at electronic chain stores and phone centers. Take the old part to the store so the salesperson can cross-check part numbers to ensure that you get the right replacement part.

Older phones have cords that are wired directly into the phone and handset. Don't try to remove these cords. Instead, install a new receiver. If this doesn't help, and you've already checked the switch-hook contacts, then the phone is beyond repair.

Weak Transmission

Do people have difficulty hearing you over the phone? Then the problem may be with the transmitting end of the handset. Unscrew the mouthpiece cover and remove the transmitter.

Unlike the receiver, there are no wires attached to the transmitter.

Inside the handset are two metal contacts. Clean the contacts and the metal surface on the back of the transmitter piece with fine emery cloth or sandpaper. Then, bend the contacts slightly to ensure that they touch the transmitter. Now tap the transmitter gently on a hard surface to loosen the carbon granules inside.

Replace the transmitter and mouthpiece in the phone. If transmission quality isn't improved, then clean the switch-hook contacts, test the cords and finally, if all else fails, replace the transmitter.

More Quick Fixes

In addition to reception and transmission problems, there are other troubles that can strike model 500 and 2500 telephones. The good news is that in most cases you can make the repairs yourself.

Here's a rundown of some of the most common problems and reliable remedies.

Constant Dial Tone. You pick up the handset, dial a number and get only a dial tone. Now what?

Disconnect the line cord from the wall jack and remove the phone's housing to expose its interior. Next, examine the network—the panel to which the tangle of interior wires are connected. Depending on the phone, the wires will be connected with either push-on/pull-off spade connectors or screws.

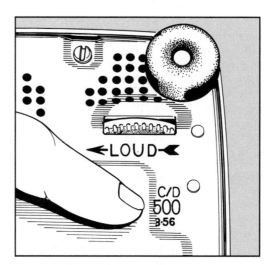

Phone's model number and date it was built are printed on the bottom plate. Note ringer's volume control knob.

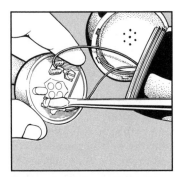

The receiver is located behind the earpiece cover. Be sure the wires leading to the receiver are fastened securely.

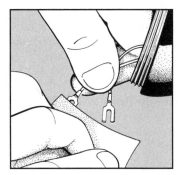

Use very fine emery cloth or sandpaper to clean Y-shaped terminals of receiver. Clean back surface of the receiver, too.

If the carbon granules inside the receiver are compacted, tap it gently against a hard surface to loosen them.

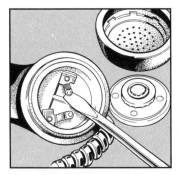

Unscrew mouthpiece and remove transmitter. Then, bend up the contacts slightly to ensure good contact with transmitter.

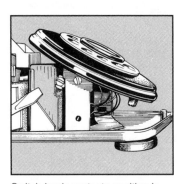

Switch-hook contacts position is shown here. The contacts are protected under a plastic dust cover.

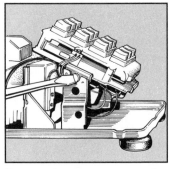

To get at the contacts, remove the push-button panel or rotary dial by loosening the screws on each side.

To test spade connectors, push down on each wire to make sure it is attached securely on the network. If the wires are fastened with screws, simply tighten each screw. Now test the phone.

If you still can't break the dial tone, switch the positions of the red and green wires on the network. This will reverse the polarity.

Be sure to switch the red and green wires of the line cord—the cord that connects to the wall jack. If this doesn't help, put the wires back in their original positions and clean the switch-hook contacts.

Irregular Dial Tone. Another annoying problem results in an on-again/off-again dial tone. Sometimes the phone works fine. Other times it's dead—no dial tone.

Replace the line cord with a cord from a phone that's known to work properly. If the substitute cord solves the problem, then buy a new line cord for your phone. If not, service the switch-hook contacts.

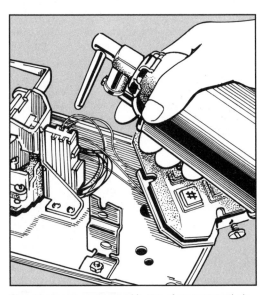

Clean between contacts with can of compressed air. Blow out all dirt and dust to prevent the contacts from sticking together.

Spade connectors are used on this phone to attach wires to the network. Push down on connectors to secure wires.

Four wires connect line cord to network. Reverse positions of red and green wires to help break constant dial tone.

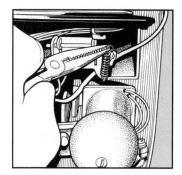

Use needle-nose pliers to connect the switch-hook spring to the arms of the switch-hook. This should restore dial tone.

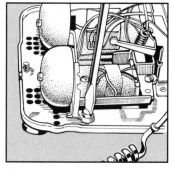

If phone doesn't ring, you may need to replace the ringer assembly. Loosen screw on each side of ringer to remove.

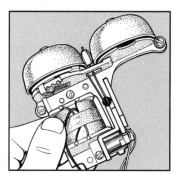

Ringer assembly consists of two bells, a clapper, spring and coil. Mark wire positions before disconnecting the assembly.

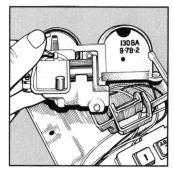

The model number is printed on the back of ringer assembly. Use this number to buy correct replacement part.

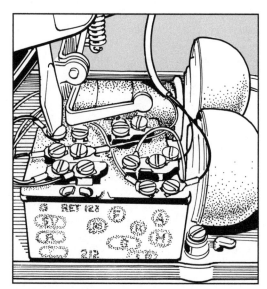

Tighten all screws on network to prevent trouble caused by loose wires. Clean away all dust and dirt that has accumulated.

No Dial Tone. When the phone appears dead—no dial tone at all—check the line cord. Be sure it's connected securely to the phone and wall jack. Try substituting another line cord.

If the line cord isn't at fault, then check the switch-hook spring. Be certain that the spring is connected to the upper and lower arms of the switch hook. Clean the switch-hook contacts.

If these repairs don't restore the dial tone, then the problem is probably a defective network. Since a network can't be replaced, the telephone must be scrapped.

No Connection. Let's say that you dial a number and the phone on the other end rings. But, when the party picks up, no connection is made and you hear a dial tone. As with so many other phone troubles, this one is caused by dirty switch-hook contacts.

If cleaning the contacts doesn't help, then check with the telephone company. A fouled circuit at their central office can also prevent the connection from being completed.

Doorbell repairs

If your doorbell has had the life rung out of it, don't despair. Defective doorbells are easy and inexpensive to fix. Since a doorbell system operates on low-voltage current, there's little of the danger normally associated with regular household electrical work.

Doorbells also have few components, which makes problem diagnosis quick and easy. Every doorbell system is made up of a button, transformer and bell, buzzer or chime mechanism. Aside from a possible break in the wiring, a problem with your doorbell will eventually be traced to the faulty operation of one of these components.

Start with the Button

Because the button gets the most physical abuse and is located on the exterior of the house where it's subjected to the elements, it's often the component that fails first. If you press the button and hear no sound at all, it makes sense to start your investigation here.

Start by removing the button from the exterior trim. Buttons are either screwed directly to the trim or snap-mounted to a base that's screwed to the trim. If you can't find the screws, you have the snap-on variety. Remove this type by gently

prying under the button housing edge with a small screwdriver to pop it free.

The button is simply a spring-loaded switch that completes the low-voltage bell circuit, allowing current to flow through the other components. You can determine whether the transformer and sound-generating unit are in working order and the wires are intact by jumping the button. On the back of the button housing you'll see two wires connected to screw terminals. Remove one wire and briefly hold it against the other wire to bypass the switch. If the bell rings, you know the rest of the system is fine and the button is at fault. Although you can attempt to clean the screw terminals and contacts, simply replacing the button is often the most practical solution. Install the new button by fastening the two wires to it and reattaching it to the trim. If bypassing the button didn't cause the bell to ring, assume for the meantime that the button is in good operating condition and the problem is located in the transformer, in the sound-generating unit or is caused by a broken wire.

Bells and Buzzers

If your bell or buzzer makes any sound at all—even a muffled, raspy hum, it's fairly safe to assume that both the transformer and button are in working order and the wires are not broken. In this case, your job is to check out the sound-generating unit.

Begin by using a thin-bladed screwdriver to pry the cover from the bell or buzzer and inspect the wiring and contact points. Some units have covers that can be popped off by simply pressing at the top or bottom. If the sound was muffled, check for grease and dust clinging to the moving parts. Use an old toothbrush and a drop of lighter fluid to clean the parts. After cleaning, resist any temptation to lubricate the moving parts. Dust has a greater tendency to cling to surfaces that are oiled than to dry surfaces and you'll only be shortening the time until the next overhaul.

Check the wire connections. If a wire is loosely connected to its terminal, tighten the screw. If the insulation on either wire is frayed, cut off the bad section, strip the wire end and connect it to the terminal. Clean the coils with the toothbrush and lighter fluid. The contact points can be checked by pulling the clapper away from its seat.

If you see a buildup of dirt and tarnish, clean the contact points with fine sandpaper or emery cloth.

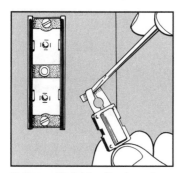

Buttons with lights often have two brass spring tabs. Be sure they're clean and make contact with the mounting plate terminals.

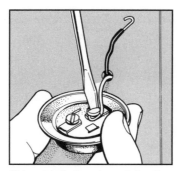

Older-style buttons mount directly to the trim. Each of two low-voltage wires is connected to a brass screw terminal.

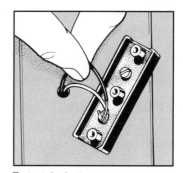

To test the button, remove one wire and touch it to the other terminal. If the bell rings, you've got a defective button.

After you've checked the wires and connections, cleaned the entire mechanism, and dressed the points, put the unit back together and try the doorbell.

Cleaning and Repairing Chimes

Many homes feature doorbells that strike chimes rather than a bell or buzzer. After years of service, chimes often sound in muted tones. In other cases, you'll hear only one note of the chime's 2- or 3-note sequence. The rest may sound more like dull thumps than clear tones. This too can be caused by dust accumulation, but more often it is the result of worn pads on the tone bar mounts.

To clean a set of chimes, pop off the cover and look for dust around the plunger springs and tarnish buildup on the tips of the plungers. Again, use a toothbrush and lighter fluid to clean the plungers and return springs.

Check the rubber pads, or grommets, on the mounts of each tone bar. These pads insulate the tone bars from the mounts so that the tone bars can vibrate freely. If you find worn, hard, or missing pads, you'll need to buy replacements. Check with a local hardware store or electrical supply outlet for the pads.

If you have trouble finding new pads, you may have to replace the entire chime. Remove the old chime by disconnecting the wires and loosening the screws in the mounting plate. Simply reverse the procedure when installing the new chime.

Checking the Transformer

Every low-voltage doorbell system has a transformer that reduces the 110-volt household current to between 8 and 16 volts, depending on the specifications of the bell, buzzer or chime unit. You'll find the transformer connected to a junction box, usually in the basement, and often near the electrical entrance panel, where it's wired to a 110-volt house circuit. Look for it on the side of one of the joists of the floor above the basement. The low-voltage wires are connected to the transformer by screw terminals and are

Gently pry off the cover of bell or buzzer with a screwdriver. Some covers pop off when you press the top or bottom.

Pull back the clapper to check the condition of the bell contact points. If necessary, clean them with a piece of fine sandpaper.

Buzzer contact points should also be cleaned. Spread them apart with a screwdriver to check their condition.

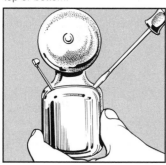

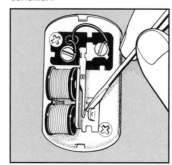

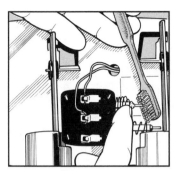

Clean the parts of a bell, buzzer or chime with a toothbrush and lighter fluid. Don't lubricate to avoid collecting dust.

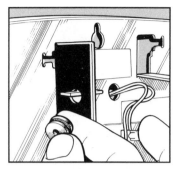

Rubber grommets in a chime unit isolate tone bar from its mounting. Get replacements if they're worn, hard or missing.

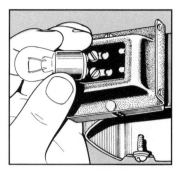

To test a transformer, remove the low-voltage wires and hold a 12-volt bulb to the terminals. If bulb lights up, all is well.

safe to handle. The connections inside the junction box carry the full 110-volt house current.

To check if your transformer is doing its job, undo the low-voltage wires and hold the terminals of a 12-volt automotive bulb to the low-voltage terminals on the transformer. Don't test the unit by jumping the terminals with a screwdriver. Some models have built-in fuses that will blow with this unsafe procedure. If the bulb lights, the transformer is working. If not, you'll have to install a replacement.

Before attempting to remove the old transformer, shut off the house circuit that supplies current to the transformer. Find the appropriate circuit breaker at the main panel and switch it off. If your panel has fuses, simply unscrew and remove the fuse. If you're not sure which circuit the doorbell is on, turn off the power to all circuits at the main switch.

Remove the junction-box cover plate and disconnect the transformer wires that connect the unit to the house current. Undo the box connector that holds the transformer to the box and pull

out the unit. Reverse this procedure to mount the new transformer and, finally, connect it to the 110-volt circuit and turn it back on.

Doorbell systems require an 8-, 10-, 12-, 14-, or 16-volt transformer. While any brand will do, make sure the new transformer has the same voltage rating as the original when purchasing a replacement.

Checking the Wires

If the three main electrical components of your doorbell system check out, and your doorbell still doesn't work, you probably have a broken wire. You can check this by disconnecting the two low-voltage wires at the transformer and holding the probes of a continuity tester to each wire while a helper holds the doorbell button down. If the tester light comes on, the wires are intact. If not, you'll need to string new wires through the basement or attic. You can often attach the new wires to the old and then pull the new wires through the walls and other blind spots.

Transformer is connected to house circuit at a junction box. After shutting off power, disconnect wires and remove.

Install new unit by connecting the transformer wires to the incoming black and white wires. Ground is screwed to box.

Fasten each low-voltage wire to a transformer terminal after you've connected the transformer to the house current.

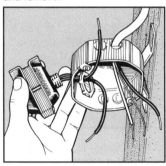

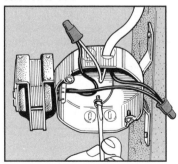

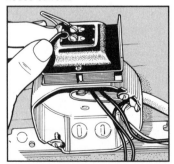

Air conditioner basics

Home air conditioning, over a relatively brief span, has erupted from an almost unheard-of luxury to a virtual necessity. In 1948, despite a multimillion-dollar promotional campaign, there was so little interest in air conditioning that major manufacturers were considering abandoning the whole idea. By the mid-'80s, about 85 percent of the new homes built came with air conditioners. In many areas, air conditioning has become the largest single user of electric power. As a nation, we now spend about $10 *billion* dollars a year—more than the entire gross national product of many Third World nations—to keep cool and dry.

What Air Conditioners Do

An air conditioner does two different, though related, jobs: cooling indoor air *and* removing unwanted moisture from that air. Both tasks require taking energy from inside and dumping it outside. It's easy to see that if an air conditioner pulls energy (in the form of heat) out of the air, the air's temperature will drop. How it removes moisture is a little less obvious.

The basic point to keep in mind is that the warmer the air gets, the more moisture it can hold. If air—at any temperature—is holding all the water vapor it can, it's said to be saturated, or to have a relative humidity (RH) of 100 percent. If it contains, say, half that amount, its RH will be 50 percent. If you lower the temperature of air without adding or removing any moisture, its capacity for holding water vapor would drop, and its RH would rise. Drop the temperature low enough, and the air can no longer hold all its moisture: that's why air conditioners sometimes drip water. If the cool air is reheated by mixing with the warmer air in the room, the air will have a lower *relative* humidity because of the water removed when the air was cold.

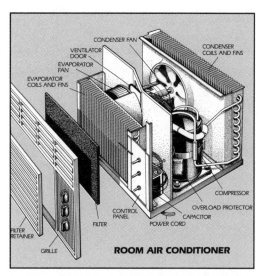

An air conditioner is a relatively simple appliance. It has four basic parts: an evaporator that absorbs heat from a room, a condenser that expels this heat outside, and a compressor to compress the refrigerant in gas form to a liquid thereby cooling it so it can absorb heat from the room again.

How Air Conditioners Work

Many people think air conditioners are mysterious gadgets. They're really not. Although they are more complicated than electric fans or space heaters, they do their job by making use of only a couple of basic principles. First, when a gas is compressed, it gets hot—think of how a bicycle pump heats up when you inflate a tire. When liquid evaporates, it gets cold—think of an alcohol rub-down. Second, a hot material gives off heat to its surroundings and a cold one absorbs heat.

The essential components of an air conditioner (or heat pump or refrigerator) are a compressor, a condenser, an evaporator and a refrigerant. The refrigerant liquefies when compressed and reverts to a gaseous form when pressure is released. Fluorocarbon compounds such as Freon are now widely used. In the past, sulphur dioxide and ammonia were used as refrigerants.

In any air conditioner, the evaporator is located indoors while the compressor and the condenser are located outdoors, where the room's heat is dumped. The refrigerant is cycled back and forth between them.

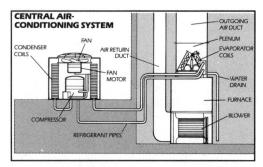

CENTRAL AIR-CONDITIONING SYSTEM

CONDENSER COILS

FAN

AIR RETURN DUCT

FAN MOTOR

COMPRESSOR

REFRIGERANT PIPES

OUTGOING AIR DUCT

PLENUM

EVAPORATOR COILS

WATER DRAIN

FURNACE

BLOWER

A central airconditioning system has the same basic components as a room air conditioner but they are positioned differently. The central system has the compressor and condenser coils located outside the house, the evaporator coils are located inside the furnace ducts and the refrigerant passes between the two locations in insulated pipes.

In the evaporator, liquid refrigerant is allowed to evaporate by releasing the pressure applied to it. Its temperature drops sharply, and the cold gas absorbs heat from the room via the fins on the evaporator's coils. The gas, somewhat warmed now, is then pumped to the compressor. There, the gas is compressed until it liquefies, becoming quite warm (about 200°F) in the process. The hot liquid then goes to the compressor's condenser coils where it loses heat to the outside air. The cooled liquid is then pumped to the evaporator, and the entire cycle starts again. The heat from the indoors is effectively absorbed by the evaporator's coils and then dumped outside the house.

Just about all air conditioners used in the home work this way, but there are some major variations in design.

Air Conditioner Designs

Probably the most popular kind of home air conditioner is the room, or unitary, type. Unitary models are so called because the entire assembly is built in a single unit, designed to be mounted in a window or through an exterior wall.

The next most popular type is the central air conditioner. This is a single unit that services a number of rooms or a whole house. Typically, the evaporator is located in a furnace duct that supplies air to many rooms of a house. The

condenser and compressor are separated from the evaporator and are mounted outdoors. Insulated tubing connects them all.

The third, and newest, type of air conditioner is the so-called split model. Introduced a few years ago by the Japanese, split air conditioners use a single condenser and compressor, much like central units. But instead of using a single duct-mounted evaporator, the split models have multiple point-of-use evaporators—one for each room that requires cooling. Instead of circulating cooled air, like the central units, the split units circulate refrigerant to the various locations being cooled.

Air Conditioner Installations

Each type has its advantages and disadvantages. Unitary air conditioners have the lowest cost—their packaged design makes for a "plug-in" installation. All that is needed is a wall or window that separates indoors from outdoors and an adequately sized electric line. Everything—compressor, condenser, evaporator and air-circulation fan—is built into the package. Unitary air conditioners cool only the area in which they're installed. If you want to cool several rooms, you must purchase several units.

Because a unitary model has its condenser and evaporator located fairly close together, it's hard to avoid heat from the hot side leaking over to the cool side, lowering efficiency. The proximity of the compressor also makes for noisy operation.

Central air conditioners, on the other hand, are more demanding in terms of installation and, as a result, cost more. Central models do, however, tend to be more efficient than unitary ones and can be designed to filter air better than the unitary type. The remote compressor also helps keep noise levels low.

The split types are a compromise between the other two. Installation problems are similar to those of central air conditioners. In homes without existing heating ductwork, the split models are considerably simpler to install than central units. But if the ductwork is in place, installation costs of split units are apt to be higher. Splits share the central model's quiet operation. They also offer the advantage of easy zoning, which central models lack. Efficiencies of split type air conditioners are typically quite high, in part because they tend to make the most of the latest technology. Since splits don't use a common air-circulating duct, they're not suited for whole-house filtered air supplies.

How to Buy

To begin with, you'll have to determine the cooling requirements of your home. If you are planning to purchase a split or central system, it's best to have a cooling contractor come to your house and do a cooling audit. Contractors will measure the volume of air in each room, the number of windows, the area they occupy and their orientation to north, south, east and west. They'll also determine the amount of insulation in the walls and ceiling and many other subtleties of the estimating procedure.

It's important to realize that any airconditioning system must be sized properly to the cooling load; otherwise, the high efficiencies of the equipment will be lost. While it is possible to do this audit yourself, it's a better idea to have at least three different contractors do it for you. Get written estimates from each one and make sure the specifications are for the same equipment.

The results of this audit will be the required cooling load expressed in BTU/hr. This is how the units are sold. If you're installing a room air conditioner, you'll have to do the audit yourself. If you don't have time to do the full-scale audit, a ballpark figure can be determined by multiplying the square footage of your room by 27 to get the estimated BTU/hr. But keep in mind that this represents the roughest of estimates. The audit is by far the best way to go.

Energy Efficiency Rating

After you've determined the number of BTU/hr. you need, shop for the unit that meets your load requirements. The two key numbers are the purchase price and the Energy Efficiency Rating. The EER is simply a measure of how much electricity an air conditioner consumes per unit of heat removed from the room. It's expressed in BTUs per watt. The higher the EER, the more efficient the air conditioner.

The EER is like a car's EPA gas mileage rating. It's a useful number for comparing air conditioners, but it's less useful for estimating just what an air conditioner will cost over a cooling season's actual operation. That's because EERs are measured under a carefully controlled set of circumstances.

The EER number appears on a bright yellow label, marked *Energy Guide*, that all air conditioners must carry. The label carries the unit's BTU/hr. cooling load rating and shows where the particular unit falls in comparison to other models of the same capacity. The label also gives the estimated costs for running the unit for a year in the area of the country in which you live. Low efficiency models generally have an EER of around 6. High efficiency models sport an EER around 9. Keep in mind that split and central units have higher EERs than room models, often between 10 and 15.

To use the chart, you'll first need to find out—or estimate—the number of hours during the year that the unit will be operating. The map shows the average number of hours for the various regions of the United States. This is a rough but serviceable number.

Next you need the BTU/hr. rating. This depends on the size and other characteristics of the room you want to cool. You can get a rough approximation by multiplying the square feet of the room to be cooled by 27. Then, you need the EER rating for the unit you want to buy. This appears on the bright yellow Energy Guide label attached to every unit. The last piece of information you need is the rate you pay for electricity. You can get this either from an old electric bill or by calling your local utility. This chart and map should help you decide which unit is the best to buy.

Hours of Operation (from map)		Air Conditoner Rating (BTU/hr.)		EER (from label)		Electric Rate ($/KWH)		Yearly Operating Cost
600	×	8000	÷	6	×	.09	=	$ 72.00
600	×	8000	÷	9.5	×	.09	=	$ 45.47

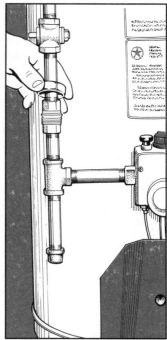

1 After turning off gas valve, loosen the union below the valve and disassemble the piping that connects to control valve.

Water heater replacement

Like all things mechanical, water heaters do break down. When it's time to have yours replaced, you can expect the installation charge to equal or exceed the cost of the heater itself. You can, however, remove your old heater and install the new one yourself. You'll need a permit to do the job and an inspection may be required in your area, but don't let that intimidate you. Just keep in mind you'll be saving $120 to $160 by doing it yourself.

When to Replace a Heater

A water heater does not usually need to be replaced until its tank begins to leak. An inoperative heater with a sound tank *can* be repaired. If your unit is several years past its warranty, however, it's probably unwise to invest more than $50 in repairs. There's no way of knowing how long the tank will last and you'd probably be better off replacing the entire unit. Remember, if the manufacturer loses faith in the heater after five years, there's probably a good reason to do so yourself.

Choosing the Right Heater

As you shop for a new water heater, you'll find a confusing array of brand names, efficiency ratings and warranties. There are many more brand names on the market than water heater manufacturers. This means that more than one brand name is being manufactured by the same company. If you're looking for an inexpensive water heater, then you probably should ignore the brand and simply shop for the best price.

The real differences occur when shopping for extended-life and high-efficiency heaters. Extended-life heaters may feature dual anode rods. These are magnesium rods that retard tank corrosion by acting as electrolytic sacrifices. Instead of your tank corroding, the anode rods corrode. While all heaters have at least one anode rod, having two can greatly increase the time before tank corrosion creates a serious problem. Extended-life units may also feature fill tubes designed to keep sediment from collecting on the tank bottom and, if your choice is electric, they may have heavier heating elements.

2 Attach a garden hose to the drain valve. Open the T&P valve or the hot-water taps in your house and drain the tank.

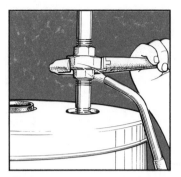

3 Disconnect iron water pipes by loosening unions with pipe wrench. Stubborn unions may require heating with a torch.

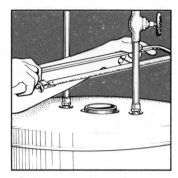

4 Copper pipes can simply be cut with a hacksaw. Leave pipe stubs in place to use as handles when carrying the tank away.

Other extended-life heaters with 10-year warranties are virtually the same as ordinary units warranted for five years. You're simply betting with the manufacturer that the heater will actually last 10 years. It's at least a $70 wager that may or may not pay off.

High-efficiency heaters have foam insulation instead of fiberglass. The extra R-factor is particularly valuable if you use your hot water only a few hours a day. High-efficiency heaters may also have two anode rods, an antisediment fill tube, and a modified burner assembly.

Base your decision on as much technical information as you can get, and pay close attention to the estimated energy cost printed on the sticker attached to the heater.

Removing the Old Heater

If you have an electric heater, shut off its circuit breaker or remove its fuse at the main panel. Remove the cover plate near the conduit entrance on the heater cabinet. Remove the wire

nuts and disconnect the wires and ground connection. Undo the box connector that secures the conduit to the cabinet and pull out the wires.

If you have a gas heater, shut off the gas valve by turning it to its cross-line position. Most codes require this valve to be within 3 ft. of the heater's control valve. Loosen the union below the valve and disassemble the piping that connects to the heater.

With the energy supply disconnected, shut off the water inlet valve and attach a garden hose to the heater's drain valve. Then open the T&P (temperature and pressure) valve at the top of the heater and drain the water into the nearest floor drain. If yours is an older model with no T&P valve, open the hot-water faucets in your home.

If your heater is not electric, then the next step is to disconnect the exhaust flue. In most cases the flue will be fastened to the flue hat with sheetmetal screws. Simply remove the screws and lift off the flue piping.

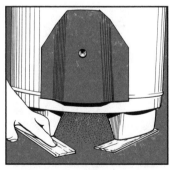

5 If the new tank is installed on a sloping floor, level the heater by shimming under the legs with wood shingles.

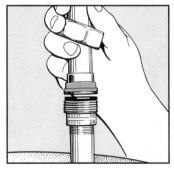

6 This dielectric union uses a rubber washer and plastic insert to keep the brass upper half from contacting the iron half.

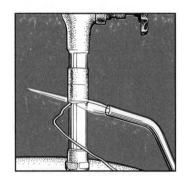

7 After soldering length of copper pipe into adapter and threading into tank, use sweat coupling to join to existing pipe.

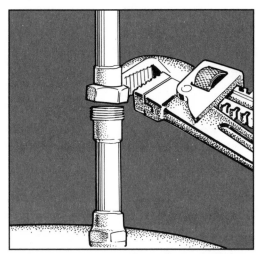

8 Copper pipes can also be reconnected with a brass union. Solder the bottom half to stub before threading into heater.

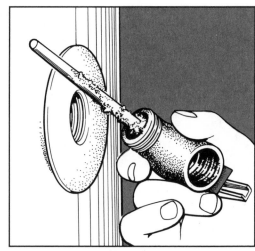

9 A clogged T&P valve means that the new one you install should be checked periodically by lifting the manual release lever.

Removing the Water Pipes

If your heater is supplied by iron pipes or you have copper pipes that are connected by unions, loosen the unions to disconnect the pipes. You can also simply cut copper pipes with a hacksaw or wheeled pipe cutter. Leave the pipe stubs connected to the heater to use as handles when carrying the old heater out of the house.

After the water heater is completely disconnected from its energy source, piping and flue, grasp the pipe stubs and rock the heater side-to-side to move it.

Connecting the New Heater

If the floor is level, simply slide the new heater under the water pipes and align it properly. If it's to be positioned near a floor drain, as many are, then you'll need to shim one side of the heater to compensate for the sloping floor. Use short pieces of cedar shingles or strap iron to shim the legs so the unit is plumb and secure.

When connecting the water inlet and outlet pipes, it's generally okay to duplicate the type and configuration of fittings that existed on your old heater. If, however, you live in an area that

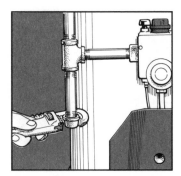

10 Before lighting pilot on gas heaters, loosen bottom cap to remove trapped air. Then air out the room to get rid of the gas.

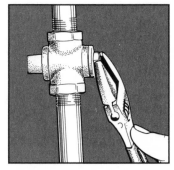

11 Gas valves often leak after being operated. After gas is turned on, tighten stem nut on the back of the valve one-half turn.

12 If you end up with two female ends on the flue pipe, crimp one end with a crimping tool or needle-nose pliers.

has prolonged high humidity or your if water has a high concentration of dissolved mineral salts and your pipes are copper, it's advisable to connect the heater with dielectric unions. Because the fittings on the heater are iron, a direct copper-to-iron connection under these conditions can significantly increase the rate of corrison in the iron pipes.

A *dielectric union* consists of a threaded iron half, a brass half and a threaded iron collar. Separating the two halves is a rubber washer. A plastic insert separates the iron collar from the brass. With this union you can join copper to iron without any direct contact between the metals. If you're unsure as to whether this union is necessary in your locality, check with a plumber or your local building code authorities.

If no dielectric unions are required, the connection is simple. Measure between the existing pipes and the heater fittings and cut two pieces of copper pipe to length, taking into account the shoulder depth of the adapters. Then, flux an end of each pipe stub and insert in the adapters. Solder them on a fireproof surface. Never solder an adapter after threading it into the cold-water inlet tube because you may melt the plastic fill tube.

When the adapters have cooled, wrap three layers of Teflon tape clockwise around the threads of the male adapters. Thread the adapters into the heater fittings and tighten. Then, clean and flux the remaining pipe ends and join them with copper sweat couplings. If you can't raise the existing pipes high enough to slide the couplings in place, use slip couplings which have no center tops. Slide the slip couplings over the pipe stubs before threading the adapters in place. As an alternative, you can use brass unions in place of the sweat couplings.

If yours is an older home with galvanized iron pipes, simply thread an appropriately sized galvanized nipple into each fitting and join the nipples to the existing pipes with galvanized unions. Apply pipe compound to the threads of each connection. Avoid any temptation to use black iron nipples or fittings as they'll rust quickly.

Installing the T&P Valve

Today, every heater must be equipped with an approved temperature and pressure relief valve. Should the control mechanism on a heater stick in the ON position, this valve will bleed off the excess steam pressure. Check the T&P valve on your old unit for sediment buildup. If it's

13 If necessary, use a vent adapter to connect the heater's 3-in. flue hat to a 4-in. vent. Secure joints with sheetmetal screws.

clogged, then make a point of checking your new valve periodically to ensure safe operation.

The critical thing to look for when buying a T&P valve is its psi rating. (The psi rating is the release pressure measured in *p*ounds per *s*quare *i*nch.) Check the rating on your new heater first, and buy an appropriate valve.

To install the valve, simply coat the threads with pipe compound and thread the valve into the heater opening. You may find the heater opening on the side or top. Most codes require that you install a drain pipe that extends from the valve to within 3 in. of the floor.

Connecting the Gas

Make sure you use only black iron pipe for the gas line. Compounds in the gas can cause the zinc coating on galvanized pipe to flake away and enter the control valve. In many cases you'll be able to use the nipple and fitting arrangement from the old heater. If not, thread an appropriately sized nipple into the control valve and thread a ½-in. tee to it. Thread a second nipple into the top of the tee and attach the bottom half of the union. Thread the short nipple into the bottom of the tee and install an iron cap on the open end. Finally, tighten the union. Typically, pipe compound is used on all gas joints. Teflon tape, however, also does the job and ensures that no compound particles work their way into the control valve.

Turn on the gas and check for leaks by brushing a solution of warm water and liquid dish detergent on all the joints. If bubbles appear, turn off the gas, take the piping apart, and start over. When all the joints are tight and the gas is on, slightly loosen the cap on the nipple below the tee to bleed air out of the line. Then tighten the cap. Because gas valves can leak after they've been used, tighten the stem nut on the back of the valve a half turn.

Install the flue pipe. Most new heaters have 3-in.-dia. flue hats, but many codes require 4-in.-dia. pipes. If so, install a step-up adapter on the flue hat to accommodate the larger pipe. Join all connections with sheetmetal screws.

If your old flue pipe is sound, you can simply put it back in. New pipe usually comes with its snap seam apart. Simply cut it to length with tin snips. Use a hacksaw to cut pipe with a closed seam. If you end up with two female ends, form a male end with a flue pipe crimping tool or needle-nose pliers.

Connecting the Electricity

Chances are the existing electrical wires can be reconnected just as you found them on the old heater. Your old wiring will need to be replaced, however, if it doesn't meet your local electrical code. The wires leading from the ceiling or wall must be encased in flexible or rigid conduit and fastened to the heater with an approved box connector. You may find that a separate disconnect box is required in your area.

Fish the wires into the cabinet and secure the cable with the box connector. Join the black wire to the black lead and the white wire to the white lead with approved wire nuts. Then screw the ground wire to the green terminal in the cabinet. Finally, make sure the heater thermostat is covered with insulation and replace the cover plate.

Before turning the power on, fill the tank and bleed all air through the hot and cold faucets in your home. Never energize a dry heating element in an electric tank. It will burn up in a matter of seconds.

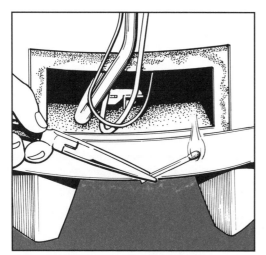

14 A wooden match held in a long pair of pliers is best for lighting the pilot. Press pilot button and slide match into heater.

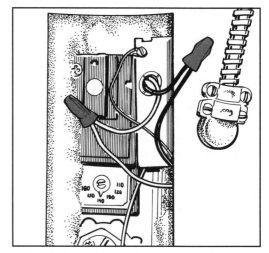

15 On electric units, secure conduit with an approved box connector. Connect wires with wire nuts and secure ground wire.

Bathroom drain repairs

Repairing a poorly working tub drain is an intimidating task for most people. All the important parts seem to be hidden under the tub or inside an adjacent partition wall. In practice, however, nothing could be farther from the truth, because the working parts can all be removed, cleaned, adjusted and installed from the outside. All you need to know is what type of drain you have.

Tub drains, usually called *tripwastes* by plumbers, come in two basic styles with the same purpose: to close off the tub opening so the water does not drain until you want it to. One type is an internal plunger. When you flip the trip lever below the faucets, the plunger slides past a drain baffle in the overflow tube and prevents the water from passing into the drain system. This type of tripwaste calls for a simple screen that covers the drain opening at the bottom of the tub.

The second type is called a pop-up tripwaste. When you operate its trip lever, it lets the drain stopper—positioned in the drain opening—to fall into the opening, closing it off and preventing water drainage.

In most cases, the tripwaste just needs to be cleaned and sometimes adjusted, as shown. Accumulations of hair and soap are the usual culprits.

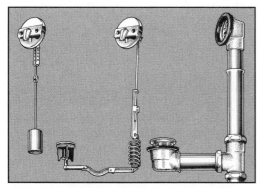

Two basic tripwastes are internal plunger (*left*) and pop-up model (*middle*). Both fit standard drain system (*right*) with vertical overflow and horizontal drain-opening tubes.

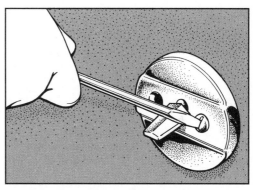

To remove plunger tripwaste—or vertical section of pop-up—unscrew overflow cover plate. It's attached to overflow tube.

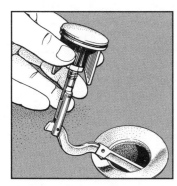

To clean pop-up type (*shown above*) just pull mechanism from drain opening. For plunger type, just remove screen.

Pull mechanism from overflow tube and clean thoroughly. Apply heat-proof grease, then install and check operation.

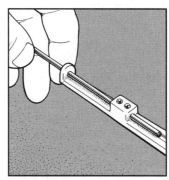

If plunger and spring arm need adjustment, move connecting rod on fitting and tighten. Install and check.

Guide to toilet repair

Most residential toilets are simple, straightforward pieces of plumbing. Because of this, they are *very* durable and dependable. Still, like every mechanical system, they will eventually break down and need repair. Fortunately, most of the repairs are not only inexpensive but also easy to do.

To begin with, there are two kinds of toilets in residential use today. By far the most common is the 2-piece tank-and-bowl type. These toilets flush primarily by the weight of the water held in their tanks. This weight, also known as *head pressure*, allows the unit to operate with very few mechanical parts.

The other type differs because it is made in one piece. These toilets are offered by a variety of companies and are generally known as silent-flush models. Aside from appearance, the main difference is that the silent-flush toilets rely less on gravity and more on control valves. Silent-flush toilets are complicated enough to require special attention, so only 2-piece toilets will be discussed here.

How a 2-Piece Toilet Works

When you flush a toilet, the flush lever pulls up a chain, or wire, connected to a rubber stopper which is shaped like a ball or flapper. This lifts the stopper off its flush valve seat, the part that connects the tank and the bowl. Basically, this pulls the plug on the stored water and sends it into the bowl. The stopper is hollow and has a trapped bubble of air inside. This air bubble holds up the stopper until the receding water level carries it back down onto its seat.

When the water level drops, a hollow float ball attached to a brass rod drops with it. The other end of the rod controls a stopper inside a water inlet valve, called a *ballcock*. The rod acts as a lever. When the ball goes down, it pulls the stopper up, allowing water from the supply system to rush through the valve and into the tank. As the tank begins to fill, the weight of the water pressure presses on the seated flush valve stopper and forces a seal, preventing the water from leaving the tank. As the rising water level carries the float ball up, the inlet valve stopper is forced back into the ballcock, shutting off the water.

The bowl, on the other hand, has no mechanical parts. In terms of design, it is little more than a vitreous china water trap, very much like the P-trap under the kitchen sink. The water you see standing in the bowl is the water held by the trap. This water serves two important functions. It keeps the bowl clean and it seals off the sewer gas that is always present in your drainage pipes.

When the flush valve opens, the water rushes into the hollow rim of the bowl by force of gravity. The rim has a dozen or so small, slanted openings and one larger, opening. The smaller openings are visible under the rim and send water coursing down the sides of the bowl in a diagonal pattern. The larger opening, about ½ in. dia., dumps a forceful jet of water into a channel inside the bowl. Although this channel is concealed, its opening is directly across from the drain opening in the toilet.

A toilet, then, is flushed by water sent from two directions. Water from the rim openings cleans the bowl and starts the trapped water in its spiral up through the trap. The water from the larger opening sends a jet of water into the drain and forces the trap.

As soon as the water spills over the trap, a siphoning action pulls the rest of the water in the bowl with it. When not enough water is left to fill the narrow passage at the top of the trap, the

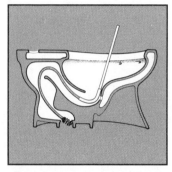

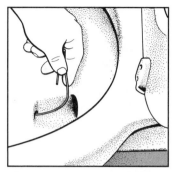

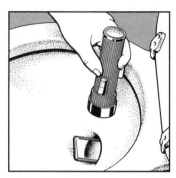

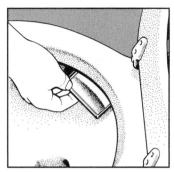

1 A 2-piece toilet is a simple mechanical device that operates on water pressure and gravity.

2 A dirty bowl usually means poor water flow from rim openings. To check clogged openings, hold mirror under rim.

3 If the bowl flushes sluggishly, check for a bacteria-clogged siphon hole. Bend a coat hanger and use it to clear the hole.

4 To check for a partial blockage at the top of the trap, shine a flashlight onto a mirror placed in the bottom of the bowl.

5 To clear congested rim holes, pour a 50-50 mixture of warm water and vinegar into the flush valve. Then ream holes with wire.

6 Use closet auger to clear large obstructions. Auger's cable is long enough to reach the soil pipe below the bowl.

siphon is broken and all the water pulled to the top of the trap slips back into the bowl. Aside from the small amount of water added through the overflow tube, the water left standing in the bowl after a flush is the water that didn't make it over the trap.

Troubleshooting Toilet Repairs

That's how a toilet is meant to work, but let one component fail and you'll be left with an often confusing array of symptoms. These symptoms are your quickest route to effective repairs.

Symptom 1. *Your toilet flushes normally but is sluggish and often needs more than one flush to clear the bowl. The sides of the bowl are also stained and need frequent cleaning.*

Toilets that flush sluggishly do so for one of three reasons. If the toilet has never flushed properly, you can count on a flawed trap or an

inadequate vent in the waste line. As these conditions are rare, save investigating them for last. Probably the trouble is a bacteria-clogged siphon hole or partial clog at the top of the trap.

Bubbles are a sure sign of a partially blocked trap. Flush the toilet and watch for air bubbles between $1/8$ and $1/4$ in. dia. They will rise out of the trap opening halfway through the flush. As the water goes down, the bubbles will come up. Items that can cause a partial blockage are toothpaste caps, cotton swabs and hair pins. A partial blockage usually means that some such obstruction rests against the side of the top of the trap.

To locate the blockage, dip the water out of the bowl with a paper cup. Then hold a pocket mirror at an angle facing into the drain opening. Shine a flashlight into the mirror so the beam bounces toward the top of the trap. This will let you see the obstruction. When you learn its

7 If replacing flapper on a flush valve that has no side pegs, slip collar over the tube. If there are pegs, cut them off collar.

8 Once collar is cut off, simply hook the flapper eyelets over the side pegs and connect the lift chain to the flush lever.

9 To remove a defective tank ball, hold the lift wire with pliers and unthread the ball. Old, brittle rubber will often tear.

shape and location, fashion a hook from a piece of wire and snag the blockage. Then, flush the toilet several times to clear the passageway.

If you see no obvious bubbles, look for a bacterial-clogged siphon hole and mineral-clogged rim openings. You will usually be able to see a buildup in the siphon hole. To clear the opening, ream it with a piece of wire. The clog should fall forward into the bowl as you work.

If your toilet seems to need cleaning more frequently, flush the toilet and watch the action of the water as it spills from the rim openings. It should course down the sides of the bowl diagonally. If the water slides straight down the sides of the bowl, the rim openings are partially clogged with calcified minerals and bacteria.

To clean the rim openings, shut off the water and empty the tank by flushing. Then, while holding the flush valve stopper up, pour a 50-50 mixture of warm water and white vinegar into the flush valve opening. Much of it will drain into the bowl, but some of it will be trapped at the clogged openings. Let it stand for half an hour. Then ream each opening with a wire. If the openings are really clogged, start with a rigid wire—a coat hanger is ideal—and work up in size to a small screwdriver. To keep the problem from recurring, install a chlorine tank treatment and use lime-dissolving bowl cleaner.

For improper venting or a flawed bowl trap, check the venting first. Each toilet in your home must have its own 2-in. vent or be within 6 ft. of a full-size vertical stack. You may need a plumber to make sure your bathroom is vented properly.

Symptom 2. *Your toilet clogs and overflows, or passes only water.*

A toilet that does not flush at all is likely to have a larger blockage at the top of its trap. Such a blockage may be caused by too much paper, but is more likely the result of a combination of foreign objects and paper. Occasionally, you will be able to retrieve a full blockage with the mirror-and-wire method or a plunger, but a *closet auger* is often a better alternative.

To use a closet auger, pull the cable back through the handle so that only the pilot spring shows at the bend. Then insert the bend into the drain opening of the toilet and push the cable through the housing until it stops against the top of the trap. When you feel the resistance of the trap bend, crank the cable in a clockwise direction. If you feel a snag, continue to crank in the same direction while you retrieve the cable.

If you can't feel a snag, continue cranking through the drain until you run out of cable. Then retrieve the cable and repeat the process several times more.

Symptom 3. *Your toilet continues to run until you wiggle the flush handle.*

This is a common problem that is almost always a quick fix. It is caused either by a lift chain that is too long or by a lift-wire guide that is poorly aligned. Start by shutting off the water and flushing the toilet. If your flush valve has a rubber flapper, look for too much play in its lift chain. To make the adjustment, unhook the chain at the tank lever and connect it in a lower link. Try for an adjustment that leaves no more than ½ in. of slack in the chain.

If your toilet has a flush valve with a lift wire and a tank ball (some are ball-shaped and some are wedge-shaped), start by removing the tank lid and watching the action of the lift wire and

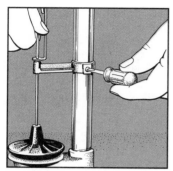

10 If the tank ball drifts to one side as it falls, loosen screw in lift-wire guide, then rotate guide until wire falls properly.

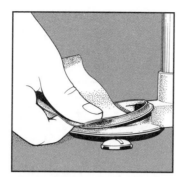

11 Before installing new ball or flapper, sand valve seat smooth with fine sandpaper. To avoid damage, use light touch.

12 If seat is damaged beyond repair, it must be replaced or retrofitted with new seat as shown. Epoxy bonds it to old seat.

13 If you find a broken overflow tube, pull old tube out, pry threads from the flush valve, and thread a new tube in place.

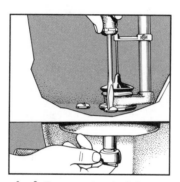

14 To separate a tank from a bowl, first unscrew the tank bolts. Hold one end with a screwdriver—use socket on the other.

15 Remove the water supply line. This can be done at ballcock connection under the tank or at the shutoff valve.

tank ball through several flushes. This should give you a good idea about where the ball is landing and how the guide should be moved.

Use one hand to steady the flush valve's overflow tube and another to loosen the setscrew in the guide. With the setscrew loosened, move the guide only slightly in the desired direction. Then tighten the screw and turn the water back on.

Symptom 4. *The water comes on in your toilet tank automatically every half hour or so, runs for a minute, then shuts off.*

This phantom operation stumps a lot of homeowners and is especially annoying in the middle of the night. In most cases, all that is required here is a new flapper ball or tank ball. If your toilet has a flapper, buy a universal replacement. A universal flapper has an eyelet opening on each side—where it hinges—and a center collar made to slide over an overflow tube.

You will need one or the other, but not both. If your flush valve has side pegs for the eyelets, cut the collar from the flapper.

In any case, empty the tank and slip the old flapper from its eyelets, or cut through its collar with a utility knife or scissors. Before installing the new flapper, run a finger around the flush valve seat. Through years of use, dissolved mineral salts in the water can calcify on the flush valve and keep the flapper from seating properly. If the seat feels rough or gritty, sand it lightly with grit cloth or sandpaper.

If your toilet has a tank ball instead of a flapper, repair will differ slightly. Start by shutting off the water and draining the tank. Then hold the lower lift wire steady with a pair of pliers and unthread the ball from the wire. Rubber tank balls deteriorate with age, so don't be surprised if the ball strips away from its threaded brass insert. If this happens, simply hold the insert with one pair of pliers and thread

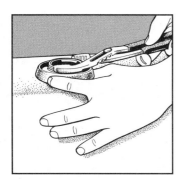

16 If you must replace a flush valve, separate the tank and bowl, then turn the tank over. Remove the nut and washer.

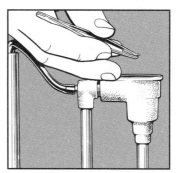

17 Sediment causes ballcock to perform poorly. To check, take off diaphragm cover. Remove particles with tweezers.

18 Ballcock seals differ by manufacturer. This one features a plastic plunger with an O-ring and a separate seat seal.

the lift wire from it with another. With the old ball removed, sand the flush valve seat and thread the new tank ball onto the lower lift wire.

Symptom 5. *Your toilet continues to come on at regular intervals, even though the tank ball or flush valve has been replaced and the flush valve seat has been sanded.*

This symptom means that your flush valve seat has a factory defect or is simply worn out. The best solution, of course, is to replace the valve, but replacement will require that you separate the tank from the bowl. If your toilet has a wall-mounted tank with a fragile chrome flush valve connecting the bowl, or if breaking your toilet in half sounds like more than you want to tackle right now, try an epoxy seat replacement kit.

Start by shutting the water off and flushing the toilet. Follow by sponging the remaining water from the tank and drying the flush valve seat. When the seat is dry, sand it lightly until it feels smooth. Remove the epoxy from the kit and press it onto the flush valve and connect the lift chain to the flush lever.

Replacing a Flush Valve. A better and more reliable solution is to replace the flush valve. You'll find both plastic and brass versions at your local hardware store. Brass will last longer and will be less likely to cause problems later.

Replacing a flush valve is not that difficult, but expect it to take an hour or more. Begin by shutting the water off and flushing the toilet. Then sponge all remaining water from the tank and disconnect the water supply tube from the ballcock. With the tank empty, remove the tank bolt nuts, lift the tank from the bowl, and set it upside down on the floor.

To remove the flush valve, pry the washer from the valve spud and undo the large spud nut. You'll then be able to pull the valve out from the inside.

Before installing the new valve, sand the area around the tank opening. Then coat the tank washer with pipe-joint compound or petroleum jelly and insert the valve spud through the tank. Tighten the spud hand tight, plus about three complete turns. Finally, slide the new spud washer onto the spud and set the tank back in place.

If your toilet is more than a few years old, buy new tank bolts and washers. Corroded bolts and brittle washers are usually more trouble than they are worth.

In any case, slide a rubber washer onto each tank bolt. Drop the tank bolts through the tank holes and through the corresponding holes in the bowl. Then start a rubber washer, a metal washer and a nut onto each bolt from below and tighten the nuts.

When tightening tank bolts, remember that vitreous china can break under too much pressure. Don't tighten any one bolt all the way down. Rather, move from bolt to bolt, tightening each only a few turns before moving to the next. Keep in mind that with most brands, the tank does not actually touch the bowl but is suspended by the spud washer. In any case, stop tightening the tank bolts as soon as you feel firm resistance. Then connect the toilet supply tube, attach the flapper chain to the tank lever and turn on the water.

Symptom 6. *Your toilet does not shut off completely but trickles a small stream of water into the bowl. You also hear a slight but prolonged hissing sound.*

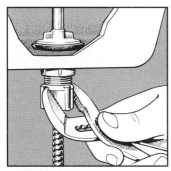

19 To remove ballcock, start by unthreading nut under tank that holds water-supply tube to ballcock shank.

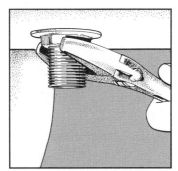

20 Loosen and remove the hexhead jamb nut that actually holds the ballcock to the tank. Hold ballcock from inside.

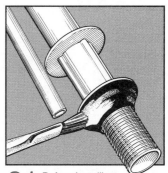

21 Before installing ballcock, clean opening. Coat ballcock washer with pipe-joint compound or petroleum jelly.

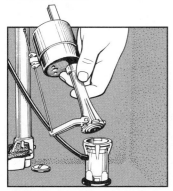

22 If sediment is a problem, a ballcock replacement like the one shown makes sense. It comes apart easily for cleaning.

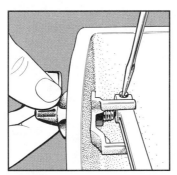

23 To replace two-piece flush lever, loosen screw and remove handle. One-piece levers have nuts with left-hand threads.

24 Wax ring gasket forms seal between bowl and waste line. Gaskets also come in rubber and wax-covered rubber.

These symptoms invariably signal trouble at the ballcock. In most cases, the ballcock needs a new seal or needs to be replaced entirely. In a few cases, the problem may only be sediment in the diaphragm. Shut the water off and remove the diaphragm screws from the top of the ball-cock. Then lift the float, float arm and diaphragm cover off the ballcock.

If the trouble is sediment, you'll be able to see it in the diaphragm. Use tweezers to pick it out. If you don't find sediment, assume there is a faulty seat or diaphragm seal. You have two choices for repair. You can either replace the seal or replace the entire ballcock assembly. The factors influencing your decision will be the condition of the diaphragm seat and the material of the ballcock.

Because imperfections in plastic ballcocks are difficult to see or feel, you will often be better off replacing a troublesome plastic model. If your ballcock is made of brass, and if the seat shows

no signs of wear, a diaphragm seal kit will save you time.

Ballcock diaphragm designs are proprietary, so your best bet is a kit made by the manufacturer of your toilet.

Replacing a Ballcock. Replacing a ballcock is not hard. You'll have to drain the tank, but you won't need to disturb the tank-to-bowl connection. Loosen the compression nut that holds the supply tube to the shank of the ballcock. Next, loosen the jamb nut that holds the ballcock in place. With the nut removed, the entire assembly should lift right out.

Before installing your new ballcock, apply pipe-joint compound to the rubber washer. Insert the shank through the tank opening, tighten the jamb nut and reconnect the supply tube. You'll probably have to adjust the float level on the ballcock. Bend the rod for large adjustments. For minor corrections, use the adjustment screw

25 When moving a toilet with the tank attached, you'll get the best balance point if you hold the bowl near the seat hinges.

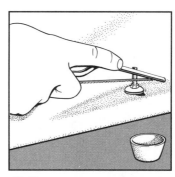

26 To secure toilet, tighten hold-down nuts until bowl doesn't rock. then cut off bolt tops and snap caps in place.

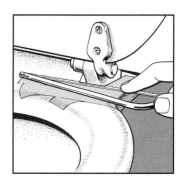

27 To replace broken seat, hinge bolts must be removed. If rusted, cover bowl rim with tape and cut bolts with hacksaw.

at the top of the diaphragm. You want the water level to be about an inch below the top of the overflow tube. The inside of many tanks is marked with a water-level line cast into the porcelain.

Symptom 7. *Tank handle falls out or is loose.*

The only trick to replacing a flush lever is to remember that it has left-hand threads. The replacement is a matter of loosening the retaining nut and pulling the lever out by the handle. The replacement handle will go in the same way. If your toilet's flush lever is made in two pieces, loosen the setscrew in the lever before undoing the nut.

Symptom 8. *Water appears around the base of the toilet. The toilet may also rock side-to-side slightly when used.*

Water around a toilet is a sure sign that a seal between the bowl and toilet flange is broken.

Bowl gaskets come in three forms: rubber, beeswax and a newer rubber covered with wax. Each has its advantages and disadvantages. Wax gaskets are by far the most popular, primarily because one size fits nearly every installation and because they are inexpensive. Rubber gaskets, on the other hand, seldom leak once installed, are reusable and cause fewer problems when the right thickness of gasket is used. The disadvantage is that the right thickness must be determined in advance, which is not always easy. Rubber gaskets are also more expensive. New, wax-covered rubber gaskets are a compromise between the two. They provide the strong seal associated with rubber and afford the minor gap-filling capabilities of the wax gaskets.

In determining which gasket to use, consider the use the toilet will get and the kind of floor supporting it. If the toilet will be used by a very heavy or handicapped person, or if the floor level has been raised by subflooring or quarry tile, rubber gaskets are a better choice. Wax gaskets will hold up well in other situations.

To reseat a toilet, drain the tank and dip all water out of the bowl. Then undo the supply tube connection, either at the ballcock or at the shutoff valve. Pry the caps from the closet bolts at the base of the bowl and undo the nuts from the bolts. Then straddle the bowl, grasp it on each side near the seat hinges and pull up. Set the toilet down on a few sheets of newspaper and gently lay it over on its side. This will expose the horn, or drain opening, of the toilet.

Use a putty knife to scrape all remaining wax from around the horn of the bowl and from the bowl flange on the floor. Next, slide the old closet bolts from the flange and replace with new bolts. Press a new gasket onto the flange so it's centered between the bolts. Then pick the bowl up and walk it over to the flange. Align it so you can see the closet bolts through holes in the base. Then settle the bowl down onto the gasket. It is best not to lift or move the bowl once the wax seal has come in contact with the flange.

Before tightening the closet bolt nuts, make sure the back of the tank sits square with the wall. Then tighten the bolts, each a little at a time. Draw the nuts down only until you feel firm resistance. Then sit or stand on the toilet to compress the gasket. This should let you draw the bolts down another two turns.

Finally turn the water back on. After a few days of normal use, tighten the closet bolts again until they feel snug. Then trim off the long ends of the bolts with a hacksaw, if necessary, and snap the caps over the bolts to complete the job.

Common bathroom repairs

This is a guide to some of the most common bathroom repairs.

Faucet Repair

The faucets in your home will eventually need repair, and because replacement parts are inexpensive and plumbers are not, it makes sense to do the job yourself. All that's required is a basic knowledge of faucet components, an adjustable wrench, a utility knife or awl, a screwdriver, heat-proof grease and assorted washers or replacement cartridges, depending on your faucet.

You are likely to encounter two types of faucets: the older valve stem-and-seat units and newer washerless cartridge types.

In stem-and-seat units, the movable valve stem connects to the handle and the valve seat is threaded into the fixture. By turning the handle counterclockwise, the stem moves off the seat and water passes through. If you turn the stem the other way, it will bear down on the seat and stop the water. To get a tight seal in the closed position, the bottom of the stem has a replaceable washer. To prevent water from leaking around the stem in the open position, cover the outside of the stem with either graphite packing or a small O-ring. Because replacing the washer and packing is easier than replacing the valve seat, undertake the repair as soon as you see water beginning to drip. Otherwise, you can damage the seat by overtightening the valve stem.

The washerless cartridge-type units work in a similar way. The cartridge simply moves up and down within the fixture to start or stop the flow. When it becomes worn, however, the entire cartridge must be replaced.

To repair either type, begin by shutting off the water. If the faucet has its own shutoff valves, just turn these off. If not, shut down the entire system at the water meter or at the valve close to

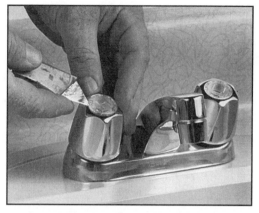

Remove decorative caps from handles with a utility knife. If there are no caps, look for setscrew at the bottom of the handles.

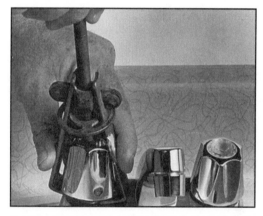

Remove faucet screw, then gently pry off handle with screwdriver. If stuck, use handle puller, as shown, to prevent damage.

To remove valve stem, slide adjustable wrench over locknut and turn counterclockwise. Valve stem should come out easily.

Remove worn washer from valve stem, then replace with a new one. Tighten screw so washer just begins to compress.

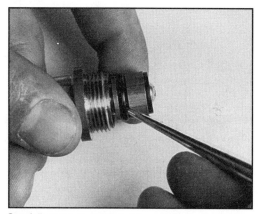

Carefully remove old O-ring from side of valve stem with awl or knife. Then replace with size recommended by manufacturer.

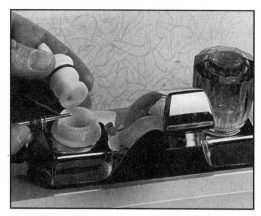

On washerless faucets, entire cartridge—including spring cup on bottom—must be replaced. Use awl to guide both.

where the water supply enters the house. Next, remove the faucet handle. To do this, you must pry off the decorative cap on the top of the handle and remove the screws underneath. Some faucets have a setscrew at the bottom of the handle that holds the handle to the stem.

If you have trouble removing the handle, gently pry under its edge with a screwdriver. If this doesn't work, then use a handle puller to remove it (see photo). With the handle removed, you will see the valve stem and its locknut. Using an adjustable wrench, loosen this nut and back out the entire stem. You can see if it's a washer-and-seat type or a cartridge model. If it's the former, remove the washer screw and discard the old washer. Replace it with a new one that fills the stem flange completely. Then replace the stem O-ring or graphite packing and apply heat-proof grease to the washer and all faucet and stem threads. This grease can easily double the life of washers and make removing the stem easier next time. Install the stem and handle.

To install new cartridges in washerless faucets, just press the new unit into place, tighten the locknut and replace the handle and cap. Some models have a spring-loaded rubber cap that seals against the bottom of the cartridge. These must also be replaced, then carefully guided—with the new cartridge—into the fixture.

Drain Cleaning

Cleaning clogged plumbing drains need not be difficult. The trick is knowing when to hire a professional and when to do it yourself. As a general rule, clean small, easily accessible drains on sinks and tubs, and leave larger toilet and sewer lines to the pros.

To do a good job, most drains require a two-step cleaning process. First, snake the drain line, then use a plunger and hot water to force debris into the larger sewer stack. A handheld snake and a plunger are good investments for this job, especially if you can share the cost with your neighbors. You can also rent these plumbing tools.

Start by removing the trap from the clogged drain line. This can be the most troublesome part of the job. Chrome traps become fragile with age and can crumble or break when taken apart. Plastic traps, on the other hand, are joined with compression fittings which are much easier to remove.

When you have the trap out, begin feeding the snake cable into the drain line one foot at a time.

Some clogs will fill the entire drain line from the trap, while others might be lodged between fittings 10 ft. away. Start cranking the cable when it no longer pushes in easily. When you do feel resistance, lock the cable to its housing with the setscrew and slowly push the snake and turn the cable at the same time.

When the snake housing is against the drain opening, stop, pull out another foot of cable and crank again. Repeat the process until you have worked through the entire line. Then reverse the steps to remove the snake. Pull it out and crank the cable one foot at a time.

When all the cable is retrieved, put the trap back in and run hot water into the line. Then plunge the drain until the water passes freely. When plunging fixtures with overflow openings, these openings must be plugged with a wet rag; otherwise, you will lose the force of the plunger.

The process for cleaning tub drains is basically the same, except you operate the snake through the overflow opening. To gain access, just remove the trip-lever mechanism as shown.

Automatic Drain Vents

It is sometimes impossible to vent a plumbing fixture that has a conventional pipe, especially on jobs when you relocate a fixture. But to keep your fixtures operating properly and to keep your house free of sewer gas, you should vent every fixture. To make this easier, manufacturers have designed automatic venting devices that are easy to install, inexpensive and almost foolproof. Keep in mind, however, that some codes prohibit their use, so check your local codes before proceeding. A typical vent has a 1½×3-in. plastic cylinder with a hooded passage on one end and male pipe threads on the other. Inside there is a spring-loaded diaphragm. When drain water rushes past the vent, suction opens the diaphragm and pulls in surrounding air instead of water from the trap. When pressure is equalized, the diaphragm closes to keep sewer gas from escaping. To install, disassemble the existing fittings and buy proper fittings and pipe for your situation.

Begin drain repair by removing the trap. Adjustable pliers will loosen plastic fittings; use a pipe wrench for chrome.

Slide snake cable into drain line one foot at a time. Tighten set-screw on cable, then turn crank and push in cable gently.

After snaking, reconnect trap, then run very hot water into drain line. Plug overflow with rag, then plunge drain opening.

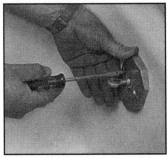

Bathtub drains must be snaked through overflow opening, not drain hole. Begin by removing trip-lever plate and mechanism.

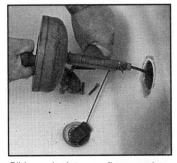

Slide snake into overflow opening and crank. Trap is within 2 ft. of opening, so you'll feel resistance almost immediately.

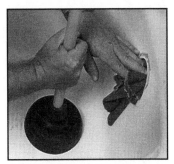

Remove snake and run very hot water into drain. Plug overflow opening with rag, then plunge drain opening repeatedly.

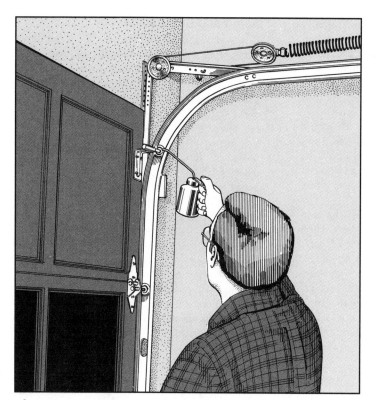

1 Remove any accumulated grime from the rollers and tracks using an oil-dampened rag. Once they're clean, periodically lubricate rollers with a touch of lightweight oil.

2 Severely clogged rollers must be removed from door by backing off retaining nuts. Be sure to remove one roller at a time.

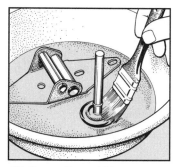

3 Once roller and hinge are removed, wash both in kerosene until thoroughly cleaned. Use old paint brush or toothbrush.

Overhead garage door repair

Lifting and lowering a heavy sectional garage door should normally be an easy task because of the built-in mechanical advantages: rollers, pulleys and counterbalance springs. But over time, this task can become very difficult because of neglect of simple maintenance or because some parts are broken, worn or misaligned. It doesn't take much time and only a few simple tools are needed to get your garage door in shape.

Lubrication

The most common cause for a door to move sluggishly is lack of lubrication—coupled with the accumulation of grime—in the roller bearings. Another possible source of friction can be traced to grime-caked or rusted roller shafts that prevent the roller hinges from pivoting freely as the door moves through its tracks.

Periodic oiling of the rollers and hinges, as well as the pulleys and the insides of the tracks, will help keep the door functioning trouble free. But keep in mind that oiled tracks tend to collect dirt so don't overdo your lubrication. Just apply a thin film of lightweight oil to the rollers and occasionally wipe the tracks clean with an oil-dampened cloth.

Removing Rollers

Severely neglected roller assemblies may well call for removal in order to do a thorough job of cleaning and lubrication. If you have to go this route, be sure to remove only one roller assembly at a time and replace it before removing another.

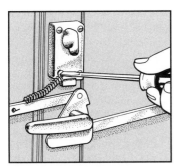

4 If return spring on lock bars has lost tension, replace it. One end of spring is hooked on bar, other is screwed to lock.

5 The lockset should be lubricated from outside the door using graphite—in dry or liquid form. Do not use oil on lock.

6 If lockbar doesn't slide into strike opening in the track, loosen guide bracket screws and adjust bracket up or down.

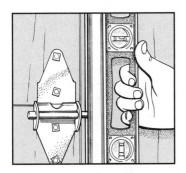

7 If severe binding between roller and track occurs, then track is probably out of alignment. Check for plumb using a level.

8 If track is out of plumb, loosen mounting-bracket lagscrews so it moves. Three or four brackets per track are common.

9 To change tension on counterbalance spring, open door completely then tighten or loosen support cable in its bracket.

When replacing the hinge, attach the bottom leaf first, then insert a thin cardboard shim between the adjacent door panels before tightening the nuts on the upper leaf. This will prevent the door panels from binding.

Track Alignment

Another trouble spot to check when the door is balky and functioning poorly is the track alignment. Hard use and abuse in operating the door, as well as the normal settling of the garage structure, can cause the tracks to become misaligned. Visual observation of the rollers in the tracks and checking for plumb with a spirit level will indicate whether an adjustment of one or both tracks is required.

Another situation that results from settling is the gradual misalignment of the lock bars. Eventually the bars can start to rub against the strike opening or miss the hole completely.

The problem can usually be solved by adjusting the slotted bar guides on both ends of the door. In extreme cases it may even be necessary to enlarge the opening with a metal file to allow free movement of the bar.

Counterbalance Springs

The counterbalance springs on the typical door shown have no built-in adjustment mechanism like some of the older doors had. The only way to adjust the springs on these newer doors is to increase or reduce the tension by tightening or loosening the connecting lift cable. If the spring has lost its tension it should be replaced. This is indicated when the spring, under no tension, does not close tightly and shows spaces between the coils. This determination, as well as the adjustment or removal of the springs, must be done with the door in the fully opened—raised—position.

Some experimentation is required to adjust the counterbalance springs. If your door is sluggish, tighten the spring slightly by pulling more cable through the locking bracket as shown. If the door lifts too quickly, loosen the cable. In either case, be sure to put the cable back on its locking bracket as shown.

In addition to these simple maintenance chores, also be on the lookout for failing paint on the exterior of a wood door. Keep it well painted to seal out moisture.

Fix a problem door

While most of us think of a house as a static structure—totally unlike a mechanically functioning object such as a car engine, houses do have moving parts. And, in the same way that an engine needs periodic tuneup, the moving parts of your house may have fallen out of adjustment and require attention. The doors are the most likely candidates for wear and tear. Changes in humidity cause them to bind against the jamb, and worn or poorly fit hinges will cause the door to sag. Perhaps it's time to perform a tuneup on your house to get those doors working like new.

Checking the Hinges

Hinges should be recessed so the hinge leaves are flush with the door edge and jamb. If a recess is too deep, the door edge can bind against the jamb before the door is completely closed. This condition can eventually loosen the screw fastenings.

Check to make sure the screws are tight by pulling outward slightly on the door. If you see any movement between the hinge and wood, try tightening the screws. If the screw continues to turn when it should be tight, the screw hole is stripped.

The easiest solution to a stripped screw hole is to replace the old screws with longer ones.

Because most jambs are ¾ in. thick, installing a 1½-in.-long screw usually will catch the framing beyond the jamb. First, bore a pilot hole through the jamb for the longer screw. Don't overtighten the new screw to avoid splitting the jamb.

You can also plug a stripped hole with a dowel and then fasten the hinge with the original screw. Begin by removing the hinge leaf. If your door is hung on two hinges, you'll have to remove the door. Check the holding power of each screw so you can fix all the problem holes at once. If your door is hung on three hinges, you can remove one of them without removing the door. Support the door with a couple of wooden shingles or other tapered wedges. Tap these under the door until its weight is removed from the hinge. Then remove the screws to free the hinge leaf.

Using the old hole as a pilot, bore a ⅜-in.-dia. hole taking care not to go completely through the jamb. Cut a plug from a ⅜-in.-dia. fluted dowel pin. Glue the plug in place and let dry before boring the new pilot hole.

If any of the hinge mortises are too deep, shim them before installing the hinges. Trim a thick piece of veneer or mat board to the size of the mortise. Then place it in the mortise, bore screw holes and install the hinge.

Proper Clearance

If the door rubs against the jamb as it closes, it must be trimmed to fit. The top and sides should show a ⅛- to 3⁄16-in. space and a 3⁄16- to ¼-in. gap should appear at the bottom. Set an ordinary compass to the correct clearance. Hold the point on the jamb edge and scribe the trim line around the door.

If you have a small amount of material to remove on the latch edge or outer corner of the top, you can do the job with the door in place

Fix stripped screw holes by boring a ⅜-in.-dia. hole and gluing a plug in place. Don't bore completely through the jamb.

If the hinge leaf sits below wood surface, the mortise is too deep. Repair by installing shims between hinge and mortise bottom.

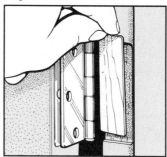

Use a compass to scribe the ⅛- to 3⁄16-in. clearance line on the latch side and top of door. Leave 3⁄16- to ¼-in. gap at bottom.

using a block plane. You may need to remove the latch set. If so, check that the latch plate is flush with the door edge when you put it back in. If necessary, deepen the mortise with a sharp chisel. Trimming the full length of the top or any part of the bottom requires that your remove the door. First, wedge the door to take the load off the hinges. Then, tap the hinge pins out. Remove the top pin last and be prepared to catch the door when it's free.

The top and bottom are trimmed by planing in from each side to avoid splitting the door stiles. If you need to remove more material than can be comfortably planed, use a circular saw for the job. Use a blade designed for making finished cuts and apply masking tape to the saw base plate to prevent marring the door. Measure the distance from the plate edge to a tooth on the blade.

Clamp a straight cutting guide to the door so the distance between the guide and the cut line equals the distance between the blade and the base edge. Scribe the trim line with a sharp utility knife to minimize tear out.

Adjusting the Stops

If the door contacts the stops before the latch engages, the stops will need to be adjusted. If the contact area is small, try tapping the stop into position with a block of wood and hammer. Once the door closes easily, nail the stop with 4d finishing nails.

If tapping it doesn't work, or the door is simply too tight all around, remove the stops by punching a nail completely through at one end of each piece with a nail set and then prying each stop off. Put them back by first closing the door and pressing gently until the lock hits the strike.

With the door at this position, the head stop can be installed with a $1/16$ in. clearance between the door and the stop. Nail with 4d finishing nails and attach the other stops with the same clearance.

In situations where the stop abuts the casing, it's simplest to adjust the clearance by moving the strikeplate. Remove it and expand the latch hole. Then, plug the old screw holes and install the strike in the correct position. Fill the remaining gap with wood filler, sand and finish.

A sharp block plane trims door to exact size. Remove door and plane in from ends when trimming top and bottom edges.

First try adjusting stop clearance by tapping the stop into position. Then, secure the stop with 4d finishing nails.

To remove stop, punch bottom nail through and pry the stop off. Pull remaining nails from back with locking pliers.

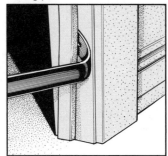

Use a circular saw to remove excessive material. Measure distance from tooth to base edge for positioning cutting guide.

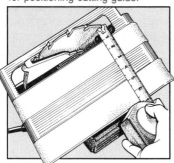

Clamp cutting guide to door spaced at the correct distance from the trim line. Score line with sharp knife to minimize tearing.

After removing stock near the latch set, check that the plate is still flush with the edge. Adjust mortise with sharp chisel.

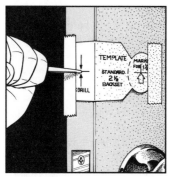

1 Begin by positioning the template supplied with your lock on the edge of your door. Use an awl to mark hole locations.

2 Bore lockset hole first using holesaw. Bore until pilot bit breaks through other side, then complete hole from other side.

3 Bore bolt hole next, making sure to keep bit aligned vertically *and* horizontally. Accuracy is crucial on this job.

Deadbolt lock installation

It seems that all of us are more security conscious than we used to be. New high-end electronic security systems seem to be springing up everywhere these days. And while many of these boast truly remarkable capabilities, it's important to remember that any good security system should start out with the installation of deadbolt locks on all your exterior doors. With a little care and the right tools you can install them yourself and save a substantial amount of money in the process.

Types of Locks

Deadbolts come in two basic styles. One requires a key to lock and unlock the door from both sides. The other requires a key from the outside but also has a turn unit knob on the inside. The type you choose will depend on the type of doors you have and on fire-safety factors.

If you have a door with a glass panel in it, an inside key lock offers more protection from an intruder who might be able to reach the turn units by breaking the glass. If your doors have no glass, locks with inside turn units will work fine. The added advantage of a lock with a turn unit on the inside is that you don't need a key to get out in the event of a fire. The choice is yours. The installation is virtually the same.

Planning the Installation

Start by deciding where you want the lock to be. If you have a hollow-core door, stay just above the lockset that is already on your door. Hollow-core doors are reinforced near this lockset and, therefore, are strongest at door-knob level. Even if you have a solid-core door, stay near the lockset for the greatest strength.

When you buy your deadbolt, you will find directions that include the exact drill bit sizes you will need. Make sure you have bits to meet those requirements. Inexpensive, adjustable holesaws work fine. You will also find a paper template to help you mark the exact hole locations.

Installing the Lock

The hole for the lock cylinder should be bored first. While you bore the hole, pay close attention to the angle of your drill and make sure that you bore straight in. Don't drift to the left or

4 Trace bolt plate on edge of door, then mortise out door edge so plate will sit flush. Be sure to use a very sharp chisel.

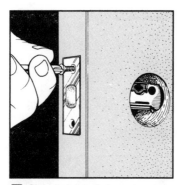

5 Slide bolt into hole and make sure it fits flush on door edge. Bore screw clearance holes, then attach with screws.

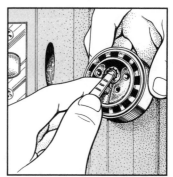

6 Deadbolt is activated by flat pin that joins both sides of lockset. Pin length can be adjusted to match door thickness.

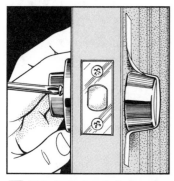

7 Slide lockset and pin through deadbolt mechanism, then tape to door. Slide other half of lockset into place and attach.

8 Test bolt for proper operation, then when satisfied, coat end of bolt with lipstick, close door and slide bolt onto jamb.

9 Using lipstick mark as guide, mortise jamb to receive dead-bolt hardware. When hole is bored, attach plates with long screws.

right. If you are working alone, block the door so that it remains steady and concentrate on a straight hole through the door. When you finish the larger hole for the lock cylinder, bore the smaller bolt hole. Use the same procedure.

After your bore the holes, press the bolt in place and mark around the plate with a knife. Then, chisel out the plate area to the manufacturer's recommended depth. Press the lock cylinder into its opening from the outside and make sure it catches the bolt. Installing a strike plate for a deadbolt is a little more involved than for a regular lockset.

Many deadbolts come with a reinforcing box to give the door frame added strength. Measuring for this box is critical. Because doors often warp when in place, simply measuring from the bolt to the edge of the door and transferring these measurements to the door jamb do not always work. A better way is to paint the edge of the bolt with lipstick and then, after closing the

door, turn the bolt against the door frame. The lipstick will mark the exact spot where the bolt will strike the frame. Determine the exact center of the lipstick mark and take all measurements off this point.

Deadbolt Reinforcing

When installing a reinforcing box, you will need to bore two holes and then trim them into a square hole for the box. If there is no reinforcing box, you will still have to chisel out a recessed area to accept the strike plate and a heavier, brass reinforcing plate. The total depth of these two plates will be near ¼ inch.

When the door frame is ready for the strike plate, reinforcing plate or reinforcing box, bore the screw holes. The reinforcing plate will come with heavy screws at least 3 in. long that will extend through the door frame and into the wall studs. Install these and the screws for the strike plate and the job is complete.

Reglazing windows

Replacing a broken pane of window glass is a relatively simple task and, for most homeowners, an inevitable one. If it is done carelessly, it can result in serious injury. Follow the shop-tested, step-by-step instructions presented here to repair shattered windows like a pro—safely and easily.

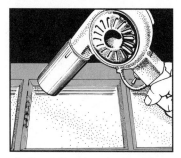

1 Use a flameless heat gun to soften old, brittle putty. Heat the putty (be careful not to char the wood) and then scrape it off.

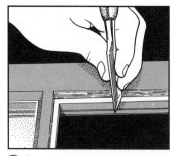

2 Scrape clean sash and muntin rabbets with a chisel. Hold chisel perpendicular and scrape down to bare wood.

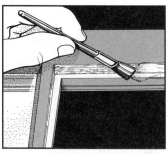

3 Apply coat of linseed oil to the clean rabbets. This prevents bare wood from absorbing oil out of the compound.

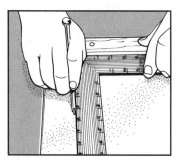

4 Hold glass cutter between index and middle fingers and score glass. Use square and board, nailed to bench, as guides.

5 Use a flexible-blade putty knife to apply a ⅛-in.-thick bead of glazing compound in the four rabbets around the opening.

6 Place new pane into the opening and press down gently. Squeeze out air pockets in compound for a good seal.

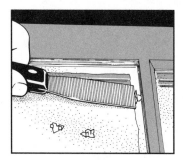

7 Install push-point glazier's points with a rigid-blade putty knife. Force the points into the wood to hold the glass securely.

8 Roll glazing compound between your palms to form ⅜-in.-dia. ropes. Lay these ropes around the perimeter of the glass.

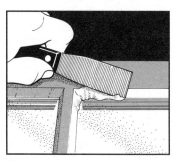

9 Hold putty knife at an angle and press compound into the rabbets to form a smooth, triangular-shaped bead.

You can get a soft, grainy effect similar to Impressionist paintings if you overexpose high speed slide film and make an enlarged print.

Fun with film

Daylight films shot in artificial light suggest warmth, romance or nostalgia.

When someone mentions special-effects photography, your first reaction might be to reach for some exotic filters. But you don't have to. One way to delve into the magic of special effects photography without filters or a home darkroom is to use ordinary film in extraordinary ways—in some cases breaking the rules of good photography.

The first effect we'll explore involves shifting the color in pictures—without the use of color filters. When daylight films are shot indoors, they record all the deficiencies of artificial light, yielding images that are warm—or yellowish red. This effect can impart a nostalgic glow to scenes, one that comes in handy when you want photos to have a sentimental mood, as in the portrait shown here. In some cases, slides gain an old-fashioned, sepia-toned look.

Conversely, tungsten films shot outdoors have a definite bluish cast, one that gives a cold, though not stern, feeling to pictures. Try this technique with landscapes made on quiet, misty mornings, or to exaggerate the frigid feelings of shots of snow-covered fields.

Another rule you can break is the one that says you shouldn't shoot color under mixed light sources. "Mixed" means scenes lit with artificial light *and* daylight, such as a room with all the lights turned on and sunlight streaming through the window. You can use either daylight or tungsten film to shoot this scene. With daylight film, you'll get the true color of the sunlight and a yellow glow from the lamps. With tungsten, you'll get natural colors around the lamps and a cold blue light streaming through the window.

The easiest way to get a high-grain effect is to start with a film that already has inherently high grain. Then expose these films at even higher speeds. There is a limit to how far you can push these films—a 1- or 2-stop push is best. Beyond that, color and sharpness rapidly deteriorate. After you shoot, inform your lab that you want the film push-processed at the ISO rating you shot at.

You can also get offbeat effects with 35mm instant slide films. These films were designed for special applications, such as the photomicrograph shot seen here. Soon after release, photographers began to explore their creative possibilities. The film is actually a black-and-white film overlaid with a single layer of primary-color filter stripes. When made into prints, the color-forming stripes read as color *patterns*. Prints made from these slides have been compared to those of antique color processes, such as turn-of-the-century autochromes.

Inner visions

Specialized infrared film allows us to picture the world through an entirely new set of eyes. Infrared light (IR) behaves very differently from natural light. Objects that normally reflect light might be totally nonreflective to IR, whereas other subjects, indistinguishable to panchromatic films, pop right out of an IR photo. IR films are available as b&w prints or color transparencies for about twice the price of conventional films.

IR b&w is ideal for dramatic shots of clouds and sky, and for cutting through haze. Pollutants that reflect IR are easily detected. Leafy plants also reflect lots of infrared under the right light. IR film renders plants as white with b&w film

Infrared lightwaves are visible to the eye,but IR film detects how objects absorb or reflect it *(above)*. Compared to conventional film *(below)*, IR reveals unusual color shifts—green sky, black water, red vegetation.

and as varying shades of red and magenta when color IR film is used with a red or orange filter. Camouflage detection with color IR film was once very popular, since many paints and fabrics reflect IR differently than visible light. It is still very popular with creative photographers because of its false color effects. Color variations within the subject, impossible to get with filters alone, are possible with IR film. It all depends on the color of the filter you use in front of the lens. For true IR photography (shown here in the aerial photo), a medium-red filter blocks violet, blue and red lightwaves—to which the film is also sensitive. For more offbeat photos, experiment with a variety of filters—or none at all.

As with visible light photography, IR films need enough light reflecting off a subject to produce an image. At night, there's not enough IR light available to shoot in total darkness. You'll need an artificial light source, such as a flash or flood light. Filters are not necessary in the dark.

A popular expectation is that IR films can illustrate differences in temperature. It is true that heat radiation is part of the IR spectrum, but IR films are made to work with the shorter IR wavelengths and not the longer heat waves. A hot iron does not emit enough short IR waves to be used as a light source in total darkness and will require very long exposures. Hot appliances, engines, castings and other objects between 500°F and 1000°F emit lots of IR and can be shot in total darkness.

Infrared photography requires little, if any, additional equipment to experiment. In fact, b&w IR photography is as easy to try as ordering the film. Conventional b&w processing at home or any lab will produce good results. Color IR film is not easy to process at home because it requires the old E-4 chemistry. IR images do tend to be a bit grainy due to their thicker emulsions. Be sure to tell the lab that it is IR to minimize handling the cassette in light.

If you have ever wondered about the purpose of that little red dot near your focusing scale, it's for IR photography. Without correction, long IR waves would focus behind the film. When using IR film, simply focus normally, note the subject's distance on your focusing scale, and move the distance measurement over to the red dot. Autofocus SLR cameras will require manual focusing. Compact, autofocus point-and-shoot cameras with lenses shorter than 40mm should work fine without focus compensation.

Use long exposures to capture a fireworks display as it cascades down.

Night shots

Summertime presents many opportunities to photograph dazzling displays of light at night. Whether it's fireworks on the Fourth of July or carnival rides at the county fair, you can create colorful pictures with a minimum of equipment and a few simple techniques.

Use either daylight- or tungsten-balanced films to shoot fireworks or neon. Tungsten films will give a cooler look to the colors. Daylight films will give a warmer rendition. Use a lens with a focal length between 100 and 200mm to fill the frame. Zooms work well here.

There's no practical way to make exposure readings of fireworks. For that reason, the techniques shown here require you to work in the manual exposure mode, according to the speed of the film.

We've all seen shots of fireworks where the colors seem to flow down through the sky. Most of these are made with exposure times of 1 second or longer. To make these shots, mount your camera on a tripod, set the shutter on B (bulb), open the shutter when you see the first hint of color in the sky, then close it after a second or two. If your camera does not have a B setting, set the shutter speed for 1 or 2 seconds.

If you can't use a tripod, you might try hand-holding the camera. To reduce the risk of vibration-induced blurs, you'll have to use faster exposures. You won't get the streaming effect as the pryotechnics drop from the sky—just the initial burst.

Exposure times are approximate. Try 1/30-second at f/2.8 with ISO 200 film, 1/30-second at f/4 with ISO 400 film, and 1/60-second at f/5.6 for ISO 1000 or higher. These are still relatively slow speeds, so steady your camera as much as possible. With auto-everything compacts, you really can't control the exposure. These cameras will expose for the overall darkness of the sky. On newer models, override the automatic flash. On older ones, trick the camera by covering the metering eye—even the flash—with black tape. Shoot only ISO 400 or faster films with these cameras.

For portraits use a telephoto lens to blur the background and emphasize the subject. Note that props are used to keep subject's hands busy. Sitting pose makes subject more relaxed.

One on one

Pictures of friends or relatives predominate in our photo albums. Portraiture attempts to project an individual's character on two-dimensional film. This is a demanding task.

The best portraits should emphasize the subject. Keep the background simple or out of focus. Short telephoto lenses (70mm through 135mm) used at larger apertures (lower f/stop numbers) will blur backgrounds for greater subject emphasis. Point-and-shoot compacts with tele lenses (or adapters) set to about 70mm make nice portrait cameras when shooting between 6 and 10 feet. Shooting with slow films, such as ISO 25 or 50, ensures larger lens openings.

The best kind of lighting for casual portraits is diffused daylight, such as that available on a bright but hazy day or in the shade or through a white curtain.

Lighting depends greatly on your subject's physical attributes. Large round faces need side lighting to thin them out. Thin faces need head-on illumination to bring them into proportion. Position your subject accordingly or use reflectors to direct light to specific areas of the face.

Subtle changes in body positioning can alter personality. People photograph much more aggressively when leaning toward the camera. You also emphasize confidence when the subject looks over the shoulder and directly into the lens. Tilting the head slightly to the side enhances femininity. Double chins can be eliminated by tilting the subject's head back, raising the camera and shooting from above (parallel to the face) for a head-and-shoulders portrait.

Highlighting the hair will help you separate your subject's head from the background—and add a touch of flattery. A small flash unit, connected to the camera with a long PC cable and positioned above and behind the subject, will do the trick. For more glamorous pictures of women, place the flash directly behind the head. Natural backlighting works too, but in all cases, be sure to meter light reading directly off the face.

Compose vertically, if you can, and fill the frame with as much of the subject as possible for tightly cropped portraits.

Shoot the moon

The moon photographs well on its own or when juxtaposed against Earth's landscapes, as in the multiple exposure shown here. You can reach the moon with a compact point-and-shoot camera, but SLRs offer more options.

A simple zoom or telephoto lens in the 200mm range will show crater details when coupled to your SLR with an inexpensive 2X converter lens. With long lenses, vibration will be more of a problem than optical resolution. Mount your camera on a tripod. For really sharp pictures, use a locking cable release instead of the camera's own shutter release button, and load the camera with slow ISO 25 slide film.

Set the lens aperture at f/16 for a telephoto lens. Lock the shutter open on the B (bulb) setting while holding a piece of black cardboard

in front of the lens. ISO 25 film at f/16 requires a 1/2-second exposure—slow enough to expose by hand with the cardboard.

Nightscapes with the moon are easily shot as multiple exposure photos. To create the picture seen here, you'll have to run the film through the camera twice. The first set of exposures is for the moon, the second for the landscape.

You can shoot your landscape in another location or at another time. Set the aperture at f/5.6 and the focal length of the lens anywhere you want—just remember where the moon was positioned in the frame when you shot it.

You can shoot the moon with an autofocus point-and-shoot camera, but you'll have to trick the camera first. Although the moon reflects light brightly, autocompacts will meter for the predominantly dark sky and set exposure accordingly, overexposing the moon. To trick the camera, use ISO 25 slide film, but before you load it cover the cassette's DX coding (the series of silver and black boxes) with tape. This will force the camera to expose for ISO 100 film, underexposing the ISO 25 slides.

Because compact cameras have short lenses, the moon won't appear large or detailed in your pictures. Set the lens for the greatest focal length possible, and try to use a tele-adapter lens.

Focus on speed

You don't have to be a professional race-car photographer to take good action shots of your favorite race or driver. At oval courses, from small dirt tracks up to Daytona or the Indianapolis 500, you can get some good photos from the infield or stands, but you won't have the kind of success available at a road-racing course. Road racing provides more photo opportunities, mainly because cars turn left and right, go uphill and down, and you can see them from a variety of angles.

Most racing photos are of the three basic types shown here.

Public access areas offer opportunity to take close-up shots of favorite car or driver.

Panning is the most commonly used and is really quite simple. You want to capture the movement of a race car as it rushes past you or around a corner. Here's all you do. Pick the angle at which you want to shoot the car. Get the car in your viewfinder well before that point, follow it along and press the shutter release when the car is at the desired angle. Follow the car *smoothly* for a second or two after you've shot.

To show the car sharply from front to back, shoot at 1/125-second. Try slower speeds, even down to 1/15-sec. for the different, often beautiful, effects of speed blur. Try panning when the cars are on straight stretches, but also get them in corners, particularly on sweeping turns where you are on the inside.

To stop a race car, especially with a telephoto lens, use shutter speeds of 1/250-sec. or faster. Pick the spot you want to shoot, and watch for a few laps. See where the cars are working—you'll be freezing the action, but you don't want the car to look like it's just parked on the track. Try to find a place where the car looks like it's a bit out of shape, as in a turn.

Frame the scene in your viewfinder, but don't start shooting until you've done a few dry runs to follow the car through the scene. Although you're not taking a pan shot, you should still follow the car into the scene, snap the photo, and follow it out again.

The overall shot can be a pan or stop-action photo, but the point is to show what the environment around the track is like. Usually, short lenses and wide-angle lenses are best for this.

It would be a mistake to go to a race and just do one of the three types of photos we've suggested.

Panning at 1/30-second keeps most of car sharp, but adds enough blur to suggest speed.

Slow, 1/5-second exposure creates an Impressionist rendition of race car at speed.

Fading memories

Its sad but true: The photographs to which we entrust our memories are neither immortal nor immutable. They can develop partial amnesia, where a color fades or changes, or chronic loss of memory, where the entire image vanishes progressively. This is especially true of prints that are left out for display, particularly color prints. But stored prints, even negatives and slides, are not immune to the ravages of time and the environment.

As good as they are, the dyes used in color films do fade, and the papers and gels used for prints, negatives and transparencies do deteriorate. Fading comes in two forms. Balanced fading is a matter of color *quantity*. The cyan, magenta and yellow dyes that make up the image diminish equally in relation to each other. The colors are no longer as rich as before, but they're still recognizable as correct. Unbalanced fading is a matter of color *quality*, and it is objectionable to most people. If one color has deteriorated out of proportion to the others, the tonal balances will be altered and appear unnatural. For example, normal flesh tones might turn boiled-ham pink or sickly yellow-green.

Light, heat, humidity, air pollutants and certain chemicals are harmful to color photos. Store developed images in a dark, cool, dry and preferably airtight environment.

The ultraviolet radiation in sunlight and fluorescent bulbs will bleach colors (incandescent light is less damaging). If a photo is permanently displayed, it should be framed and located away from direct lighting. Glass will filter some ultraviolet, but plastics sold to protect photos are better.

Heat and humidity, together or separately and especially in combination with chemical fumes, will accelerate the deterioration of a photo. This can happen even in dark storage. Moreover, humidity can breed damaging mold. This means attics, basements and garages are not the ideal repositories for your photos. If you have to compromise, a warm and dry location is better than a damp one—even if it's cool.

Airborne pollutants are difficult to avoid—and they'll damage otherwise stable black-and-white photos. Besides automotive and industrial emissions, harmful fumes emanate from gas stoves, paints and solvents, mildew inhibitors insecticides, unfinished and unaged woods, newly finished woods and glued-wood products.

There's hope for that faded portrait you might find in an old family album. If the negative's in good shape, routine reprinting should yield a sharp new print. But if the negative has deteriorated, you'll need customized service. If the negative isn't totally spoiled, the lab can reconstitute key elements such as flesh tones in a portrait.

If you want to spare future generations from the expense and disappointment of faded photos you have taken, store you photos well and make duplicates for cold storage while the negative or slide is young.

Modern processing salvaged much of the original quality of this poorly stored 32-year-old print and its negative.

Harsh flash yielded an over-exposed print *(left)* of this child's face, but the print was corrected by the lab *(right)*.

Developing strategies

Be aware of the services—and service—your photo processor can and should provide. Generally, we accept whatever the lab gives us. If the colors are off, or the print is too dark, we allow the lab to blame our technique or equipment. In fact, when it comes to color and b&w prints, about the only thing a lab can't fix is a poorly focused picture. A little extra effort on the part of a lab can make most pictures turn out right.

If you're like most people, the roll you send in for processing contains a variety of subjects photographed under diverse lighting conditions. Though modern printing machinery accommodates for these changes and corrects printing accordingly, many labs still have equipment that is geared mainly to normal negatives—ones exposed in daylight with an overall balance of colors and tones. These printing machines also have channels—specific filter packs balanced for the more popular brands of color films. When your images don't match these programmed conditions, the operator still has the option to program in more or less exposure to shift the color balance to normalize what labs call oddball

negatives. If the lab doesn't take the time to do this, you might get less than optimal prints.

For example, let's say you've taken a picture of your child sitting on a red rug. When the automatic printing machine views the negative, it sees a large field of red and tries to balance it out in the print. The result is untrue colors on the rug, and a child with a purple face. This is known as subject failure, and it can be corrected.

Pictures made with flash can also present a problem. If the flash is too close to the subject or too powerful, the face often prints in a highly over-exposed fashion, as in the example shown here. All the operator has to do is print one button darker to get a well-exposed face. This will sacrifice the darker tones in the print (notice the carpet), but at least your principal subject will turn out right, as shown in the print on the right.

For the most part, today's color negative processing is standardized and mechanized and should yield good results—barring glitches in the processing machinery. If your negatives appear off-color, or if you see streaks and scratches spaced randomly throughout the roll, chances are you're looking at a lab-related problem. Unfortunately, poorly developed film can only be salvaged, not made right. You're lucky if you get an image at all.

When film *develops* properly but *prints* poorly insist on corrected prints. Insist firmly. Labs hate to remake prints. Once you let the lab operators know that you know they can do a better job, they might pay more attention next time.

Folding stairway installation

Perhaps you're fortunate enough to live in an older home that's complete with a full staircase to the attic. If so, you've probably found that the attic is a great place to store seasonal items and memorabilia. Homeowners without easy access to the attic either don't use the space or are forced to haul out the stepladder when they do. There is an alternative, however. A folding attic stairway allows you convenient access to this otherwise unused space without compromising the floor plan below. All that's needed are a few basic tools, some framing lumber and a friend to help out downstairs when you're in the attic.

Keep in mind that the ceiling framework in most homes without attic access was primarily designed to support the ceiling only. If you plan to use this space for heavy storage, make sure you put the heavy items above a load-bearing or partition wall.

Lay Out the Opening

The first step in a folding stairway installation project is to inspect the spacing, direction and size of the ceiling joists. The ceiling illustrated here was framed with 2×6 joists on 16-in. centers and the stairway unit was to lie parallel with the joists. Only one joist had to be cut to achieve the required 22-in.-wide rough opening. Installing a folding stairway at right angles to the joists involves a similar operation, but more joists will have to be cut and the framing will be more complex.

1 Complete framing includes headers for supporting the cut joist and the trimming joist placed at width of rough opening. Components are joined with metal hangers and nails.

When considering the placement of your stairway, keep in mind that besides providing space on the floor below for unfolding the stairs and moving around the unit, you'll need headroom at the top of the stairs.

Once you've determined where to place the stairway, climb into the attic and remove any insulation over and around the intended opening. Remember that the ceiling itself will not support your weight. Step only on the joists. After removing the insulation, tack-nail wide boards or ¾-in. plywood on the joists around the area where you'll be working to give you a better work surface.

If possible, plan to use an existing joist as one side of the rough opening framework. You'll need to find the position of this joist and mark it on the ceiling of the floor below. Install a ³⁄₁₆-in.-dia. bit in a drill and bore test holes through the ceiling in the rough opening area to locate the joist. Use a straightedge to mark the joist line on the ceiling. Then, lay out the rough opening with a framing square and straightedge.

The term "rough opening" refers to a size ½ in. wider and longer than the unit to be fit. This allows for small errors in laying out and squaring the framework and requires that shims be fit between the unit and the framework before you fasten it in permanently. It's a good idea to double check the actual size of the folding stairway case to make sure it will fit in the specified opening.

2 Before cutting the center joist, erect temporary 2×4 support partitions about 3 in. away from each rough opening end.

3 Use framing square to lay out for cutting joist. Actual cut line is 3 in. outside rough opening to allow for doubled header.

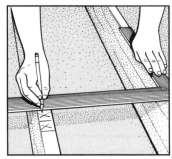

4 Set blade on your circular saw to maximum depth and cut the joist on inside of the line at each end of the opening.

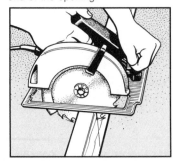

5 A sharp handsaw finishes cut. Because the cut line is outside the rough opening, make sure you don't cut through ceiling.

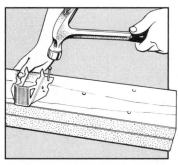

6 Construct both doubled headers to fit between the joists and install metal hangers to support the ends of the cut joist.

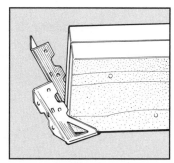

7 Before setting the headers in place, slip double joist hangers on the header ends for fastening to the ceiling joists.

With the rough opening marked, bore $^3/_{16}$-in.-dia. holes at each corner so you'll be able to find the defined area in the attic.

Framing the Ceiling

In any situation where you find that you have to cut through ceiling joists, you'll need to prepare temporary support partitions to carry their load before they're cut. Starting at one end, cut two pieces of 2×4 to a length that spans two joists on either side of the opening. These serve as a top and bottom plate for the temporary support partition. Then, cut three studs so the combined height of the plates and studs equals the ceiling height. Nail the top plate to the stud ends with 16d common nails. Lift up the top plate and studs so the plate is positioned about 3 in. to 4 in. away from the opening. Wedge the bottom plate under the studs and tap the assembly in place so it's plumb. Toenail the studs into the bottom plate. After the first partition is in place, install another at the other end of the opening.

With the temporary supports in place, climb back in the attic and use the holes bored at the layout corners to mark the rough opening. Carry the marks squarely up the side of the joist faces and across their top edges. Double check to be sure your marks are square and properly dimensioned. The section of the joist that runs through the rough opening must be removed and the cut ends supported with headers made of doubled joist stock. To find the correct cutting lines, add 3 in. to the layout marks at each rough opening end on the joist to be removed. This allows for the thickness of the doubled 2×6. Mark a square line down the face of the joist at these points.

To cut the joist, first set your circular saw blade to maximum depth and carefully cut on the inside edge of each cutoff line. Then, complete each cut with a small handsaw. Try to keep the handsaw from cutting through the ceiling.

This is a difficult operation, especially if the joists are closely spaced. If you do go through the ceiling, simply patch the hole after the stairway is installed.

8 Replace headers between joists and nail through to header ends. Install nails in hangers and toenail with 10d nails.

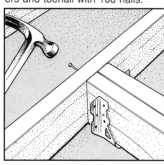

9 Mark position of trimming joist so its inside face is on the rough opening line. Install support hangers on headers.

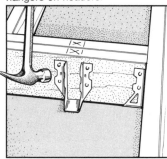

10 After cutting the trimmer to length, slip it in the hangers and nail. Complete by toenailing with 10d common nails.

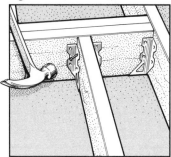

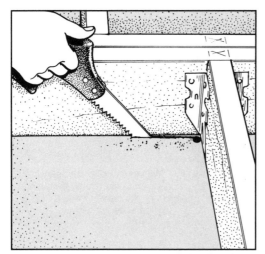

11 When cutting opening, have a helper on hand in room below. Then, nail the ceiling to the new frame.

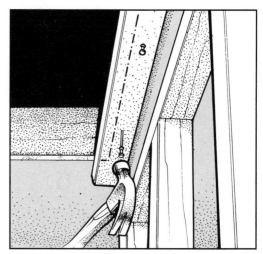

12 Install temporary ledgers to support folding stairway while it's being attached. Double-headed nails permit easy removal.

After you have made the cuts, remove the joist section and measure the distance between the outer joists at each end of the opening. Cut new joist stock exactly to length for the doubled headers at each end and nail together with 12d common nails. Make sure their ends and edges are flush.

Mark the positions of the cutoff joist ends on the headers and lay out a square line at the mark to indicate the metal hanger placement. Then, install the hangers that support the joist ends. Slip double joist hangers on each end of the headers, but don't nail them in place yet. Slide

13 Position stairway unit on ledger and use 8d nails to temporarily secure fixed end. Use shims to square unit, if necessary.

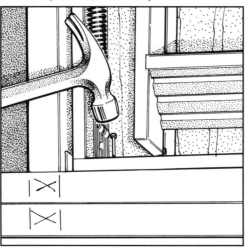

the headers in place and align them squarely with the layout marks and flush with the existing joists. Then secure them with 16d nails driven through the joists into the header ends. Install hanger nails or 1½-in. roofing nails in the hangers and toenail with 10d common nails.

Because the rough opening is narrower than the width left between the remaining joists, the completed framing will include a section called a *trimming joist* that spans the headers and serves as one long edge of the rough opening frame.

The opening layout indicates the position of the trimming joist. Carry the mark squarely up on the header faces and install hangers to carry the trimming joist. Nail the trimming joist in place.

After the framing is completed, you're ready to remove the ceiling. With a helper below to catch the cut-out section, cut around the opening with a compass or keyhole saw. Then move downstairs and nail the ceiling around the rough opening to the new framework.

Installing the Stairway

Tip the stairway on its side, lift it through the opening into the attic, and set it aside. Then install temporary ledgers on both sides of the opening to support the stairway case while it's being positioned and fastened. The unit shown here required the hinge-end ledger to extend ½ in. into the opening and the ledger on the opposite end to extend ⅞ inch. Use 2×4 stock for the ledgers and secure with 16d common nails.

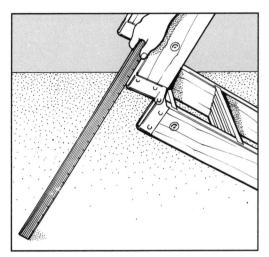

14 Open stair midsection while keeping lower section folded. Use straightedge to measure cutoff length of lower sections.

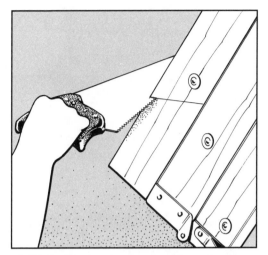

15 Transfer length to lower section and mark cutoff line. Saw each stringer to the waste side of the line with handsaw.

Set the stairway into the opening and let it rest on the ledgers. With the unit still folded, place shims between the stairway case and the headers to straighten and square the unit. Check that it's level and temporarily nail the case ends to the headers with 8d common nails. Leave the heads exposed for easy removal.

Have your helper unfold the mid-section of the stairway down but keep the bottom section folded back. Bore pilot holes to prevent splitting and nail through the stairway case to headers with 16d common nails. Nail through the holes provided in the hinges and complete the fastening by spacing nails 16 in. apart around the entire case. Be sure there's a shim to fill the space between the case and framework where you nail.

Cutting to Length

With the unit still partially unfolded, place some weight on the stairs so you're sure the hardware is fully extended. Lay a straightedge along the top of one stringer and slide it down until it touches the floor. Mark the length on the straightedge. Then, line up the straightedge with the back of the stringer, extend it to the floor and mark that length. Repeat the procedure on the other stringer to ensure that the legs will seat firmly on the floor even if it's not perfectly flat. Fold the staircase so you can mark and cut the lengths on the bottom stringers. Unfold the stairway and have your helper stand on the

second or third step. Check that the stairway sections form a straight line and there are no uneven gaps between them. Complete installation by first removing ledgers and temporary support partitions. Install mitered case molding around the opening, leaving a 3/16-in. reveal between the stairway case and the molding edge. Attach the molding to the case with 4d finishing nails and to the framework with 6d nails. Set the nails, sand with 120-grit sandpaper and prime. Finally, fill the nail holes and paint.

16 Cut mitered trim for opening and attach to the stair casing with 4d finishing nails and to the headers with 6d nails.

Floor tile installation

Installing a resilient tile floor is a simple, straightforward job that gives you a terrific return on time and money spent. Floor tile manufacturers have come up with a remarkable variety of tiles. The different styles and colors offer hundreds of possibilities. But the results you get will be only as good as your surface preparation because the tiles are flexible enough to show serious irregularities in the floor beneath them.

Resilient floor tiles are made of asphalt, solid vinyl or vinyl reinforced with mineral fibers (vinyl composition). The preparation process is similar for all of these floors, though the adhesive you'll need varies according to the type of tile and the floor to which you'll glue the tile.

Your local flooring dealer can provide the proper adhesive for your situation. No matter what tile you choose, plan to warm the room in which you will install the floor to 70°F for 24 hours before beginning, and keep it at that temperature for 24 hours after installation. Be sure to keep the tiles warm for at least one day before laying them down.

Room and Floor Preparations

If you are working in a kitchen, remove the refrigerator and range, and place them in another room. Built-in gas or electric ranges can be left in place. If you have an electric range, simply slide it out and unplug it from the wall

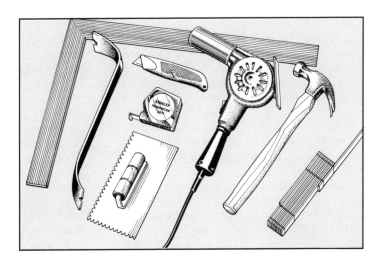

The minimum tools required for installing floor tile include a framing square, pry bar, utility knife, tape measure, notched trowel, heat gun, hammer and folding rule. A chalkline and linoleum roller may also come in handy.

socket. If you have a gas range, make arrangements with the gas company to disconnect the appliance before you begin work. If you have a built-in gas range, be sure to shut off the gas before you use any flammable adhesive, since the pilot light could ignite fumes.

Remove any shoe molding from the bottom of the baseboard. Pry off the molding with a flat pry bar, then pull out nails from behind with locking pliers to avoid damaging the wood. The shoe molding can be reused. Manufacturers claim you can install new tiles over old tiles or linoleum under certain conditions. Your present floor covering should be firmly stuck to the floor, have a smooth surface (not an embossed one) and have no foam backing.

If your floor meets these requirements, first remove wax and floor finish by scrubbing with cleaner and steel wool. (Never sand a resilient floor, since it may contain asbestos fibers.) If you have a few slightly loose areas, nail them down with underlayment nails, sinking the nailheads just below the surface. Fill over the heads —and any other depressions—with patching compound.

If your existing floor is in poor condition, you have two alternatives. The first is to cover it with ¼-in. underlayment-grade plywood. Fasten the underlayment with underlayment nails in a 6-in.-sq. pattern (every 3 in. along the edges). Sink the heads just below the surface. You can rent a floor stapler especially made for stapling underlayment. It drives and sets staples in one motion. Lay out the plywood to minimize seams in doorways and other heavy traffic areas. Stagger the sheets so the seams at the ends are not continuous. Fill the depressions over nailheads and seams between sheets with patching com-

pound. When dry, sand the compound flush with 100-grit sandpaper, and clean the dust very thoroughly.

Your second alternative for repairing a bad floor is to lift the existing floor covering and start fresh. This method has the advantage of giving you access to the subfloor, which may also be in need of repair. You will also not be raising the floor height, making the finish work later that much easier. To lift the tiles, use a flat pry bar or wide putty knife. Then, do your best to scrape away any backing paper and adhesive left on the floor. Some adhesives are water soluble, so it's a good idea to dampen the floor first.

Once the old tiles or linoleum have been removed, examine the floor underneath. Replace any broken boards with new wood of equal thickness, making sure to begin and end your new boards over floor joists. Nail down any loose boards and fill any cracks between boards with patching compound. Sand the compound flush and remove the dust. For resilient tile installation, glue 15-pound asphalt felt to the wood. Your flooring dealer can supply the proper adhesive for this job. Be sure to butt the edges of the paper, and keep the lines on the paper facing up. Roll each row of paper with a linoleum roller or rolling pin before setting the next piece.

Once the surface is ready for the tile, you can take a step that will save some time later. It is possible to cut and fit the tiles around any door stops and casings, but it is easier to cut off approximately ⅛ in. from the bottom of these trim boards to allow the tiles to slide underneath. Place a tile next to the stop or casing, then cut the wood with a sharp handsaw, using the flat tile as a guide.

Laying Out the Floor

The layout is figured from the center of the room so the tiles around the perimeter are balanced and at least one-half tile wide. If your floor is to include a pattern which continues from one tile to the next, balance the pattern on the exposed surface, disregarding the areas that will be covered by appliances. You might find it helpful to draw out your pattern to scale on graph paper before you begin. The easiest way to get an idea of the eventual appearance of your floor is to lay the tiles dry. At this point you can experiment freely with patterns and borders.

Find the centerline between two opposite walls and mark the floor at this point at both ends. Snap a chalkline on the floor between these two marks. Place the tongue of your framing square on the chalkline at the center point of its length and make a pencil mark along the blade, perpendicular to the chalkline. Using the mark as a guide, snap a perpendicular line on the floor. These lines are reference lines and can be used to find your actual starting point.

Lay the tiles dry and move them one way and another until you find the placement that yields the best results. Use cardboard patterns of appliances to get a true picture of the floor that will be exposed to view. Shift the starting point in the center of the room until you find the point which will yield the biggest border tiles. Once you've found your starting point, snap new lines in the proper position, parallel to your original reference lines. The new lines should intersect at one corner of your first tile and extend to the walls.

The adhesive you use is determined by the tile you buy. Many of the reinforced vinyl tiles are available with adhesive backing. If you go this route, be very careful when laying the tiles, as they can't be adjusted once they've been pressed down. Do any trimming before you remove the paper backing.

If you are using adhesive, keep in mind that different types require different methods of application. You can apply some with a paintbrush or short-nap roller, while you spread others with a notched trowel. Instructions for spreading glue, as well as any cautionary notes, are printed on the can. Be sure you read and follow the instructions on the label.

It's a good idea to do the room in sections to allow yourself room to move. Plan to cover one quarter of the room at a time. Cut a 2×2 ft. piece of plywood to kneel on so you won't be kneeling on freshly laid tiles.

Laying Resilient Tile

Begin by spreading the adhesive along one of the starting lines, then work into the corner and back to the other line. Spread the adhesive just over the line. The colored chalkline will be seen through the adhesive.

Set the first tile at the intersection of the guidelines as carefully as possible. If this first tile is crooked, the whole pattern will be off. Then, set the edge of the next tile against the first tile so the corners are perfectly aligned, and lower the tile into the adhesive. Work out along the two lines, then fill in between in a pyramid fashion. Avoid sliding the tiles in place, as this will force glue in between the edges. If you are installing solid vinyl tiles, roll the tiles with a linoleum roller or rolling pin as you install them. After you have laid 20 or so tiles, go back and roll them again. Use firm pressure to ensure that the tiles are pressed into the glue. For other tile types, simply press them firmly into place with both hands.

Installing Border Tiles

Set only the full tiles at first, then go back and cut the border tiles. For the most accuracy, scribe the border tiles to the wall. To do this, place a loose tile upside down over a tile in the last row installed. Line up the tile perfectly with the tile beneath it, and be sure that the pattern runs in the proper direction. Then, place a full tile over the loose tile, with one edge against the wall. Run a pencil along the upper tile, marking the tile beneath. Heat the tile along the cutline with a heat gun. When the tile softens, lay it on a smooth surface and cut it with a utility knife and straightedge.

Finishing Up

Once all the tiles are installed, remove any adhesive spots on the surface with mineral spirits or the solvent recommended on the label of the adhesive can. Install any shoe molding, then move the appliances and fixtures back in place.

If necessary, cut down any doors that swing over the tile. Allow $3/16$- to $1/4$-in. clearance between the bottom of the doors and the new floor. Then, rehang them. Apply metal trim strips where the resilient vinyl tiles meet other floors, nailing them in place with the special nails provided. Finally, avoid washing your floor for three days so the adhesive will have a chance to set.

Begin work by removing any base-board shoe molding with a flat pry bar. Pull out the nails from the back using locking pliers.

If floor is covered with heavily damaged tiles, remove these with a flat pry bar. Begin by driving the pry bar under one corner.

Once old tiles are removed, scrape glue from floor. Try dampening the floor because many old glues are water soluble.

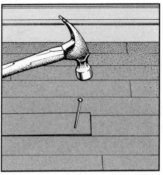

Replace severely damaged floor boards with new ones and nail any loose board ends. Set nailheads below floor surface.

If existing floor boards are in bad shape, cover with underlayment. Stapler drives and sets staples in one operation.

Fill seams between underlayment sheets, and cover staple heads with patching compound. Spread compound with putty knife.

Once compound is dry, sand it flush to surrounding surface using 100-grit sandpaper. Be sure to vacuum up all dust.

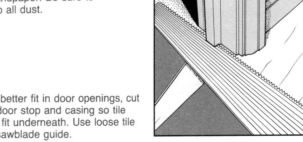

For better fit in door openings, cut off door stop and casing so tile can fit underneath. Use loose tile as sawblade guide.

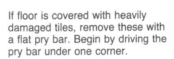

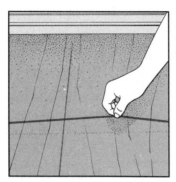

Draw initial reference lines on floor, then distribute tile to check for fit. When satisfied, snap final chalklines onto floor.

Spread adhesive onto floor according to manufacturer's instructions. Most adhesives require use of notched trowel.

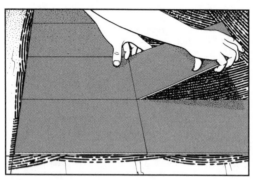

Lower tiles into place as shown. Make sure all edges align.

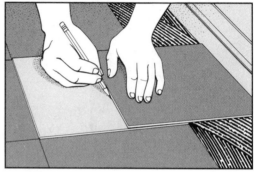

Place border tile upside down on last row then mark tile.

Once the cutline is drawn, heat the back of the tile with a heat gun. Direct the warm air along the cutline until tile is soft.

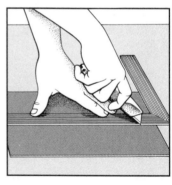

Lay heated tile on smooth surface, then cut along the line with a sharp utility knife. Use a framing square as a straightedge.

When laying out tiles—especially notched ones—be sure to lower them into place. Sliding a tile will force glue into cracks.

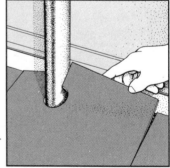

To fit around a pipe, first cut a matching diameter hole in the middle of the tile and then make a straight cut to the edge.

Installing slate tile floors

In many ways, slate is the perfect material for a foyer floor. It's durable, easy to maintain and has an elegance that tastefully accents just about any adjacent floor material. While slate may not be suitable for some rooms in your house because of its cold feel and unyielding surface, it is entirely appropriate for a foyer which is used primarily for entering and leaving the house and is often exposed to a great deal of moisture.

Traditional slate floors are set in concrete, and the subfloors that support them must be lower than the surrounding floors to accommodate this extra thickness. The floor framing must also be strong enough to carry the extra weight. Because of this, a traditional installation is a difficult and expensive remodeling project. Fortunately, today's slate floor tiles are available in a fairly uniform ¼-in. thickness and can be installed successfully over a standard wood or plywood floor using mastic instead of concrete. As such, slate becomes a relatively low-cost, high-quality floor option for the do-it-yourselfer.

Floor Preparation

The preparation for a slate tile installation does not differ too much from what you would do in preparing the floor for resilient tile. Keep in mind that slate tiles are rigid and, therefore, any resilience in the floor below can cause trouble later on. The slate may crack if the floor gives a great deal, and if the floor moves just a little, the grout can crack.

If you're laying slate tile next to a carpeted room, you'll have to cut the carpet where you want the slate to begin. Use a sharp utility knife and a straightedge guide. Then, pull the carpet off the tack strips and pry the tack strips off the floor.

Installing Slate Tiles

Before you begin actually putting down slate tile, open a package of the tile. Usually the manufacturer will supply a drawing of a "random" pattern. Feel free to create a pattern of your own. Keep in mind that traditional methods call for grout lines that are 3/8 to 1/2 in. wide, though you can reduce or enlarge this spacing for special effects. Scatter tiles of a different color to maintain a random appearance.

Cut small wood spacer blocks that match the thickness of the grout joint you prefer. Beginning at your reference lines, lay the tiles across the floor in both directions. Slide the wood spacers between the tiles to maintain straight, even grout lines. Adjust the tiles as necessary to make the borders as uniform as possible. Once all full tiles are in place, and you like the pattern, measure the pieces that are required to fill in the floor. Cut the tiles with a circular saw and masonry cutting blade, being sure to wear eye protection and a respirator, as the dust from the slate is noxious. If you can, do all of your cutting outdoors.

When satisfied with the fit of all tiles, pick them up and lay them out in the same pattern in an adjacent room. By doing this, you can avoid searching for the tile you want after you've applied the mastic to the floor.

Mastic

Begin in one corner, spreading the mastic in a 2- to 3-ft.-sq. section. Hold a 1/4-in. notched trowel at a 45° angle to the floor and work the mastic onto the floor with a sweeping motion. Press the appropriate tiles firmly into the mastic with a slight twisting motion. Place your spacer blocks between the tiles to maintain straight and even grout lines, and remove them once the tiles are down. Work backward toward an open room or doorway to avoid kneeling on the tiles. Continue spreading the mastic and installing the tile until everything is in place. Let the tiles set for 24 hours before continuing.

Grout

Begin grouting by cleaning all joints and the surface of the slate with a damp cloth. Then, read the mixing directions on the grout container. Keep in mind that the Building Stone Institute recommends the use of a latex grout for slate floors. Slowly add water to the grout while mixing until it is the texture of damp sand. Then carefully begin working the grout into the spaces between the tiles with your flat pointing trowel. Be sure to fill all of the spaces completely, then smooth the surface of the grout with the trowel. As you work, clean the grout from the adjacent slate surfaces with a sponge and clean water. Change the water often, and rinse the sponge frequently.

Be sure to clean the tile as you go, before the grout has a chance to dry. If the grout dries on the slate, you can remove it only by washing the surface with an acid bath, so try to avoid this step if you can. Be familiar with the open time of the grout, and mix only as much as you can use in this allotted time.

After the grout is dry to the touch, sprinkle sawdust over the tile. Then rub the surface briskly—in a circular motion—with a clean burlap cloth. Let the joints harden for three days before you walk on the floor.

Wash the floor again with clean water and wipe it dry. If you still have grout stains on the floor, you will have to resort to the acid bath.

Acid Bath

Begin by saturating the joints with water to prevent the acid from penetrating the grout. Mix one part muriatic acid to nine parts water. Be sure to wear rubber gloves and eye protection for this entire operation so you won't get burned by the acid. Wash the surface of the slate thoroughly, but don't work the solution into the grout. After the floor is cleaned with the acid, wash the floor several times with clean water to neutralize the acid.

Finishing the Job

It is not necessary to seal the slate, but many people choose to apply a chemical sealer to help protect the grout from stains. Sealers are available in a matte or gloss finish and are easy to apply.

Simply allow the floor to cure for 30 days, then apply the sealer to a clean floor with a large cloth or paintbrush. Apply a thin, uniform coat, then let the floor dry for 2 hours before adding a second coat. Be sure to stay off the floor for a full 24 hours after the second coat to avoid leaving marks.

When everything is dry, install any baseboard and shoe molding you may have removed. Set the nailheads, fill the holes and touch up all marked surfaces with paint.

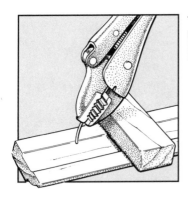

To avoid damaging trim boards, pull out nails from back side with locking pliers using small wood block for leverage.

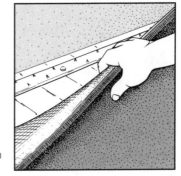

To remove carpeting, cut it to line where tile will end using a sharp utility knife. Then pull it away from tack strip border.

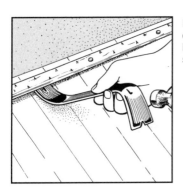

Pry tack strips off floor and discard. Resilient floor tiles and linoleum must also be removed to install slate tile.

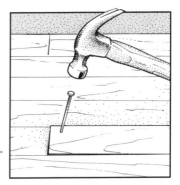

Be sure to nail any loose subfloor boards or sections of plywood subfloor panels. Use 8d common or box nails.

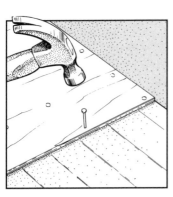

In most cases it's best to cover subfloor with underlayment plywood. Install with flooring nails driven in 6-in.-sq. pattern.

Set nailheads below surface. Fill holes and seams with patching compound. Let dry and sand smooth with 100-grit paper.

Bottom edge of casing must be cut off to accommodate slate tile. Place tile against casing and scribe cutline on surface.

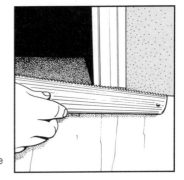

Cut casing board using a sharp handsaw. Be sure to keep blade parallel to floor and on waste side of scribed line.

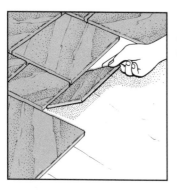

Lay out tiles on dry floor to match manufacturer's pattern or one of your choice. Be sure to balance border tiles.

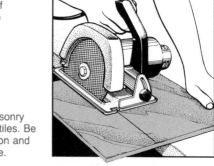

Use circular saw with masonry blade to cut slate border tiles. Be sure to wear eye protection and respirator while cutting tile.

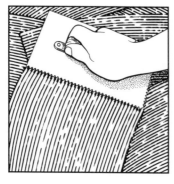

Apply mastic in small sections using notched trowel hold at 45° angle. Use sweeping motion to get best coverage.

Set slate tile into mastic and press into place with slight twist. Use wood spacer blocks to maintain uniform grout spacing.

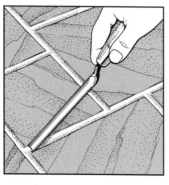

Let mastic dry, then fill joints with grout using pointing trowel. When voids are filled, smooth surface with trowel.

While grouting, keep surface of tiles clean. Wipe with damp sponge to prevent grout from hardening on surface.

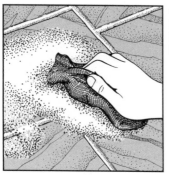

When grout is dry to touch, sprinkle sawdust on tile and rub with burlap cloth. This removes residue from grouting job.

If you want to seal the floor, wait 30 days then brush on a thin coat of commercial sealer. Let dry and apply second coat.

Bow window installation

You don't have to be an architect to know that a properly sized and placed window will add light to a room and affect your perception and, therefore, your use of the space. It's not unusual for a window to be the focal point of a room. In the project featured here, an obsolete picture window, located in a formal dining room was replaced with a new, energy-efficient bow window. The results were dramatic.

A bow window has a slightly curved, bow-like frame that adds style and dimension to a home. Inside, the window floods the room with natural light from four different angles. The window frame, projecting slightly from the house, offers a perch to the outdoors with sweeping views that no other window can match. The seat board presents a quiet place to sit and watch the world—or at least the neighborhood—go by.

You can buy bow windows ranging in size from about 3×6 ft. wide to 6×13 ft. wide. The bow window shown here measures roughly 5 ft. tall by 8 ft. wide. When purchasing a bow window, be sure to order a head board, seat board and the extension jambs. These usually don't come with the basic unit. You must also order the screens and grilles separately. Most window manufacturers also offer a choice of insulated glass (two panes) or triple glazing.

In many areas, installation of a new window such as this will require building permits. Be sure to check with local authorities before you begin.

Out With the Old

The first step is to remove the old window. Using a flat pry bar, carefully pry the window from the house. Be sure to wear long sleeves, gloves and eye protection. Try to avoid twisting the window frame because the glass may break.

Prepare the rough opening to accept the new window. Every window comes with instructions that list the rough-opening dimensions.

If the bow window is the same width as the old window, but taller, then simply lower the sill plate to accept the taller window. If the bow window is wider *and* taller than the old window, then you must frame-out the entire opening and install a longer header. When removing a header, it's necessary to install a temporary wall in the room to support the ceiling until the new header is in place. Make the header from two 2×10s separated by ½-in. plywood. This produces a 3½-in.-thick header equal to the 2×4 wall stud width.

1 The first step is to remove the old window. Duct-tape strips on the glass help to prevent shattering if the glass breaks.

2 Make a plunge cut—3 in. below rough opening dimension—into each stud. Use reciprocating saw to cut stud completely.

3 Remove studs and nail down a double 2×4 sill plate. Use a reciprocating saw to cut sheathing and wallboard flush with sill.

4 Install new header, if needed, for the bow window. Make header from two 2×10s separated by ½-in. plywood spacer.

Mark the sill plate position on the exterior wall. Then measure down 3 in., the thickness of a double 2×4 sill plate, and snap a chalkline. Use a portable circular saw and then a reciprocating saw to cut through each stud located in the rough opening. Try *not* to cut through the interior wallboard. The short studs left in the wall, called *cripple studs*, support the sill plate. Install two more cripple studs to support each end of the sill plate. Nail the two end cripple studs to the nearest full-length wall studs. Position a double 2×4 cripple stud in the center of the opening to attach the knee brace.

Cut a 2×4 sill plate to fit across the bottom of the rough opening and nail it to the cripple studs. Double-up the sill plate by nailing another 2×4 to the first sill plate. Using a reciprocating saw, trim the exterior sheathing and interior wallboard flush with the sill plate.

Make up the header and cut it to fit between the two nearest full-length wall studs. Have someone help you lift the header into place and toenail it to the wall studs on either end. Then, cut jack studs to fit between the header and the sill plate. Nail a jack stud to the full-length wall stud at each end of the header. Toenail two more jack studs—to the header and sill plate—flush with the sides of the rough opening. These two additional jack studs are necessary only if the first jack studs are set back away from the opening 1½ in. or more. For example, if the first jack stud is ¾ in. away from the rough-opening edge, then nail a ¾-in.-thick by 3½-in.-wide board to the jack stud to build out the stud and establish the side of the rough opening. Regardless of how you frame out the rough opening, be sure that the jack studs are positioned *under* the header.

In With the New

To lift a window this size, you need at least four people. Once it's in place, two people must hold it until it's secured. Move inside and drive cedar shake shims under the window to raise it against the header. Position the shims in several places to support the entire unit. Check that the window is plumb, square and level. Next, nail up through the top platform and into the header with 10d coated or ring-shanked nails. Nail down through the bottom platform and into the sill plate, placing the nails through the cedar shake shims. Now move outside and drive 1¼-in. roofing nails through the vinyl flange on each side of the window. Fill any gaps under the window with fiberglass insulation.

To support the projecting unit, attach a knee brace to the house under the center of the window. The 4-unit bow window shown needed only one center-mounted brace, but wider windows, which project farther from the house, need two or, in some cases, three knee braces. Using 2×4s, make an L-shaped brace. Secure the brace with lagscrews.

With the window fastened securely, all that's left is to install the exterior trim and finish the window's interior.

Exterior Trim

The exterior of the window shown was trimmed with 5/4-in.×5½-in.-wide pine boards painted white. First, install trim around the top and bottom of the window and then attach the vertical side pieces. Fasten the trim with 10d galvanized finishing nails.

Crosscut the top and bottom trim pieces to a 5° angle so they will meet at 10° and match the bow of the window. Screw 1×2 wood cleats to

5 After rough opening is framed-out, install the window. Two people must hold unit while it's secured from inside.

6 Nail exterior trim along top of window. Cleats attached to soffit provide nailing surfaces. Note insulation behind trim.

7 Nail trim boards along window bottom. Note brace bolted to wall, under center of window, to support projecting unit.

8 Unit has factory-fitted seat board. Apply stain or paint before installation. If needed, rip seat board flush with interior wall.

9 Nail a scrap wood block to jack stud on sides of window. This is necessary to provide solid nailing for extension jambs.

10 Fit extension jamb into routed groove to build out wall jamb flush with finished wall. Shim jamb, if necessary.

the house soffit above the windows to provide solid nailing for the trim. Then, fill the area above the window with fiberglass insulation and nail the trim in place. Before attaching the bottom trim, screw 2×2 nailing strips to the underside of the window. Install the trim by nailing into the 2×2 strips and the edge of the window platform. Glue rigid insulation, such as Styrofoam, to the underside of the window. Finally, attach the trim to the sides of the window.

Interior Trim

Start the interior trim by nailing $5/8 \times 1 1/4$-in.-wide plywood strips around the window's sill platform. Cover the platform with $1/2$-in. rigid insulation. Be sure to fit the insulation between the strips. Insulate the head platform, at the top of the window, the same way.

Install the head and seat boards which are made of pine-veneered particleboard. The boards come cut to fit a $5 1/4$-in. or $7 9/16$-in.-

thick wall. If necessary, trim the boards flush with the interior wall. Slide the seat board into position and secure it with 4d finishing nails. Install the head board the same way. Nail blocks to the wall studs to provide backing for the extension jambs. Extension jambs build out the window jambs flush with the interior wall. If necessary, trim the extension jambs to fit flush. Fasten extension jambs with 8d finishing nails.

Install the inside stop moldings and mullion casings that fit around the inside of the four windows. The parts with the window usually come precisely milled and factory fitted for easy installation. Simply nail them in place with 4d finishing nails—no cutting is usually required. Now install casing molding to the wall around the window as the final trim.

In the window shown, snap-in-place grilles divide each window into 10 panes. The plastic grilles have a special polymer coating that accepts paint or stain. Finish the grilles to match the interior wood trim.

1 Old wood-framed door was nailed through casing. Use cat's paw to pull nails. Remove door and jamb from opening.

2 Use a level to mark rough opening height of new door unit. Then, draw a plumb line to establish right side of opening.

Entry door installation

Front entry doors often need replacement sooner than you think. They often battle cruel winters, have no lights resulting in dark, shadowy foyers. Cold air howls in from around the ill-fitting door bringing snow and rain with it.

A new entry door should provide security, energy efficiency and quality construction. The entry door shown here is a combination door and sidelight. The sidelight creates a slightly larger looking entrance while providing more light from the window in the foyer.

Door's Features

This door's construction starts with solid wood stiles and rails forming the perimeter frame. A sheet of closed-cell polystyrene fills the core of the door and provides insulation. Rust-resistant galvanized steel sheets form the interior and exterior surfaces of the door. The two steel sheets are separated by a thermal break—a rubber gasket inserted in the door's edges—that stops the transmission of cold or heat from one side of the door to the other.

To help create an air-tight seal around the door, the unit is fitted with a magnetic weather strip, similar to a refrigerator's, that effectively blocks out wind and rain. A flexible, 5-finger weather strip along the door's bottom makes firm contact with an aluminum adjustable sill. The sill has a unique built-in weep (water removal) system that directs water away from the threshold via an integral pan.

This door comes factory-primed and should be painted within six weeks after installation with a good-quality, exterior-grade paint.

The real beauty of this door, though, is its foolproof, perfect-fit installation system. If every rough opening, sill and door jamb were perfectly level, plumb and square, then door installations would be easy. But in the real world, of course, this is simply not the case. This door has a system called *Jamb-Jacks* that allow you to adjust the door jambs *after* the unit is screwed into place. In fact, with this system, you can easily fine-tune the door's fit next year or in 10 years, if necessary.

A Jamb-Jack is basically a lagscrew fitted with a threaded, cylindrical-shaped head. These Jamb-Jacks fit into holes—three per jamb—and are concealed with push-in plastic caps. A special tool is provided for driving the Jamb-Jacks into the studs with a ratchet wrench. Reverse the drive tool and use its other end to adjust the door jambs in or out.

Wall Preparations

Start by removing the old door. Wood doors are usually nailed through the exterior casing. Pull the nails and remove the door and frame as one unit. Next, extend the opening to accept the wider door/sidelight unit. Using a level, mark the new rough opening on the house wall. Before cutting, measure the new unit just to be sure that the rough opening dimensions are correct. Use a portable circular saw to cut through the siding and sheathing. Pull off the siding and sheathing and remove the studs and insulation.

Install a new header, if necessary, and frame the side of the rough opening that was just cut. On this particular installation, the existing double 2×8 header extended beyond the rough opening so there was no need to replace it. Also, it just happened that a wall stud was only ¾ in. away from the edge of the rough opening. Therefore, the opening was closed with only a strip of ¾-in. plywood. In most cases, however, you'll have to replace the old header with a longer one,

3 Double check your measurements of the rough opening. Use circular saw to cut through the exterior siding and sheathing.

4 Cut away the interior wall with a reciprocating saw. Hang a drop cloth on inside wall and execute cut from the outside.

5 Wall stud here was ¾ in. away from rough opening, so plywood was added to fill void and provide base for fastening door.

6 Check sill for level. It must be level for door to operate properly. Also, check to be sure sides of opening are plumb.

7 Apply two parallel beads of butyl caulk along the sill and up the sides about 3 inches. This will stop air and water infiltration.

8 Position unit in the opening, sill first, and then tilt in the top. Note that door and sidelight come assembled as one unit.

add a full-length wall stud and a jack stud. Be sure to fit the jack stud *under* the header. Nail through the sheathing and wallboard to secure the new framing members. Build up the sill opening, if necessary, flush with the floor. A strip of ⅜-in. plywood will usually do the trick.

Door Installation

With the rough opening framed, it's time to install the door. Note that the door and sidelight for this door come assembled as a prehung unit. Apply caulking to the wall first and then install the unit, putting the bottom in first, then tilting the top into position. Use the hex-shaped screwdriver to screw in the first Jamb-Jack fastener. The driver fits a 10-mm socket or you can use an electric drill. Note that the ends of the driver are slightly different. A hexagonal hole is milled in one end and the opposite end has a round hole drilled in it. Use the hexagonal-hole end to drive the fasteners into the studs and the round-hole end to adjust the jambs.

Check the door-to-frame alignment. Using the drive tool, turn the Jamb-Jacks clockwise to pull the jamb out, and counterclockwise to move the jamb in.

Once the door jambs are adjusted, install the latch and deadbolt, and mortise the strike plates into the jamb. For additional support and security, insert a wood block between the jamb and the stud at the strike plate locations. Then fasten the strike plates with long screws. Use two more long screws to secure the top door hinge. Drive the screws through the hinge holes located closest to the weatherstripping. These 2½-in.-long screws will help prevent sagging and binding.

Close the door and check the sill plate. The 5-finger door-bottom cap should fit snugly against the sill to seal out wind and rain. Loosen the screws to raise the sill; tighten them to lower it.

Apply two coats of paint to the door unit. Avoid getting paint on the weatherstripping, and don't paint in temperatures below 50°F.

9 Close-up view of a Jamb-Jack. Lagscrew shank is driven into studs and cylindrical head threads into door jamb.

10 Adjustable Jamb-Jacks secure the door. Use a ratchet wrench and special driver to screw bolt into stud.

11 Reverse the special driver in the wrench and use it to adjust the jambs in or out until the door and frame align perfectly.

12 Mark the strike-plate location on door jamb and bore a hole for the dead bolt with a spade bit.

13 Door features and adjustable sill that stops drafts. Loosen screws slightly to raise sill. Then, close door and check seal.

14 Test sill height with a dollar bill. Close door on bill and tug gently. If the bill can be moved freely, adjust sill for a tighter fit.

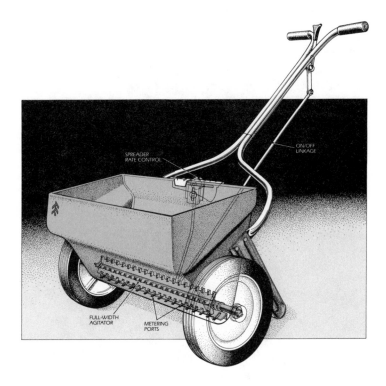

Drop-type spreaders feature a full-width agitator that feeds material through the accurately controlled metering ports. It's best for lawns with shrubs and flowerbeds.

Lawn spreader selection

At the top of the list of basic tools for a lush, healthy lawn is the lawn spreader. This machine is designed for spreading granular fertilizers, insecticides, herbicides and grass seed uniformly and quickly. It can also spread ice-melting materials in the winter.

You have a choice between two distinct spreader designs, each having certain benefits and each suited to your specific requirements.

Spreader Models

Lawn spreaders are distinguished by the way they disperse the material. Drop-type spreaders feature a hopper to hold the product being applied and a full-width agitator for uniform dispersal rate. The material flows out through a row of small slots below the agitator. These slots, also called *metering ports*, can be adjusted to provide the optimum feed rate for the specific

product you're applying. A properly maintained and operated drop spreader will provide a very uniform dispersal pattern over the entire width of the swath.

Rotary-type spreaders have a drum to contain the product and an impeller that spins as the spreader is pushed. The spinning impeller broadcasts the material over the area as you walk. Rotary spreaders also feature adjustable metering ports, but they disperse the product over a much wider swath than a drop spreader. While they don't offer the precise control that a drop spreader does, they're faster and easier to operate.

Making a Choice

Before you shop for a spreader, take some time to determine the specific requirements of your lawn and the amount of use the machine will get. If your lawn contains numerous ornamental shrubs or flowerbeds, you'll want a spreader that offers the greatest control over application of chemicals. Some chemicals designed for lawn treatment can damage or kill other plants in the yard. You must make sure the application is confined to the grass only. Because drop spreaders treat only the area directly under the metering ports, they are a good choice for this type of lawn. They do, however, require a short lawn. Taller grass, especially if it's wet, can be a problem due to the low ground clearance of this design. Also, some fertilizers are granules that are too large for the port size of drop spreaders.

On the other hand, if your lawn is large and fairly free of obstructions, a carefully operated

SPREADER
RATE CONTROL

IMPELLER

GEAR ASSEMBLY

The rotary spreader drops material through adjustable metering ports onto a spinning impeller that's driven by the wheels. An agitator inside the drum keeps the granules moving. Swaths can be as wide as 8 ft. but narrower passes give more control.

rotary spreader will get the job done in far less time. Depending on the manufacturer, rotary spreaders will apply fertilizer in a 2½ to 8-ft. swath. The wider swaths tend to provide a less uniform application and you'll probably find it best to adjust the swath and sacrifice some speed for a uniform pattern. Because the broadcast pattern of rotary spreaders tends to feather out at the edges of the swath, it's easier to get an even dispersal over the entire lawn than with a drop spreader. Chemical particles, however, are also more likely to fall on areas where you don't want them. A rotary spreader should *not* be used to apply pesticides unless it throws a narrow swath or the lawn area is open and free from bordering ornamentals or vegetables.

After you've decided on which type of spreader best fulfills your particular needs, take a close look at the actual construction of the model of your choice. The precision metering components of drop spreaders demand steel construction, which is prone to corrosion. Some models offer an epoxy coating on these parts. The epoxy coating will at least double the life of your drop spreader, regardless of your maintenance schedule. Although drop spreaders with corrosion-resistant plastic components are available, they don't achieve the metering accuracy of those with steel or coated steel parts. Rotary spreaders, however, can make effective use of plastic metering components without sacrificing precision because of their large port openings.

Spreader Use and Care

Each lawn-treatment product is designed to be spread at a specific rate. Too heavy a coverage can injure the lawn and too light a coverage reduces the product effectiveness and may have no effect at all. Make sure you observe the coverage requirements specified for the product you're using and set the spreader rate accordingly. Unfortunately, spreader settings vary from one manufacturer to the next and can vary from one model to the next of the same make.

If you have questions about the rate setting for a particular application and spreader, ask your dealer. It's best if you buy your spreader from the same company that will be supplying your material applications. This assures you that the coverage specified with the material is compatible with the rate settings on your machine.

Before filling the spreader, turn off the spreader control and adjust the rate setting appropriately. Fill the spreader on the driveway or sidewalk, clean up any spills and roll the machine to the lawn. Always have the machine moving when you turn on or stop the spreading control and turn off spreading when you make turns. This helps avoid dropping excessive material that may burn the lawn at the beginning and end of a pass.

When finished, empty any remaining material and hose down the spreader to reduce corrosion. Then, oil axle bearings and control linkage.

Starter pull-rope replacement

Without that pull-rope wound and waiting, even the best maintained small engine becomes a useless lawn ornament. All ropes wear out eventually. The wise homeowner will keep an eye on the condition of the pull-rope so it can be replaced *before* it breaks. The following rope replacement procedures cover most of the pull-rope starters found on Briggs & Stratton and Tecumseh engines.

Varying engines and applications require different length ropes, so make sure you get an exact replacement. To protect against unraveling, burn both ends of the new rope and use a cloth to wipe them smooth while they're still hot.

Briggs & Stratton Starters

First, disconnect the sparkplug cable from the plug. Use a jumper cable with alligator clips on each end to ground the cable to a metal part of the engine. This is a precaution against accidental starting.

Unscrew the securing clip that holds the throttle cable to the housing. Remove the housing bolts and take off the housing. On the underside of the housing you'll find the starter assembly.

Cut the rope near the handle, pry out the metal rope-retaining pin and remove the old rope. Pull the remaining rope out of the starter as far as it will go. Then, while holding the pulley in place with your thumb, pry the knotted end out of the pulley and cut off the knot. Remove the rope slowly and allow the pulley to return to its unwound position.

Tie a knot in one end of the new rope. Turn the pulley counterclockwise as far as it will go, back off two turns and thread the unknotted end through the hole in the pulley while holding the pulley in place with your thumb. Then, pull the rope through the hole in the housing. Stretch the rope tight to engage the knotted end and slowly let the pulley rewind the rope. Thread the other end of the rope through the handle and tie it to the rope-retaining pin.

To reach the starter mechanism on Briggs & Stratton engines, first remove the throttle cable clip on the housing. Ground sparkplug and remove the housing.

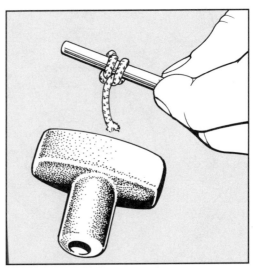

Cut the pull-rope near the handle, pry out the metal retaining pin that secures the rope. Untie and throw away the rope end.

Tecumseh Pull-Starters

Many Tecumseh engines feature a starter that's similar to the type found on Briggs & Stratton engines.

Other Tecumseh engines use side-mounted vertical-pull starters. The following describes the procedure for the most common side-mounted starters manufactured over the past 8 to 10 years.

Ground the sparkplug cable as described for the B&S engines. Then, remove the gas tank by prying back the retaining clips and sliding the tank upward. Unbolt the air filter and remove the housing.

You'll see the starter assembly mounted in a bracket that's secured to the engine side. Check the bracket for a notch in the center of the upper edge. This notch facilitates removing the old rope without disassembling the starter. If your unit lacks this feature, simply shape an approximately ¼-in.-deep × ½-in.-wide notch by carefully breaking away the bracket material with a pair of pliers.

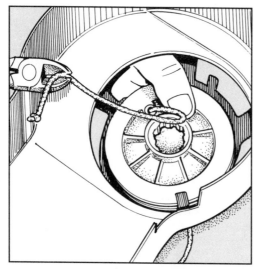

After stretching the rope out from starter, hold spring in place, pry out the end and cut off the knot. Remove the old rope.

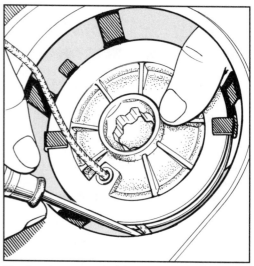

After knotting one end of the new rope, hold pulley with spring tensioned and thread rope through hole in pulley.

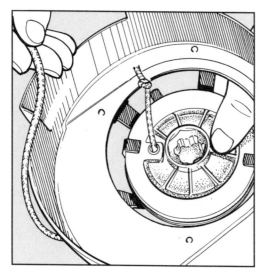

Thread rope through the housing and stretch it tight. Let the pulley slowly wind up and then secure the handle.

To remove the housing on Tecumseh engines, first unbolt the air filter and slide off the gas tank. Then remove the housing bolts.

Pull up on the rope until the staple that secures it to the pulley is centered in the notch. Hold the pulley in position and use a narrow-blade screwdriver to pry the staple out. Then, pull out the remaining rope. Hold on to the pulley when unwinding the rope. When it's free, wedge a large screwdriver between the bracket and pulley to hold the pulley in place with the spring tensioned.

Remove the rope from the handle by prying out the staple in the handle stem. Thread the new rope through the handle, tie a knot in the end and pull it tight.

Feed the other end through the housing. Turn the pulley as tight as it will go. Then, back it off while looking down into the pulley until you see the rope hole. It should be about 180° from the old staple position. Line this hole up with the notch and wedge the pulley in place. Thread the rope under the wire rope clip, through the hole, and out the side of the pulley. Tie a knot in the rope end, pull it tight into the pulley cavity and let the rope wind onto the pulley.

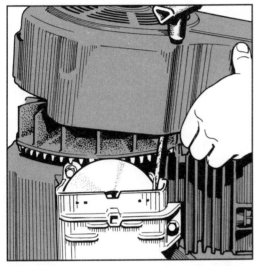

Lift the housing off the engine, pull out rope and set housing aside. The starter assembly is mounted on the engine side.

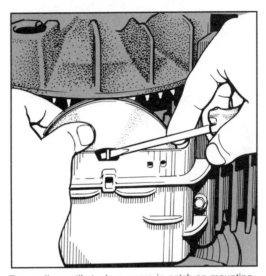

Turn pulley until staple appears in notch on mounting bracket. Remove staple with narrow-tip screwdriver or awl.

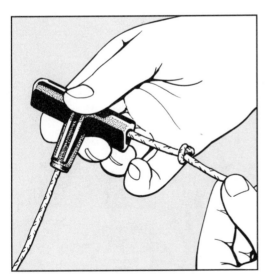

After removing old rope from the handle, thread new rope through, knot the end, and pull tight to seat rope in handle.

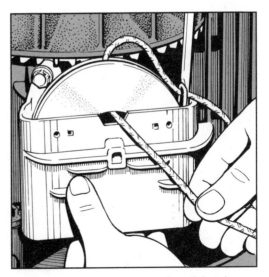

With spring tensioned, pass rope through housing, under clip and through hole in pulley. Knot end and pull snugly.

Service the foam air filter element by washing it in detergent, letting it dry and giving it a light coat of engine oil.

Small engine overhaul

Overhauling engines for lawnmowers, snow-throwers and tillers may well be within the range of skills of the do-it-yourselfer. To determine just how far you'll need to tear down your engine, spend the time to troubleshoot its problems. There's no sense going to bare bones just to find out that the carburetor clogged up with fuel deposits after a winter of storage.

Troubleshooting Engine Problems

Some of the disassembly steps shown here are actually part of a normal maintenance procedure. Manufacturers point out that a small engine can lose as much as 30 percent of its power after 100 hours of use. Their recommendation is to remove the cylinder head as part of the 100-hour maintenance service—also called a *power tuneup*. This will let you clean up the head, piston top and valves, removing any buildup of carbon deposits.

Unbolt and remove the top engine cover, which usually contains the pull starter mechanism, for access to the flywheel.

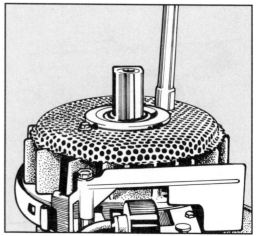

Remove the perforated metal screen on top of the flywheel. Its purpose is to keep large debris from getting inside the engine.

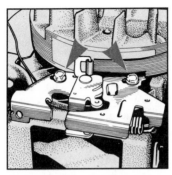

Don't touch the two adjustment bolts on the brake-band stop so you won't have to adjust it when the flywheel is put back.

Using needle-nose pliers, disconnect the brake-band stop spring. Then bend out the lever tang at the other end of the band.

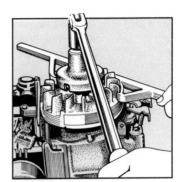

Flywheel removal requires a special holding tool to grab the fins and a wrench to remove the starter clutch and washer.

Once loosened, lift off the starter clutch and washer. Then, loosen the flywheel nut but leave it in place to protect threads.

Remove the flywheel with a puller, tightening the two bolts alternately to break it loose from the crankshaft.

Lift the flywheel off the crankshaft and check the condition of the indexing key which positions it on the crankshaft.

Curing other engine ailments requires different degrees of engine teardown. In most cases, refusal to start is caused by ignition or fuel supply problems which can be solved without a complete overhaul. Failure to restart after a sudden stop—such as hitting a rock with the lawnmower blade—can often be traced to a sheared flywheel key. Remedy this by removing no more than the top engine housing and flywheel. If it's an older engine, built before electronic ignition modules, remove the flywheel to replace the breaker points.

Rough running, backfiring or a distinct lack of power could indicate deeper problems which will require complete engine disassembly to replace worn piston rings or burned valves. The standard troubleshooting procedures apply here—a compression test, inspection of the sparkplug for oil fouling and checking for a strong ignition spark. As always, the repair manual for your engine model is the best source of instructions, and it will come in handy for valve lash and bolt torque specifications.

Disassembly and Power Tuneup

Here's a step-by-step guide to disassembly and the power tuneup, complete with short-cuts.

Step 1. Disconnect and ground the sparkplug cable. Remove the air cleaner, wash the foam filter element in a detergent solution, and let it dry. Pour a small amount of clean engine oil over the foam element, squeeze out the excess, and set it aside for reassembly. Drain oil and gas. (It will probably be easier if you unbolt the gas tank from the engine.)

Step 2. Disconnect control cables or linkage, wires and hoses. Unbolt the engine from the lawnmower, snowthrower or tiller and place it on your workbench. Wipe off any dirt or grease, particularly around the sump cover, that could later fall into the engine. Make life easy for yourself by constructing a stand for the engine. All you need is a simple cradle built of 2×4 lumber which supports the engine case and lets the crankshaft extension hang free.

Step 3. Unscrew and remove the blower housing. Remove the cooling air-intake screen over the flywheel. Now remove the sparkplug.

Step 4. If you need to replace the ignition points or if you will be removing the crankshaft, the flywheel has to come off. To do this on recent model Briggs & Stratton engines, you need to replace the brake-band stop.

The brake-band stop is used to comply with Consumer Product Safety Commission rules for a positive engine stop that is activated when the operator of equipment releases the handle. The purpose is to have the engine shut itself off if there's a chance it will be left unattended. The point to remember about the brake-band stop is this: Save yourself the job of having to readjust the brake band (which requires a special tool) by not loosening its two adjustment screws. To release the band without upsetting the adjustment, use needle-nose pliers to disconnect the brake spring. Then bend out the break lever tang with a bending tool to free the brake band.

Step 5. To remove a flywheel, put a flywheel holder in position over the flywheel's fins so the flywheel won't move. Lay a clutch wrench over the starter clutch. Attach a breaker bar to the clutch wrench and remove the starter clutch and washer beneath it.

Important: As you remove each part, identify it with a self-adhering label. You can lose a lot of time searching for a place to put a bolt that later you can't identify.

Use an open-end or crescent wrench to loosen the flywheel nut—if there is one—but don't remove it. If there is no flywheel nut, take any nut that is either the same size as the crankshaft threads or is oversize and put it over the crankshaft threads. This is to protect the crankshaft threads as you remove the flywheel.

Locate the two holes on top of the flywheel for the flywheel puller. If this is the first time the flywheel is coming off the engine, these holes may not be threaded. But that's okay. The flywheel puller has self-tapping screws.

Connect the flywheel puller and tighten each of the bolts and nuts on top of the puller alternately, a little at a time, until the bolts bottom. You should hear a pop when the flywheel breaks loose. If the flywheel comes loose without a pop, it means either it wasn't installed correctly or the inside of the hole where the flywheel fits on the crankshaft is dirty or oily. When you take off the flywheel, clean the hole and shaft and be sure to retrieve the flywheel key. Take care not to damage the engine speed governor's plastic air vane.

Caution: Never hit the flywheel with a hammer to loosen it. You will shatter magnets, break flywheel fins or crack the part altogether. You might also damage the crankshaft.

Removal of the flywheel will expose the ignition components of engines with breaker points.

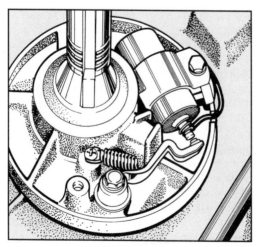

Flywheel removal reveals the ignition breaker points on engines built before changeover to all-electronic ignitions.

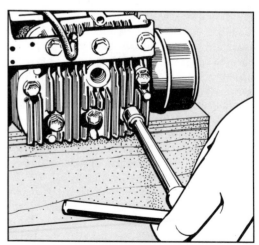

When removing the cylinder head bolts, note different length bolts so they can be installed in the proper position.

Wiggle the head or tap it with a soft mallet to free it from the cylinder, but do not pry against soft aluminum.

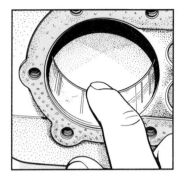

Take the piston down to the bottom of its travel and inspect the surface of the cylinder wall for scoring and gouges.

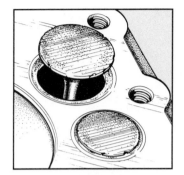

Any sign of pitting, burning or material loss around the edge of either valve is grounds for replacement of both.

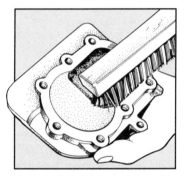

Cleaning the carbon from the cylinder head, piston top and valve area is recommended after 100 hours of operation.

Sump cover removal is only possible after unscrewing all bolts. One may be located under power take-off gear cover.

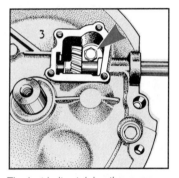

The last bolt retaining the sump cover is concealed on engines with power takeoffs as used in self-propelled equipment.

Always replace the condenser when you replace the points. Be sure to apply a thin coat of lubricant to the cam which actuates the breaker points.

Step 6. Remove the cylinder-head bolts. Then, wiggle the cylinder head until it comes off. If the head is aluminum, don't pry it off, as this could damage the soft material. If the head is cast, prying is okay.

You now have a view of the vital working parts inside the engine. Examine the condition of the cylinder by turning the crankshaft until the piston is at the bottom of the bore. Run your finger up and down the cylinder wall, checking for scratches or scoring. If the surface is smooth and you don't intend to replace the rings, leave it alone. Should the rings be replaced, though, the glaze deposited on the cylinder wall in normal service must be removed by honing.

More serious damage to the cylinder requires boring out the cylinder to the next oversize and installing a cylinder liner to match. This work is best left to a properly equipped machine shop. Make sure to bring the replacement piston along when you drop off the engine block.

Inspect the valves—which control the intake and exhaust gas flow—for burning or pitting. This type of damage will ruin the engine's ability to seal compression. Turn the crankshaft to lift each valve off its seat for a thorough looking over. When valves are replaced, it is necessary to seat them with valve lapping compound and measure the lash to ensure that it meets manufacturer's specs as listed in the repair manual.

Step 7. Wire brush the cylinder head to get it clean. With a straightedge, check the head for warpage on the piston side. If you can slide a .003-in. feeler gauge under the straightedge anywhere along the gasket mating surface, the head will have to be machined flat or replaced.

Turn the crankshaft to bring the piston to top dead center (TDC) and clean the carbon deposits off the piston and valves with a wire brush. This step is the essence of a power tuneup.

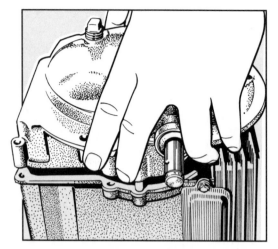

Gently lift off the sump cover to prevent damage to the crankshaft, its bearing surface and the oil seal.

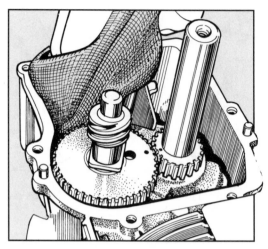

Wipe the engine sump clean of all grit and sludge before moving on to further disassembly of lower-end components.

Step 8. If your inspections indicate that removal of the piston or crankshaft is necessary, you must remove the sump cover on the bottom of the engine, though this is not a normal part of the power tuneup.

Turn the engine over and remove the bolts attaching the sump cover. If the sump cover won't come off and the engine is from a self-propelled implement, look for a hidden bolt under the power takeoff cover. Unbolt the power takeoff cover and you will find another sump cover bolt inside. Remove this bolt, then lift off the sump cover carefully.

By the way, check the length of the "hidden" bolt. You'll discover that it's shorter than the others—a bit of information you'll find useful when you put the engine together again.

Step 9. Wipe any accumulated sludge or metal filings out of the engine crankcase. Before you fiddle around inside the sump, remember that the plastic gear that seems to be just lying in the sump is an oil slinger. Lift it out.

Look for timing marks on the crankshaft gear and power takeoff gear. Rotate the shaft until the two marks line up. Then remove the power takeoff gear and retrieve the thrust washer that's attached to it. This will give you access to the connecting rod cap bolts, tappets and crankshaft for further disassembly. Consult the engine maker's repair manual for these major overhaul procedures on your engine.

Reassembly of the Engine

After finishing the power tuneup, it comes time to put things back together again. Basically, parts will go back in the reverse order from the way you took them out. But here are a few other tips to help you avoid potential problem areas:

During reassembly, lubricate all metal-to-metal parts (except cylinder head bolts) with SAE-20 engine oil. Give head bolts a shot of high-temperature lubricant.

Before you install the sump cover, turn the crankshaft several revolutions to make sure it turns freely without binding. If it doesn't turn, get back inside to find out why it doesn't.

Put a loop of paper around the crankshaft to protect it in case you accidentally hit against it with the sump cover. Then, carefully lower the cover over the sump.

Don't forget to install a new flywheel key after you install the flywheel. Match the slot in flywheel to the slot in the shaft and push in the key.

Get bolt torque specifications from a small-engine parts dealer or by writing to the manufacturer. With a torque wrench, tighten all bolts to specifications.

Always install a new head gasket and tighten cylinder head bolts in a crisscross pattern to avoid warping the head. The first time around, tighten them until they just catch. Go back over them and tighten them snugly, then go back and tighten them to the manufacturer's specifications.

Home video

Super VHS (S-VHS) represents a quantum leap in home video picture quality. Camcorders, too, are becoming more sophisticated and offer better pictures in even the poorest light conditions. These are just part of the developments that are carrying home video into the next century.

Super VHS camcorder uses full-size cassettes.

Super VHS VCR has picture resolution that exceeds broadcast standards.

Super VHS

Super VHS does provide a dramatic improvement in picture quality over other home video formats. It could open the door to even more stunning improvements in broadcast and cable television.

While this is encouraging news, it does mean that your current video equipment is to some extent obsolete. But before you rush to trade in your system, take a good look at that "to some extent." At this stage, S-VHS is definitely not for everybody. To determine whether S-VHS is right for you—and to know how to take advantage of the new format if you do decide to commit to it—you should understand how S-VHS works.

S-VHS Picture Quality. Although many new video fans don't realize it, the picture quality of most home VCRs today is really only fair—not even as good as a live TV telecast. Engineers measure resolution by counting the vertical bars or lines of a test pattern recorded by the camera system and displayed left to right on a screen. The greater the number of lines reproduced, the

finer detail of the image. (The specification described as "lines of horizontal resolution" shouldn't be confused with the 525 standard scanning lines that deliver the TV picture.) U.S. television broadcasts can transmit up to about 330 lines of resolution, and today's best TV monitor/receivers can reproduce more than 400 lines. But the average VHS VCR offers about 240 lines at best. S-VHS offers a crystal-clear 440 lines of resolution, nearly twice the detail of older VHS VCRs.

Like the original VHS format, S-VHS was largely developed by Japanese engineers. Their goal was to produce a radical improvement in VHS picture quality while changing the VHS operating system as little as possible in order to minimize any incompatibility between S-VHS and VHS. To do that, they retained the same cassette size, tape speed and method of audio recording. The method of video recording (frequency modulated, or FM, "color encoder" recording) is also similar, but the engineers have made one big change: They shifted the luminance signal (the black-and-white portion of the TV signal) to a much higher frequency.

Conventional VHS records the luminance signal in a frequency band between 3.4 and 4.4 megaHertz (MHz). The S-VHS signal is recorded in a band from 5.4 to 7.0 MHz. The S-VHS signal is not only higher, but it also occupies a band that is 60 percent broader (1.6MHz compared to 1.0MHz) than conventional VHS. That broader bandwidth means it can handle far more picture information, especially high-frequency signals.

This is seen in the fine details of the picture: skin texture, hair, foliage, woven fabrics and other delicately featured surfaces and shadow areas stand out crisply in S-VHS, whereas they blend into flat, cartoon-like strokes in conventional home video images. In addition to this expanded frequency bandwidth, S-VHS VCRs also boast a new form of video noise reduction. The system uses a digital delay circuit to boost the picture information relative to the background noise.

Videotape Compatibility. The high-frequency recording of S-VHS would never have been possible without the enormous progress magnetic tape manufacturers have made in improving videotape. Although the new S-VHS tape uses essentially the same kind of iron-oxide material employed by regular VHS tape, manufacturers have refined the familiar material for better performance. The magnetic particles in the new tape are substantially finer than those of ordinary tape so more particles can be packed on the tape. This combination reduces noise and is better for recording high frequencies.

All S-VHS VCRs can play and record regular VHS tapes, so you won't have any problem playing back tapes from your existing collection or from the local video store. You can also record on conventional cassettes, but not at the same high picture quality. And, since S-VHS cassettes have a special identifying hole, the new decks will be able to distinguish between the two types of tape. An S-VHS cassette will also work fine if you use it to record in a regular VHS deck (it won't give you an S-VHS picture, but it will perform like an excellent high-grade tape).

The one thing you can't do is play back a *recorded* S-VHS cassette in a conventional deck. Because of the shift in frequency, your old VCR won't even pick up the S-VHS signal. That's going to complicate tape trading among friends and family: if you have an S-VHS model but your friends don't, you can play back their tapes but they can't play the ones you record unless you record in the conventional mode.

Monitor/Receiver Compatibility. Some prospective S-VHS buyers might worry that after spending all that money on a new Super VCR they will have to turn around and buy a new TV, too. Fortunately for most buyers, that won't be the case.

Monitor/receiver TV sets (models with direct video and audio jacks on the back and comb filters for improved pictures) have improved dramatically in recent years. Almost all offer picture quality far better than that delivered by

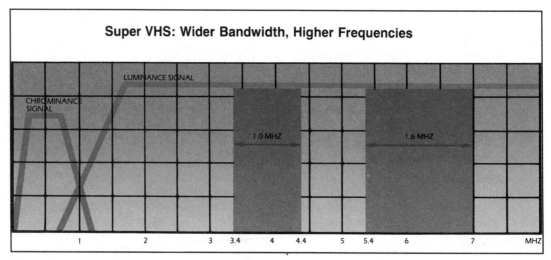

Super VHS: Wider Bandwidth, Higher Frequencies

LUMINANCE SIGNAL

CHROMINANCE SIGNAL

1.0 MHZ   1.6 MHZ

1   2   3 3.4   4 4.4   5 5.4   6   7   MHZ

The 1.6MHz bandwidth that super VHS *(right)* uses to store luminance signals captures more detail-bearing high frequencies than VHS.

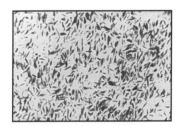

Compared to conventional video-tape, Super VHS tape *(right)* has finer particles, and more of them, to capture greater details. These electron microscope photographs show standard VHS *(left)* and Super-VHS *(right)* particles magnified 42,000 times.

today's TV transmissions. In a sense, S-VHS is simply catching up with the high standard already set by current TV monitor technology. If you purchased your monitor in the past three years, you should be able to take advantage of virtually all the quality boost in S-VHS.

The compatibility question is a bit more complicated. In addition to direct video jacks, S-VHS manufacturers include a new type of connection, specifically for S-VHS called an "S-connector."

The new hookup actually contains two separate signals in a single cable. All VCRs record the luminance (or black-and-white) portion of the TV signal separately from the chrominance (or color). Normally, these two signals are combined in order to travel through the cable to the TV set. But the S-connector keeps them separate. This is a common feature with professional video equipment—the pros call it a "Y/C" connector (the Y stands for luminance, C for chrominance). Keeping these signals separate helps prevent the interference or "crosstalk" between them that can cause minor picture problems such as graininess or vibrating moiré patterns. The S-connector helps improve the already excellent picture of S-VHS, but it is by no means necessary.

Super-VHS Cameras. For many video enthusiasts, the camcorder is the most exciting aspect of S-VHS. So far, every company offering an S-VHS VCR also plans to introduce a Super camcorder. The home moviemakers come in two types: full size (using a full-size VHS or S-VHS cassette) and VHS-C (using the cigarette-pack-sized cassette in either its VHS or S-VHS form. Either type can play back high-resolution S-VHS images directly to your TV set.

Interestingly, the S-VHS-C camcorders offer one striking advantage over their conventional counterparts. All VHS-C camcorders give you the choice of shooting the SP (standard play) speed which allows 20 minutes of taping on the miniature cassette, or shooting in EP for 1 hour of recording on one cassette. With conventional

of recording on one cassette. With conventional VHS-C camcorders, the 1-hour speed offers barely acceptable picture quality, but the new Super models should deliver stunning quality even at the slower speed. Preliminary tests have shown surprisingly little difference between the SP and EP performance on S-VHS VCRs. That translates into an hour of high-quality S-VHS recording with a camcorder that weighs under 3 pounds. In fact, in terms of picture quality the new S-VHS camcorders have actually leap-frogged some costly professional video systems.

Prerecorded S-VHS Tapes. Even more than with home movies, VCR owners are in love with the Hollywood variety. So what about prerecorded movies in S-VHS? The technology to mass produce S-VHS prerecorded cassettes already exists. U.S. movie studios probably will release S-VHS titles as soon as the number of S-VHS VCRs in use passes the 1 million point. Owners of ordinary VHS decks can rest easy, though. With well over 100 million VHS VCRs in homes around the world, and hundreds of millions of VHS cassettes in video stores and home collections, conventional VHS will carry on as the mainstream home video format for quite some time.

Camcorder Shutter Advances

One of the hottest features in video camcorders these days sounds like a holdover from film cameras: a high-speed shutter. Several VHS and VHS-C camcorders, and at least one manufacturer of 8mm camcorders, already include this new shutter technology.

These video-age shutters are quite different from those used with film movie cameras. For one thing, they're completely electronic—no mechanical curtains or other moving parts. They work by feeding the video signal from the solid-state sensor in tiny bursts of up to 1/800th of a second instead of using the normal 1/60th of a second conventional video.

These shutters offer slightly sharper moving images and drastically better slow-motion pictures. With an ordinary video camera, fast moving objects in the picture tend to blur due to the relatively slow rate (1/60-sec.) at which the camera "captures" each new image. Trying to view the tape in freeze-frame or slow-motion is nearly pointless.

With a high-speed shutter, each video field contains a crisp, clear image because it represents only a tiny instant of the object's travel. (Of course, this also requires plenty of light. In low-light conditions, the camera returns to normal shutter-speed operation.)

Obviously, not everyone needs crystal-clear slow-motion in their home movies, but anyone interested in shooting any type of sport will love it. Imagine being able to analyze the arc of a golf swing or tennis backhand with step-by-step video precision.

A closely-related development is called "flash motion" by one manufacturer of camcorders.

Accessing the flash motion feature results in a picture that is viewed as a series of successive stop-motion frames. The speed at which you can view these stop motion frames can be adjusted in intervals from 1/8-second to 4 seconds. While flash motion presents images sequentially, the "multistrobe" feature puts as many as nine or 16 separate images on the screen at once, either manually or automatically, at selected time periods.

On TVs with digital zoom (a feature that enlarges a designated area of the picture to four times normal size) you can bring one of the nine or 16 images to full-screen for closer analysis.

3-D Camcorders

Sooner or later home movie-makers are going to have as much gear available to them as Hollywood directors have on a film set. Of note in this growing list of equipment is a 3-D camcorder.

We remember 3-D as a joke from the 1950s, but in reality 3-D still has the power to stir our imaginations. Until now, filmmakers have used 3-D to entertain. Because video is easier to work with than film, 3-D will be used not only to entertain but also for education and health care.

The 3-D camcorder achieves its stereoscopic effects with two CCD image pickups fed by two lenses spaced apart like human eyes. You'll view the images with LCD glasses. Doubling the TV scanning rate from 60 to 120 frames per second eliminates any flicker. You should be able to use a conventional VCR for playback of most 3-D recorded images, but you may need an extra component that contains an analog-to-digital converter to eliminate the flicker and a frame memory and scanning-speed converter.

Many 8mm camcorders have high-speed shutters for sharp slow-motion.

You can make 3-D videos with this dual-lens, dual pickup camcorder.

DAT cassette is half the size of today's analog cassette, yet holds two hours of sound. Tape uses a high-density metal formula.

Digital audio tape recorder has controls and displays similar to today's conventional analog decks.

Digital audio tape developments

Digital audio tape (DAT) promises to be the music medium of the future. It renders sound quality on a par with digital compact discs but in a smaller package. Moreover, DAT provides the opportunity of digital recording—a feature which the playback-only CD lacks. This very asset might prevent DAT decks from reaching American homes. The proposed embargo on the import of these units is prompted by the music industry's contention that DAT makes mirror image copies of CDs, and that this ability will precipitate revenue-robbing private copying and criminal piracy.

This contention may well be uninformed and unfounded. Indeed, DAT can sound splendid—but it doesn't make bit-for-bit clones of CDs any more than today's conventional analog cassette decks do.

The DAT Recorder

Operationally, the DAT recorder is both familiar and strange. Though the front panel sports the recording controls of a conventional deck, the tape transport system resembles that of a video-cassette recorder. The machine shares the digital storage format with CDs. In actual recording, this entails different parameters than those we've become accustomed to with analog decks.

Like a VCR, the DAT recorder requires a few seconds for the tape to exit the cassette and load into the record/play tape transport system. Also like a VCR, it will disengage the tape and enter the STOP mode if the transport is left in PAUSE for an extended time.

The functional similarity to a VCR is most apparent when accessing individual tracks on the DAT cassette. Like VCRs that reverse up to 15 units on the tape counter before moving

DAT—How It Works

Digital audio tape's transport system *(right)* works just like that of a videocassette recorder. The tape is extracted and wrapped 90° around the head-bearing drum. As the tape moves past the drum from left to right at 1/3 inch per second, the drum rotates counterclockwise at 2000 rpm *(middle right)*. This combination yields a recording speed of 123 inches per second—65 times faster than today's analog cassette decks. The drum's two magnetic heads write and read information in diagonal tracks across the width of the tape *(far right)*. Because each of the two heads is mounted at a different azimuth, the information-bearing tracks are laid down in an alternating pattern.

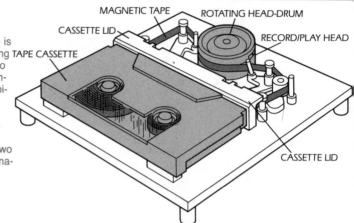

MAGNETIC TAPE
ROTATING HEAD-DRUM
CASSETTE LID
RECORD/PLAY HEAD
TAPE CASSETTE
CASSETTE LID

forward in the PLAY mode, the DAT overshoots the desired selection by 28 units, swiftly rewinds to the 8-unit mark, then counts down to zero, at which point the music begins.

The tape's fast-advance and rewind speed is awesome—200 times normal playback speed. That's not as fast as the access time between selections on a CD, but it's more than 12 times faster than an analog deck.

Just like the CD, the deck gives you direct access to each music track. Simply punch in the selection number (even by remote control) and the tape speeds to the designated point. You can program selections to play in any order you like.

Helical Recording

DAT acts like a VCR because it shares the same helical-scan recording scheme. The type of digital cassette deck available today is called R-DAT, for *rotary*. Just like a VCR, the DAT deck's magnetic heads are mounted in a rotating drum that ''writes'' data in *diagonal* tracks across the *width* of the tape—instead of along its length, as in fixed-head analog decks. Though the tape in an R-DAT deck moves at only 0.815 centimeters per second (about 1/3-in. per second), the head-bearing drum rotates at 2000 rpm. This yields a *writing speed* of 3.133 meters per second, or 123 in. per second.

That's fast compared to analog cassette decks which record and play tape at 1-7/8 in. per second. Consequently, R-DAT provides two hours of record/play time on a matchbox-size cassette. The tape measures the same 15/100-in. wide as today's analog cassette tape. But the use of high-density metal formulation permits more information to be stored.

At this standard record speed the R-DAT decks sample the music at a rate of 48kHz (48,000 times per second) and assign each sample a 16-digit code comprised of on-off pulses (the ones and zeros of the binary numbering system so familiar in computers). Though the sampling rate differs from the 44.1kHz used for CDs, theoretically the results are just as good. DAT yields flat frequency response from 4Hz to 22kHz (beyond audible range) with an impressive 96 dB (decibels) of signal-to-noise ratio. The best analog cassette decks have around 75 dB.

Sampling Variance

DAT records at 48kHz and plays back tapes sampled at that rate. But the machines also have a playback sampling rate of 44.1kHz—just like CD's—for prerecorded DAT cassettes that music companies might or might not sell.

What DAT doesn't have is the ability to record at the 44.1kHz sampling rate. This means a CD can't be copied in direct, digital form, because the machine has no way to convert the incoming 44.1kHz signal for recording at the 48kHz sampling rate. Therefore, the digital signal emanating from a CD must be converted to an analog signal (within the CD player) which is then re-recorded digitally by the DAT machine.

Even if the CD player has direct digital outputs (some do) and the DAT player has direct digital inputs (some might), the disparity in sampling rates would still prevent direct cloning. Even the improbable insertion of a sampling-rate converter between the two components would not work. That's because most CDs are inscribed with a Copy Prohibit code. This code triggers a mechanism already built into every

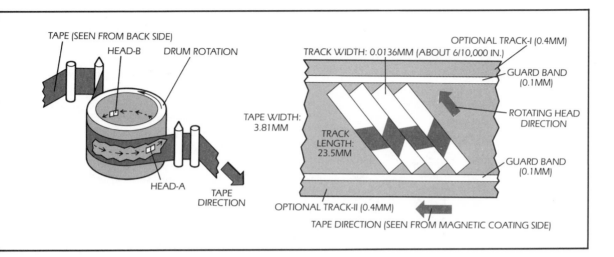

TAPE (SEEN FROM BACK SIDE)
HEAD-B   DRUM ROTATION
HEAD-A
TAPE DIRECTION

OPTIONAL TRACK-I (0.4MM)
TRACK WIDTH: 0.0136MM (ABOUT 6/10,000 IN.)
GUARD BAND (0.1MM)
TAPE WIDTH: 3.81MM
TRACK LENGTH: 23.5MM
ROTATING HEAD DIRECTION
GUARD BAND (0.1MM)
OPTIONAL TRACK-II (0.4MM)
TAPE DIRECTION (SEEN FROM MAGNETIC COATING SIDE)

DAT deck that prevents the machine from recording the encoded material.

The DAT deck's inability to make direct digital-to-digital dubs is intentional. It represents an attempt on the part of hi-fi manufacturers to address the music industry's concern that DAT decks will facilitate widespread copying, either for personal use (in car DAT players, for example) or for criminal trafficking in bootleg dubs. The music industry remains apprehensive and is lobbying for the incorporation of an anticopying device that would prevent the recording of CDs.

Home Recording

While politicians debate the propriety of home digital recording—or any home recording at all—practical experience with DAT indicates it's far from the clone-maker some think it to be.

Because digital-to-digital recording isn't possible, the input signal must pass through an analog stage. The quality of the analog electronics will determine how good a signal the DAT deck will record, but some deterioration is inevitable, possibly in frequency response and definitely in signal-to-noise ratio. You can think of

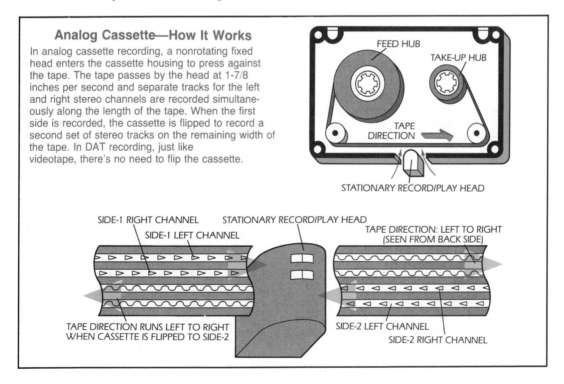

Analog Cassette—How It Works

In analog cassette recording, a nonrotating fixed head enters the cassette housing to press against the tape. The tape passes by the head at 1-7/8 inches per second and separate tracks for the left and right stereo channels are recorded simultaneously along the length of the tape. When the first side is recorded, the cassette is flipped to record a second set of stereo tracks on the remaining width of the tape. In DAT recording, just like videotape, there's no need to flip the cassette.

FEED HUB   TAKE-UP HUB
TAPE DIRECTION
STATIONARY RECORD/PLAY HEAD

SIDE-1 RIGHT CHANNEL   STATIONARY RECORD/PLAY HEAD
SIDE-1 LEFT CHANNEL
TAPE DIRECTION: LEFT TO RIGHT (SEEN FROM BACK SIDE)
TAPE DIRECTION RUNS LEFT TO RIGHT WHEN CASSETTE IS FLIPPED TO SIDE-2
SIDE-2 LEFT CHANNEL
SIDE-2 RIGHT CHANNEL

this like the process used to make a photo print, with the CD's digital signal being the negative. If direct digital recording were possible, the DAT copy would be a print made from the negative. But because the CD's signal must be converted to analog before recording, the DAT dub has the imperfect resolution of a print made from a print.

Operator Error

As with analog cassette recordings, the DAT dub's fidelity to the original depends a great deal upon the skill of the person whose hands are on the controls. Though the DAT deck's input-level dials and displays are the same as those on analog decks, it's harder to make a good digital dub. This is partly because of the digital recording process and partly because of the deck itself.

Unlike analog recording, digital is quite precise and doesn't leave room for error—especially the error of recording at too high an input level.

When you record an analog cassette, it's okay for the input signal to reach the 0-dB level—and even beyond for brief periods. The red-colored zone beyond 0-dB indicates that you're saturating the tape and warns of distortion. When the input level meters of a DAT deck flash red, it's not a warning—it's a fact.

Analog distortion results when the tape simply can't absorb any more signal. A saturated tape will sound muddy. The high, treble frequencies disappear and the bass becomes boomy rather than punchy. This distortion, however, is created by music. The natural balance of frequencies present in the original has been altered, but the distorted balance remains music. (Some rock musicians intentionally saturate their recordings to achieve a warm, buzzy sound.)

Digital distortion is completely different. Created by the machine, it sounds terrifyingly otherworldly.

Digital Distortion

Tape saturation from too high an input level plays no part in digital distortion—which sets in when the input level meter hits 0-dB.

Instead, distortion is caused by the inability of the 16-bit digital quantization system to assign a 16-digit code to the too-high input signal. The system has simply run out of bits, and it frantically attempts to assign some code to the overload signal. The scrambled-up bits it assembles, when played back, produce a noise that's horrid and distinctly unmusical. The edgy, broken-up

sound of a phonograph needle dragged across a record is pretty close to the mayhem digital distortion engenders.

To make good DAT recordings you must find the optimum input level below the 0-dB "brick wall." That takes trial and error and is difficult because of the wide dynamic range of CDs. Just when you think you've found the correct input level, a powerful passage of music jumps out; it's the brick wall, and it crashes your recording.

It helps to know the musical selection you're dubbing. This way, you can test-record the hot spots to find the input-level limits. If you don't know the music, today's DAT decks don't make your job very easy. Unlike 3-head analog cassette decks, there is no way to monitor the recording audibly as you make it. All you can do is watch the input-level meters in order to catch a mistake, correct your levels and re-record immediately. If you don't set the levels correctly and don't watch the meters, you won't be aware of any distortion until you play it back.

Sound Quality

For the most part, DAT dubs can duplicate CDs with dead accuracy, note for note. But they are not sonically authentic. Missing is the transparent or airy quality associated with CD. DAT copies do sound better than analog copies of the same material—and would be very satisfying if not compared directly to the original CDs. For that matter, so would the analog dubs!

Digital audio tape cassettes are half the size of current tapes and store two hours of music. Loading is as easy as loading a CD.

Band saw users guide

UPPER WHEEL (Guard Removed)

WORKLIGHT

BLADE GUARD

ARM

BLADE GUIDES

SAW BLADE

WORKTABLE

TILTING TABLE LOCK KNOB

LOWER WHEEL GUARD

STEEL BASE

ON/OFF SWITCH

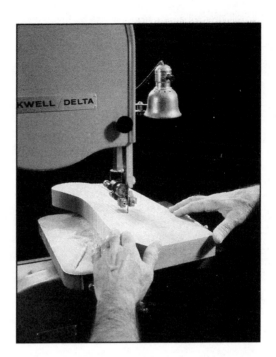

When woodworkers have to cut curved, irregular-shaped pieces, the tool they turn to first is the band saw. This saw's thin, flexible blade lets you maneuver wood easily and accurately along a winding line-of-cut and in and out of tight corners. The ability to perform these difficult cuts so effectively has, ironically, hurt the band saw's reputation as a versatile shop tool. In many workshops, the band saw is used *only* to cut curved pieces.

The band saw is capable of performing a wide variety of cuts including such *straight* cuts as rip, crosscut, miter and, if the saw has a tilting worktable, bevel and compound miters. It's also an excellent tool for resawing—cutting a thick board into thinner ones. Also, when fitted with an appropriate blade, the band saw can cut various metals and plastics. Some band saws will even accept a sanding belt.

It's important to know basic band saw practices and to see how, through various sawing techniques and shopmade jigs, you can expand your use of this tool to make many workshop procedures easier—including cutting curves.

The Band Saw

The band saw is named for its saw blade that is a continuous loop, or band of steel that has teeth on one edge. The blade rides over two wheels that are rimmed with thin rubber tires. Some benchtop band saws have three wheels. The tires provide nonslip traction to drive the blade in a down-cutting direction. The belt-driven lower wheel powers the blade. The free-spinning upper wheel is an idler wheel. The blade passes through a slotted insert in the center of a worktable.

A band saw has a few simple adjustments that are important to ensure accurate, trouble-free cutting. These include saw blade tensioning and tracking, and upper and lower blade guide adjustments. The upper, idler wheel adjusts up and down to permit installing the saw blade and applying the proper amount of tension. The upper wheel can also be tilted in or out to adjust the tracking so that it runs on the center of the tires.

A band saw has two saw blade guide assemblies—one above the worktable and one below. Each guide consists of a ball-bearing wheel that supports the back edge of the blade and a left and right guide block that supports the sides of the blade. The back support wheel prevents the blade from being pushed off the rubber tires as the workpiece is advanced into the blade. The two side guide blocks keep the blade from twisting as the workpiece is manipulated along the line-of-cut. Adjust the side guide blocks so they just clear the sides of the blade and are back far enough to clear the blade's teeth. The upper guide assembly, which also includes a blade guard, is adjustable up and down to accommodate stock of varying thicknesses. In use, adjust the upper guide so that it's ¼ in. above the top of the stock. (Note: for clarity, some photos show the guide adjusted slightly higher than it should be.)

Band saws are sized according to their approximate cutting capacity as measured from the blade to the arm. For example, the 14-in. saw shown has a cutting capacity of 13¾ inches. The maximum stock thickness that a band saw can handle is determined by the distance between the worktable and a fully raised upper edge guide. A typical 14-in. band saw has a maximum thickness capacity of about 6¼ inches.

Saw Blades

Band saw blades are commonly available in widths ranging from ¹⁄₁₆ in. to ¾ inch. You can choose from various tooth sizes and styles. Selecting the correct blade depends on the material being cut, the thickness of the material and the type of cut.

Generally, the more teeth a blade has, the smoother it will cut. To obtain smooth cuts, use a fine-tooth blade. For rough, fast cutting, choose a coarse-tooth blade. Coarse-tooth blades work best on soft, resinous or wet wood and for cutting thick stock. For extremely fast and rough cutting, use a skip-tooth blade. This type of blade has large, widely spaced teeth with deep gullets that expel sawdust and wood chips effectively.

To saw curves, use a narrow blade. The narrower the blade, the tighter a radius it can cut. For example, a ¹⁄₁₆-in.-wide blade can cut a minimum radius of about ⅛ inch. A ⅛-in-wide blade cuts a ¼-in. radius. A ¼-in. blade has a ½-in. radius. A ⅜-in.-wide blade, however, will cut only about a 1½-in. radius. A ½-in. blade: 2¼-in. radius; ¾-in. blade: 3½-in. radius.

When two curves meet at a sharp, inside corner, first cut straight into the corner. Then, saw the two curved cuts to free the waste.

To saw corners neatly, first cut into the corner. Then, backtrack slightly and saw around it. Come back later and finish it up.

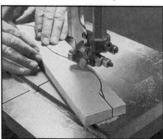

To cut curves with a wide blade, make tangential cuts or cut to the line several times and then saw away waste (background).

This setup shows how to use a shop-made V-shaped cradle and a miter gauge to saw round stock, such as pipe and tubing, safely.

Here's an easy way to cut several identical parts. First, saw the stock to the desired shape and then re-saw stock as shown.

To make resawing easier, use a simple shop-made pivot block. Clamp the block to the worktable and guide the board against it.

A band saw is an excellent metal-cutting saw when it's equipped with the appropriate blade. Metal cutting should be practiced on saws that are capable of operating at the required reduced speed. To cut metal effectively, the saw must be able to operate at about 300 fpm (feet per minute) or slower. The standard speed for wood-cutting is 3000 fpm.

Basic Band Saw Cuts

Most band saw cuts are made freehand —without the aid of a fence or guide. Freehand sawing is a two-hand operation. Use one hand to push the work into the blade and the other to steer it along the line-of-cut.

Cutting Curves. Before starting a curved cut, visualize the work being sawed along the cut line. This may help prevent interference with the saw's arm as the piece is maneuvered through the cut. Starting the cut from the other end of the line will often provide clearance for the piece. Try to avoid getting the blade trapped so you have to backtrack to free the blade. When you must backtrack, do so slowly to avoid pulling the blade away from the guides.

Cutting Intricate Designs. When executing an intricate cut, it's not usually possible to make the cut in a single, continuous pass. Instead, make a series of shorter cuts to minimize back-tracking. It's often easier to bypass small, detailed areas and come back later, after a majority of the waste has been sawed away, and finish them with short cuts.

Cutting Acute Corners. When two curves meet to form an acute, inside corner, you must first cut through the waste area directly into the corner. Then, cut along one of the curved lines and into the corner. Repeat the same cut along the remaining curved line to complete the cut.

Cutting Thin Material. When band sawing thin material, such as wood veneer or sheetmetal, the underside of the material often splinters or forms burrs. This is caused by the clearance space around the blade as it passes through the slot in the table insert. It's this lack of support right at the blade that allows the work to splinter. To ensure smooth cuts, make an auxiliary worktable surface out of a piece of ¼-in. plywood or hardboard. Cut about halfway into the

A simple wrap-around pushblock ensures safety when executing tricky cuts. Make block from three pieces of ½-in. plywood.

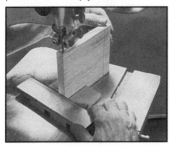

Complex work often requires compound sawing. Mark the profiles on two adjacent surfaces. Then make the first series of cuts.

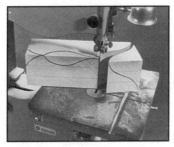

Tack-nail the first cut-off parts back onto workpiece. Rotate work and make the next series of cuts on the adjacent face.

V-shaped cradle is used to cut centering kerfs in ends of turning blanks. Clamp cradle to table and advance blank into blade.

Tilt the saw table 45° and use the rip fence to cut off the corners of the blank. Octagon-shaped blank is now ready for the lathe.

Try template-cutting to make identical parts. Tack-nail template to workpiece. Guide template against guide-arm clamped to table.

plywood panel and then secure it to the saw's worktable with masking tape. Because the saw blade now has very little clearance as it passes through the plywood panel, you can saw thin stock with virtually no splintering or burring.

Straight Cuts On a Band Saw

Crosscuts. Crosscuts can be made freehand, but for really straight, accurate cuts, use a miter gauge. The miter gauge slides in a slot milled in the top of the saw's worktable. Also use the miter gauge for making miter cuts. Most miter gauges adjust up to 60° left and right.

Rip Cuts. Accurate rip cuts are possible with the aid of a rip fence. Much like the fence found on a table saw, the band saw's rip fence can be positioned anywhere on the worktable and then locked in place. If your band saw doesn't have a rip fence, a straight-edged board clamped to the worktable works just as well. When ripping stock, be sure to use wood pushsticks to keep fingers clear of the blade. Most worktables tilt 45° to the right and 10° or 15° to the left for making angled rip cuts and compound miters.

Resawing. A band saw, with its thin blade and great cutting capacity, is an ideal tool for resawing. For best results, use as wide a blade as possible. This is especially important when resawing wide stock. To help guide the board and keep the cut on-line, use a simple shopmade pivot block, as shown. Clamp the block to the worktable at the desired distance from the blade. Then, feed the board into the blade while guiding it against the block.

Shopmade Accessories

To increase the versatility of your band saw, there are plans here showing you how to build two handy accessories: an extension table and a circle-cutting jig. Both of these accessories are designed to fit the saw shown. They can, however, be altered to fit your specific saw.

Extension Table. The extension table is a simple ½×36-in.-dia. plywood table that wraps around the saw's existing worktable. It's indispensable when cutting long or very large workpieces. The extension can also be removed easily.

Band saw extension table wraps around saw's existing worktable. Use it to cut long or very large workpieces. It removes easily.

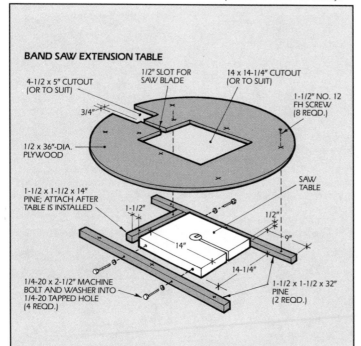

Bolt 2×2s to opposite edges of the saw table to support the plywood extension table. Add thin cardboard shims for clearance.

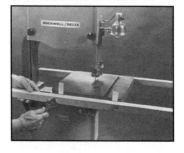

Glue and screw the plywood table to long 2×2 supports. Then attach crosspiece to plywood underside with screws only.

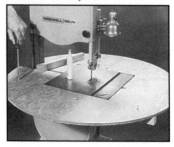

The plywood table is supported by an H-shaped frame that is bolted to the saw's worktable. Cut the frame parts from 2×2 stock. Drill and tap the edges of the saw's table to accept 1/4-20 machine bolts. Bore the holes to secure the two long frame parts 1/2 in. below the top of the saw's worktable. This 1/2-in. offset accepts the plywood table. Bolt the two long frame parts to opposite edges of the table. Place a thin cardboard shim between the frame and the table, as shown, to provide clearance for removing the extension table.

Cut out the plywood table as shown. Be sure to cut a 1/2-in.-wide slot in the table for the saw blade. Glue and screw the plywood table to the two long frame parts. Attach the short crosspiece of framing with *screws only*. Hold the crosspiece against the left edge of the table and secure it by screwing down through the plywood table.

Circle-Cutting Jig. The adjustable circle-cutting jig lets you cut perfectly round parts—up to 30 in. dia.—accurately and consistently. The jig consists of a 1-in.-thick plywood table, made from two layers of 1/2-in.-thick plywood, fitted with an adjustable pivot bar. A hardwood strip, attached to the underside of the plywood table, fits in the saw's miter gauge slot.

The pivot bar houses the pivot pin—a 3/4-in. No.6 screw sharpened to a fine point. The dovetail-shaped pivot bar slides in a matching slot and is locked in place by a lock cam mechanism. Slide the bar until the distance between the pivot point and saw blade is equal to the circle's radius. Push down on the lock cam handle to lock the pivot bar in place. The jig also has an adjustable stop cam, located at the end of the hardwood strip, that is used to align the pivot pin precisely with the saw blade teeth—regardless of the blade's width. Slide the jig forward until the stop cam hits against the edge of the saw's worktable. Then, rotate the cam until the blade teeth and pivot pin align. Tighten the wingnut to secure the cam.

To make a circular cut, first slide back the jig and place the workpiece on the pivot pin. Next, turn on the saw, slide the jig forward into the blade until it comes to a stop and then rotate the work slowly one full revolution.

Easy-to-make circle cutting jig fits over the saw's table. The bar extending from the jig to the right adjusts for various size circles.

Adjustable circle-cutting jig fits in miter gauge slot and lets you cut perfectly round parts accurately and consistently.

With the workpiece rotating on the pivot pin—a sharpened screw—a perfect circle is cut. The jig shown cuts circles up to 30 in. dia.

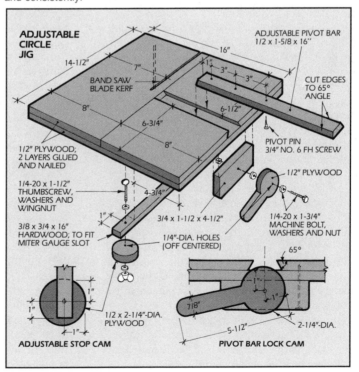

ADJUSTABLE CIRCLE JIG

14-1/2"
7"
BAND SAW BLADE KERF
8"
6-3/4"
8"
16"
3"
3"
6-1/2"
ADJUSTABLE PIVOT BAR 1/2 x 1-5/8 x 16"
CUT EDGES TO 65° ANGLE
PIVOT PIN 3/4" NO. 6 FH SCREW
1/2" PLYWOOD
1/2" PLYWOOD; 2 LAYERS GLUED AND NAILED
1/4-20 x 1-1/2" THUMBSCREW, WASHERS AND WINGNUT
3/8 x 3/4 x 16" HARDWOOD; TO FIT MITER GAUGE SLOT
4-3/4"
1"
3/4 x 1-1/2 x 4-1/2"
1/4"-DIA. HOLES (OFF CENTERED)
1/4-20 x 1-3/4" MACHINE BOLT, WASHERS AND NUT
65°
1"
1"
1"
1/2 x 2-1/4"-DIA. PLYWOOD
ADJUSTABLE STOP CAM
7/8"
1"
1"
5-1/2"
2-1/4"-DIA.
PIVOT BAR LOCK CAM

Saber saw users guide

The saber saw's unique design and versatility have made it one of the most popular portable power tools in use today. Do-it-yourselfers like the tool's user-friendly design and relatively safe style of cutting. Professionals find saber saws valuable for use both in the workshop and at the job site. Saber saws are also known as jigsaws or bayonet saws.

The saber saw's most outstanding features are its ability to make curved cuts and, when fitted with the appropriate blade, to cut a wide variety of materials including wood, metal, plastic, brick, leather and ceramic tile, to name just a few.

Regardless of the saw model, all saber saws operate basically the same way. A motor-driven gear assembly powers a shaft up and down. A blade clamp, attached to the end of the shaft, holds the saw blade securely.

Saber Saw Specifics

Saber saws are typically rated according to amperage, blade speed and stroke length—the distance the blade travels.

Generally, the current rating is a good indication of power. The more amps a tool draws, the more powerful it is. Most saber saws range between 2 amps and 4½ amps. The speed that the blade moves up and down is measured in strokes per minute (spm). Saber saws are available in single-speed, two-speed and variable-speed models. A variable-speed saber saw operates from 0 to about 3200 spm. This feature lets you adjust the blade's speed and cutting efficiency to the type and thickness of the material being cut.

Blade stroke length ranges from ½ in. to about 1 in., depending on the saw. The longer the blade stroke, the more saw blade teeth that will be doing the actual cutting.

Most saber saws cut with a straight up and down reciprocating action. Other saws offer orbital-action cutting. The blade cuts into the work at a slight angle on the upstroke and then moves away from the work on the noncutting downstroke. Orbital action means faster cutting with less chatter and increased blade life since there's practically no friction on the downstroke. Most orbital-action saber saws feature a 3- or 4-position switch for selecting the desired cutting motion from straight reciprocating through various degrees of orbital action.

Another worthwhile feature found on some saber saw models is a scrolling mechanism. This lets you rotate the blade 360°—while cutting—to gain superior control when sawing intricate scrollwork and highly detailed shapes.

Other convenient features worth looking for include electronic speed control, ball-bearing blade guides, a built-in sawdust blower, large stable base, blade wrench storage and a base insert that minimizes splintering. There are also cordless saber saws.

Saber Saw Blades

Saber saw blades are available in a wide variety of styles, shapes and sizes for cutting virtually every material. The blade you choose depends on the type of material being cut, the speed of the cut and the smoothness required. The blades are listed here according to their designed cutting purpose and the number of teeth per inch (tpi). As with most blades, the more teeth a saber saw blade has, the smoother and slower it will cut. Fewer blade teeth will produce a rougher, faster cutting blade. Blade lengths typically range from about 2½ to 4 inches. Blades, up to 12 in. long, are also available.

To cut sharp corners and tight curves in wood, try a narrow scrolling blade. For ultrasmooth cuts, use a taper-ground blade that has no-set teeth. Saw directly up to a perpendicular surface with a flush-cutting blade. The blade is offset so that the teeth extend to the front edge of the base. Wood cutting blades commonly range from 3 tpi (very roughcut) to 15 tpi (smooth cut). Metal cutting blades range from about 14 tpi to 32 tpi.

For extra durability, try bimetal saw blades. These blades feature tough high-speed steel teeth welded to a resilient spring-steel blade.

There are also a couple of *toothless* blades that are worth mentioning. A carbide-grit blade is available for sawing a variety of very hard,

Some saws have a tilting base to cut bevels. Use a straight board to guide saw. Block clamped to guide supports saw at the start.

A flush-cut saw blade lets the saw cut right up to a perpendicular surface. It's best to start the cut with a standard saw blade.

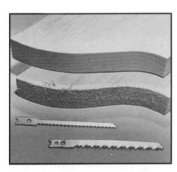

Fine-tooth blades give smoother cuts. Top board was cut with a 20-tpi taper-ground blade. Lower board, with a 6-tpi saw blade.

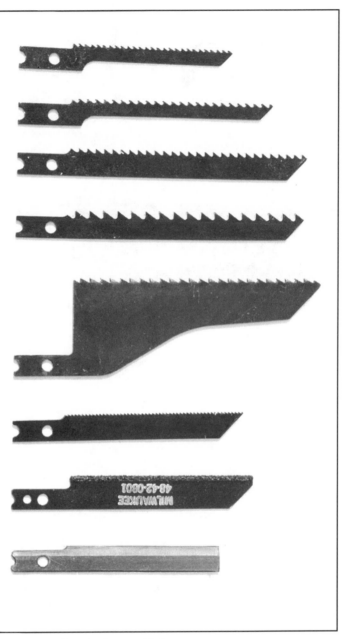

Here's a sampling of saber saw blades 14-tpi scrolling, 12-tpi scrolling, 10-tpi taper ground, 6-tpi rough cut, 10-tpi flush cut, 24-tpi metal cutting, carbide grit and knife-edge.

abrasive materials such as ceramic tile, slate, steel, plaster, brick and fiberglass. The blade is made up of thousands of tiny tungsten-carbide particles bonded to an alloy-steel blade. Another valuable toothless blade is the knife-edge blade. Use it to cut rubber, leather, cork, vinyl, cardboard and foam rubber.

Most saber saws accept a standard ¼-in. straight-shaft blade. Some saws, however, will accept only blades with a specially shaped shaft. While this type of saw works well, the blades are often a little difficult to find. Standard straight-shaft blades are sold at virtually every hardware store, home center and lumberyard.

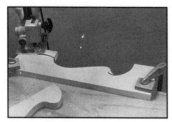

Cut out sharp inside corners in stages. First saw into the corner, back out the blade and then come back and make the finishing cuts.

To ensure straight freehand cuts, use a relatively wide blade and support the workpiece close to the line of cut with two 2×4s.

To make a plunge cut in the center of a board, tilt saw on its nose, start motor and then slowly lower the rear end of the tool.

Metal cutting blades are similar to hacksaw blades with small teeth ranging from about 14 tpi to 32 tpi. Cut metals at slow speeds.

To obtain clean, chatter-free cuts in sheetmetal, place it between pieces of cardboard or ¼-in. plywood. Support work on 2×4s.

A tungsten-carbide-grit blade will cut ceramic tile, slate and other very hard, abrasive materials. Apply slow, steady pressure.

Sawing Basics

A saber saw is most often used freehand to make curved and straight cuts. For more precise straight cuts, run the saw against a straightedge guide. Since a saber saw cuts on the upstroke, any splintering that results will appear on the top surface of the workpiece. Whenever possible, saw the work with its good side facing down. If this isn't possible, there are alternative methods to reduce splintering. Use a fine-cutting, taper-ground blade on a saw fitted with a base insert and advance the saw slowly. Another trick is to score the line of cut with a sharp utility knife before sawing. At least one manufacturer makes a reverse-tooth saw blade that cuts on the *downstroke* to eliminate top surface splintering.

When cutting curves freehand, use a narrow scrolling blade. Steer the blade slowly and tangent to the line. Try to avoid the common error of applying side pressure to steer the blade. The best way to handle sharp, inside corners and angles is to saw into the corner first, then back the blade out and bypass the corner to continue along the cut line. Then, come back later to clean up the corner.

Metal cutting is done at a slower blade speed than wood cutting. When sawing thin metal, it's important that at least two teeth of the blade make contact with the edge of the piece. Otherwise, the cut will be extremely rough and the blade teeth may be sheared off. Check the blade package for the type and thickness of the metal it's designed to cut.

A saber saw is especially useful for making plunge or pocket cuts in the middle of a board. Tilt up the saw on the front edge of its base so the blade clears the workpiece. Start the saw and then slowly lower the rear of the tool until the blade cuts through the work. It's important to keep a firm grip on the saw with *both* hands. The photo shows the plunge cut being made with one hand on the saw. This was done for photo clarity only.

A straight wood strip, tack-nailed in place, ensures straight cuts. Note that strip extends beyond board to align saw at start of cut.

Customized cutting guide requires no measuring. Simply place edge of guide on the line of cut. Saw blade will cut along guide edge.

Form edge half-lap joints with this U-shaped jig. The jig guides the saw for the two outside cuts. Interior kerfs are made freehand.

Break out the waste with a chisel. The two parts lock together and form a clean, invisible joint, as shown in the right foreground.

Cut end half-lap joints with a short blade. Wood plate under saw's base controls depth of cut. Strip nailed to work guides first cut.

Using a chisel, break out the waste and scrape the joint smooth. Assembled half-lap, (shown at right) form a clean, strong joint.

Guided Saw Cuts

Although it's used freehand a majority of the time, a saber saw can make precise cuts with the help of various jigs and straightedge guides. Some saws come with a T-shaped rip guide that is adequate for some small cuts. An easy-to-make straightedge guide provides a better way to ensure straight, accurate cuts. Make the guide from a straight piece of wood such as a strip of plywood. Clamp or nail the straightedge guide to the work and run the saw along it. The distance from the guide to the line of cut must equal the distance from the blade to the edge of the saw's base.

To eliminate the need to measure from the line to the guide, make a customized cutting guide from two pieces of ¼-in. plywood or hardboard. Glue and nail a 1½-in.-wide plywood strip to another wider strip (about 5 in. or 6 in. wide). Then, guide the saw along the edge of the narrow, top strip to trim the bottom strip to the proper width. To use the guide, simply align its edge with the line of cut, clamp it in place, as shown, and make the cut.

A saber saw is also quite handy for making lap joints. For edge-lap joints, make a simple U-shaped jig out of plywood as shown. The inside dimensions of the jig depend on the width of your saw's base and the size of the notch you need to cut. The jig controls the saw to form the width and depth of the notch. Make several freehand cuts in the middle of the notch. Use a chisel to break out the waste in the notch, as shown.

Make end half-lap joints by attaching a plywood plate to the saw's base. This shortens the blade's stroke length and determines the depth of cut which should equal one-half the thickness of the stock. Nail or clamp a board to the workpiece, as shown, to guide the first saw cut and establish the shoulder of the joint. Then, make several freehand cuts through the waste area. Use a chisel to break out the waste and trim the joint smooth.

To ensure accurate guided cuts, use a set-tooth blade, not a taper-ground blade. Also, check that the saw's blade holder and ram shaft have no side play.

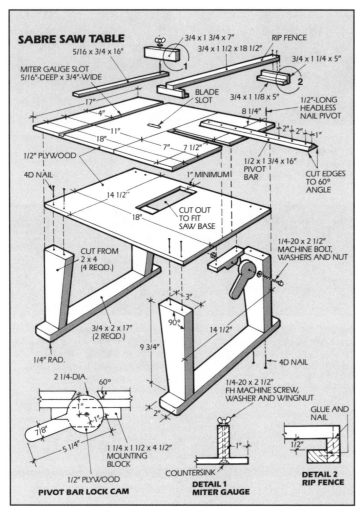

SABRE SAW TABLE

5/16 x 3/4 x 16"

3/4 x 1 3/4 x 7"

RIP FENCE

3/4 x 1 1/2 x 18 1/2"

3/4 x 1 1/4 x 5"

MITER GAUGE SLOT
5/16"-DEEP x 3/4"-WIDE

BLADE SLOT

3/4 x 1 1/8 x 5"

1/2"-LONG HEADLESS NAIL PIVOT

17"

4"

8 1/4"

11"

18"

2" 2" 1"

7" 7 1/2"

1/2" PLYWOOD

1/2 x 1 3/4 x 16" PIVOT BAR

CUT EDGES TO 60° ANGLE

4D NAIL

1" MINIMUM

14 1/2"

CUT OUT TO FIT SAW BASE

18"

1/4-20 x 2 1/2" MACHINE BOLT, WASHERS AND NUT

CUT FROM 2 x 4 (4 REQD.)

3/4 x 2 x 17" (2 REQD.)

90°

14 1/2"

9 3/4"

1/4" RAD.

4D NAIL

2 1/4-DIA.

60°

1"

1"

1/4-20 x 2 1/2" FH MACHINE SCREW, WASHER AND WINGNUT

2"

GLUE AND NAIL

7|8"

5 1/4"

1 1/4 x 1 1/2 x 4 1/2" MOUNTING BLOCK

1/2" PLYWOOD

PIVOT BAR LOCK CAM

1"

COUNTERSINK

DETAIL 1 MITER GAUGE

1/2"

DETAIL 2 RIP FENCE

Convert saber saw to a stationary power tool table by following these plans. Table has miter gauge, saw fence and circle-cutting jig.

Shopbuilt table converts the portable saber saw into a stationary tool. For accurate rip cuts, clamp the wood fence to the tabletop.

Execute square and angled cross-cuts with a miter gauge. Gauge slides in a $^{5}/_{16}$-in.-deep × $^{3}/_{4}$-in.-wide slot.

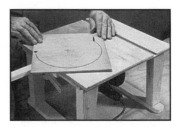

A sliding pivot bar adjusts for cutting circles from about 5 in. to 36 in. dia. Note that a blade access hole is bored in the work first.

Shopbuilt Saber Saw Table

Convert your saber saw to a stationary power tool by building the saw table according to the plans provided. The table features a 17×18-in.-wide work surface, miter gauge, saw fence and circle-cutting jig. The saw is mounted to the underside of the table. The saw blade protrudes from the table's surface and lets you guide the workpiece with two hands.

Note that the 1-in.-thick tabletop is formed by two layers of ½-in. plywood. The top layer is made of three pieces of plywood. This is necessary to form the dovetail-shaped pivot-bar

groove. The pivot bar houses a ½-in.-long pivot pin that is cut from a finishing nail and ground to a sharp point. Bore eight $^{5}/_{16}$-in.-deep holes in the pivot bar to house the pivot point. To cut perfect circles, the pivot point must align exactly with the front edge of the blade's teeth.

The pivot bar slides in the groove and is held in place by a wood handle, called a pivot-bar lock cam, that's situated under the bar. Note that the lock cam is bolted off-center to create a cam-action lever. Therefore, when you turn the handle the cam wedges against the bar and holds it securely.

A do-it-yourselfer's guide to the versatile saber saw begins on page 136. You'll find this tool user-friendly and relatively safe for cutting. Professional tradesmen find saber saws valuable for use both in the workshop and at the job site.

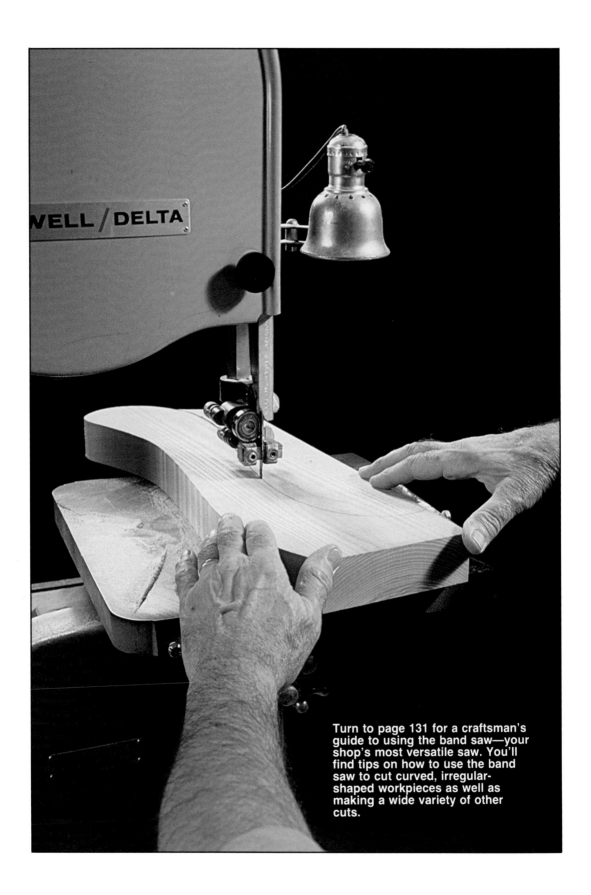

Turn to page 131 for a craftsman's guide to using the band saw—your shop's most versatile saw. You'll find tips on how to use the band saw to cut curved, irregular-shaped workpieces as well as making a wide variety of other cuts.

Compact and portable, this small-parts cabinet uses clear plastic cups for storing nails, screws, nuts and other hard-to-find items. Cabinet houses 120 cups. Plans for construction begin on page 150.

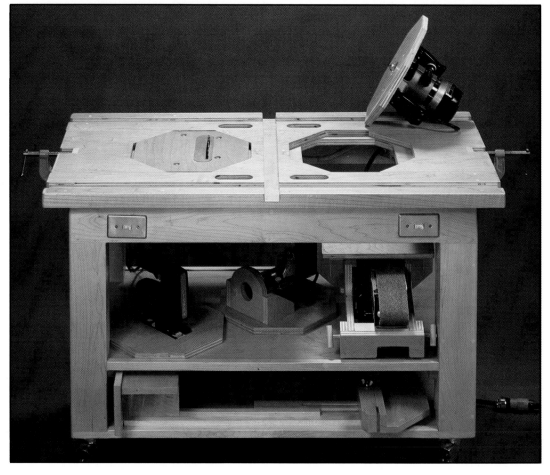

Benchmark workbench

In the old days, the construction of a workbench was a project that demanded all the skills of the accomplished cabinetmaker. Well-dried hardwood stock for the top had to be carefully joined and surfaced to be flat and true. Because a good workbench top is a guide, then and now, and reference for all the objects to be built in the shop, the supporting framework would be braced against racking and strong enough for the heaviest work. To give the bench the weight needed to stay put, heavily dimensioned stock would be used throughout.

For most do-it-yourselfers, the expense of the wood alone would be enough to deter them from making a quality workbench. Add to this the time and effort necessary for preparing and joining the heavy stock without expensive machinery, and it's no wonder that most workshops make do with a sometimes rickety, and often inadequate, work surface. The workbench shown here was designed to overcome all these problems—with a few added attractions to boot.

Designed around a torsion-box top, this bench is economical to make and, with a little care, will rival the best traditional benches for flatness and strength. Further, because it's not solid wood, it will stay flat. It can be built using portable power tools and constructed of commonly available materials. The hefty legs eliminate the need for a

This workbench features a heavy-duty vise, bench dogs and replaceable work surface.

complicated framework while adding great rigidity. This means the space underneath is completely open for roll-away storage—a feature impossible to find on conventional benches. Heavy-duty levelers let you adjust the bench to any floor. On top, there's a replaceable hardboard work surface. This bench also features a quick-action vise, bench dogs and long-stock support pin in the front leg opposite the vise.

The most interesting feature, however, is the torsion-box top which, simply, is a structure designed to resist twisting and bending. It's constructed by sandwiching a square-grid structure, or egg-crate, between two surfaces, much the same way that hollow-core doors are made. You end up getting maximum strength with minimum materials.

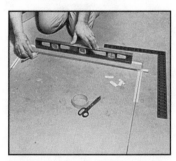

Prepare a flat assembly surface by securing leveled cleats to the floor. Scribe each cleat to fit surface irregularities.

The inner cleats are trued by spanning the end cleats with a straightedge. Mark the correct height on each inner cleat.

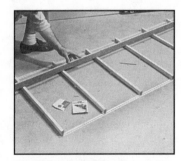

Check the assembly surface to be sure it's absolutely flat. If necessary, fine tune the cleat upper edges with a plane.

Preparing for Assembly

The flatness of a torsion-box depends entirely on the flatness of the surface that it's assembled on. So, you'll have to begin by preparing an absolutely flat surface on your basement or garage floor. This step is time consuming, but the results make it all worthwhile. First, you'll need to lay down a series of softwood cleats which can be trued up for accurate assembly.

Unless you have a wood floor that you can screw the cleats to, fasten them down with double-faced tape. Make sure you get tape with sufficient holding power. The 1-in. mounting squares sold for hanging pictures on walls will do the job nicely. If you can't find these at a hardware store, try your variety store.

Start by drawing an outline of the benchtop on the floor. Use a large framing square and an accurate 7-ft. straightedge. (You might be able to rent one of these long straightedges from a wallpaper store.) You'll need seven cleats to support the top assembly. Cut each cleat to 30⅝ in. long. Mark seven equally spaced cleat locations along the benchtop outline. It's a good idea to lay masking tape around the outline to make your pencil marks easier to see. Number the cleats and cleat locations. Each cleat will be tailored to fit one specific location and you don't want to mix them up.

Most workshop floors are not flat enough to fasten the cleats to without first scribing them to the contour of the floor. Place the first cleat in position at one end of the benchtop outline. Place a level on top and shim the cleat until the bubble centers. Scribe the contour of the floor on the lower edge of the cleat and cut to the line. When placed back in position, this cleat should now be level. Cut the cleat for the opposite end (cleat No.7) in the same way and fasten both down with three adhesive tabs each.

Scribe and trim the remaining cleats to fit the floor at their correct positions. Don't worry about leveling them at this point. Place cleat No.2 in position and temporarily secure it with the tabs. Cut three spacers (about ¼ in.) and place one of them on the end of the first cleat and

Use a spacer block and straight-edge ripping guide to accurately rip the plywood for the webs and inner aprons.

Rip enough stock for all the webs to *identical* width. Then crosscut to length, making sure the cuts are square.

Hold benchtop components in place with pipe clamps and drive one staple at each web joint. No glue is needed.

Using a long straightedge, transfer the egg-crate pattern to the panel top to be used as a guide when driving nails.

After one side of the egg-crate is stapled together, check for square, and apply slow-setting hide glue on all edges.

Instead of using clamps to hold the panel in place while the glue sets, drive finishing nails between each intersection.

one on the end of cleat No.7. Lay your long straightedge on these spacers and use the third spacer to scribe the correct height of cleat No.2. Repeat this on the other side of the benchtop outline. Then remove cleat No.2, connect the marks with a straight line, and trim to this line. Repeat this procedure for the remaining cleats and then lay them all in position and check them with the straightedge. When you're satisfied that the top edges of all the cleats are true and flat, fasten them down with adhesive tabs.

Building the Benchtop

Start construction of the benchtop by cutting the plywood webs. Use a straightedge ripping jig to cut the webs straight and to the same width. Then cut the maple webs to size and prepare the vise support block as shown in the drawing. Cut the long inner aprons to size and rout the recesses for the maple inserts. These inserts accept the front lagscrews that hold the vise. Finally, cut the top and bottom particle board panels about ¼ in. oversize.

Lay one of the panels on the cleats and temporarily fasten it in place with four 4d finishing nails. Position the inner aprons and the end web pieces and use pipe clamps to hold them together. Now begin assembling the egg-crate pieces, fastening each to the next with a staple driven across the joint. No glue is necessary. The staples only serve to hold the pieces in place until the box is completed.

Mark the remaining panel with the grid pattern as reference for nailing. Run a bead of slow-setting hide glue on the top edges of the egg-crate and lay the panel in place. Drive 4d finishing nails between each intersection to clamp the panel in place. Let the glue set overnight. When the glue is dry, lift off the partially completed torsion box and carefully pry the base panel away from the cleats. Lay the glued-up section face down on the cleats and drive staples at all joints. Spread glue and attach the other panel. After the glue has dried, use a router with a flush-trimming bit to trim the excess from panel edges.

When the glue has dried, remove the benchtop and pry up the base panel. Then lay the top, face down, on the cleats.

Glue and nail the second panel in place and use a router with a flush-trimming bit to trim the panel excess.

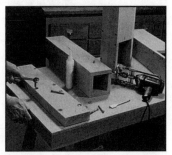
Maple ledgers connect the leg assemblies to the top. Secure these with lagscrews that extend into the maple webs.

Clamp the leg pieces together and counterbore pilot holes for the screws and plugs. Glue and screw together.

Glue plugs in the counterbored holes and dress with a belt sander. Then rout a ⅜-in. round on the outer leg corners.

Screw adjustable levelers to the mounting blocks and glue the mounting blocks to the support cleats in the legs.

The Support System

Cut the maple ledgers to size and fasten them in place with 3/8×3-in. lagscrews. Be sure they're positioned so the lagscrews enter the maple webs in the benchtop. Next, cut the stock to the correct length and width for the legs. Bore the 1-in. holes for the stock support pin as shown in the drawing.

Fasten the short cleats which hold the leveler support blocks in place before assembling the legs. Clamp the leg pieces together and bore the screw pilot holes and counterbores for the plugs. Apply glue and assemble the legs as shown in the drawing. Bore a hole in each leveler support block and screw the levelers in place. Then glue the blocks to the support cleats mounted in the legs. Glue the plugs in place and, when dry, dress them down with a belt sander. Then rout the 3/8-in. round on the outer leg corners.

Adding Final Touches

Position the hardboard top leaving 1/16 in. all around and fasten it down with 3/4-in. brads on roughly 8-in. centers. Cut the maple outer aprons about 1/4 in. oversize in width and glue and screw in place. Trim the edges with a router and flush-trimming bit. Use a 3/8-in.-rad. rounding-over bit to soften each corner of the bench.

Turn the bench upside down and place the vise in position to mark the holes for the lagscrews. After the vise is secured, lagscrew the legs to the ledgers. Be sure to check that the legs are square with the bench.

To make use of the retractable dog in the vise, bore 3/4-in.-dia. holes across the bench on the vise centerline to accept a 3/4-in. bolt bench dog. Bore the holes completely through the bench on 6-in. centers. Finish up with three coats of satin polyurethane varnish.

After nailing the hardboard top in place, glue and screw the maple outer aprons. Use a router to trim the excess.

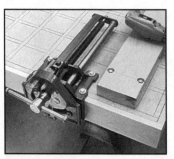
Place the vise in position to mark the lagscrew holes. These holes extend into the vise support block and inserts.

A drill guide helps in boring the 3/4-in. holes for the bench dog. Use a 3/4-in. bolt—threaded end cut off—for the dog.

MATERIALS LIST
WORKBENCH

Key	No.	Size and description (use)	Key	No.	Size and description (use)
A	13	3/4×2 1/2×28 7/8" lauan plywood (long web)	R	4	13/16×5 5/8×28 3/4" maple (crossmember slab)
B	10	3/4×2 1/2×2 1/2" lauan plywood (web)	S	12	13/16×5 5/8×29 1/4" maple (outer leg piece)
C	5	3/4×2 1/2×3 3/4" lauan plywood (web)			
D	8	3/4×2 1/2×3 13/32" lauan plywood (web)	T	4	13/16×5 5/8×21 7/8" maple (inner leg piece)
E	5	3/4×2 1/2×3 5/8" lauan plywood (web)	U	4	13/16×4×28 3/4" maple (crossmember inner rail)
F	5	3/4×2 1/2×4" lauan plywood (web)			
G	50	3/4×2 1/2×4 1/4" lauan plywood (web)	V	4	13/16×7 3/8×19 1/8" " maple (crossmember outer rail)
H	2	3/4×2 1/2×82 3/8" lauan plywood (apron)	W	4	13/16×3 15/16×5 5/8" maple (leveler support)
I	4	1 1/16×2 1/2×28 7/8" maple (web)			
J	3	1 1/16×2 1/2×22 7/8" maple (bench dog web)	X	8	13/16×2×5 5/8" maple (support cleat)
			Y	2	1/2×3 3/4×9 1/8" plywood (vise pad)
K	2	13/16×3 3/4×84" maple (apron)	Z	1	1" dia×12" dowel (stock support)
L	2	13/16×3 3/4×30 3/8" maple (apron)	AA	80	2" No. 12 fh screws
M	2	3/8×2×2 1/2" maple (insert)	BB	28	1 1/2" No. 12 fh screws
N1	3	3/4×6×10" plywood (vise block)	CC	108	1/2" dia. plugs
N2	1	1/4×6×10" plywood (vise block)	DD	28	3/8×3" lagscrews and washers
O	2	1/2×30 3/8×82 3/8" particle board (top)	EE	4	6" leveling jacks
P	1	1/4×30 1/4×82 1/4" hardboard (top)	FF	1	vise
Q	2	1 3/4×5 5/8×28 1/2" maple (cleat)			

WORKBENCH

32" WIDE X 34" HIGH X 84" LONG

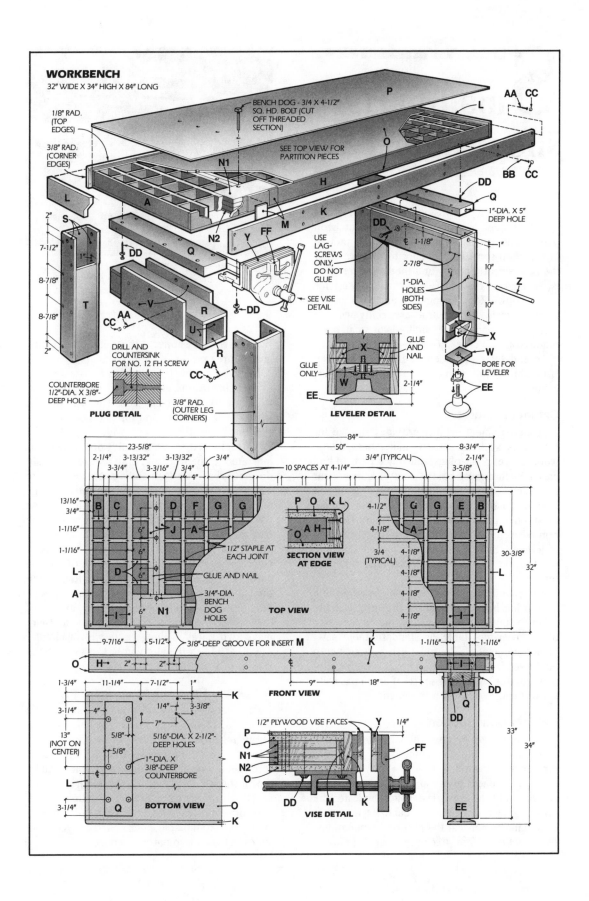

BENCH DOG - 3/4 X 4-1/2"
SQ. HD. BOLT (CUT
OFF THREADED
SECTION)

SEE TOP VIEW FOR
PARTITION PIECES

1/8" RAD.
(TOP
EDGES)

3/8" RAD.
(CORNER
EDGES)

1"-DIA. X 5"
DEEP HOLE

USE
LAG-
SCREWS
ONLY,
DO NOT
GLUE

1"-DIA.
HOLES
(BOTH
SIDES)

SEE VISE
DETAIL

BORE FOR
LEVELER

2"

7-1/2"

8-7/8"

8-7/8"

2"

1"

DRILL AND
COUNTERSINK
FOR NO. 12 FH SCREW

COUNTERBORE
1/2"-DIA. X 3/8"-
DEEP HOLE

PLUG DETAIL

3/8" RAD.
(OUTER LEG
CORNERS)

GLUE
AND
NAIL

GLUE
ONLY

2-1/4"

LEVELER DETAIL

84"

23-5/8"
2-1/4"
3-3/4"
3-13/32"
3-13/32"
3-3/16"
3/4"
3/4"
4"

50"

10 SPACES AT 4-1/4"

3/4" (TYPICAL)

8-3/4"
2-1/4"
3-5/8"

13/16"
3/4"

1-1/16"

1-1/16"

4-1/2"

4-1/8"

3/4
(TYPICAL)

4-1/8"

4-1/8"

4-1/8"

4-1/8"

4-1/8"

30-3/8"

32"

1/2" STAPLE AT
EACH JOINT

**SECTION VIEW
AT EDGE**

GLUE AND NAIL

3/4"-DIA.
BENCH
DOG
HOLES

TOP VIEW

6"

6"

6"

6"

6"

9-7/16"

5-1/2"

3/8"-DEEP GROOVE FOR INSERT

2"

2"

9"

18"

1-1/16"

1-1/16"

FRONT VIEW

1-3/4"
11-1/4"
7-1/2"
1"

3-1/4"

4"

13"
(NOT ON
CENTER)

1/4"
3-3/8"

7"

5/8"

5/8"

5/8"

5/16"-DIA. X 2-1/2"-
DEEP HOLES

1"-DIA. X
3/8"-DEEP
COUNTERBORE

3-1/4"

BOTTOM VIEW

1/2" PLYWOOD VISE FACES

1/4"

VISE DETAIL

33"

34"

Small-parts shop cabinet

How often have you wasted time searching for a specific box of screws or the brass escutcheon pins you bought last summer—you know they're in the shop somewhere—only to discover that the box is nearly empty and the hardware store is, of course, closed. Take heart, because for most shopworkers, keeping organized is an on-going struggle. This is true especially when it comes to organizing the hundreds of small parts required for all types of shopwork.

To end some of the chaotic clutter, you can build this simple 6-drawer roll-around storage cabinet.

Cabinet Features

This easy-to-build cabinet provides storage for 120 items such as screws, nails, nuts, bolts, wood dowel pins, plugs and other hard-to-find parts. Each drawer holds twenty 9-ounce clear plastic cups. The inexpensive cups are available at supermarkets and convenience stores. Unlike most small-parts cabinets, this system lets you remove a cup and bring it right to the workbench or job site. Since the caps are clear, it's easy to identify the contents and determine when to refill.

The cabinet also features a built-in adjustable steel roller housed behind the drawers. Use the roller to support workpieces on the outfeed side of a power-tool table or standard table saw, planer and jointer. The roller can be adjusted to hold oversize stock. The compact portable cabinet requires less than 4 sq. ft. of floor space and stores neatly against a workbench.

Cabinet Construction

This cabinet can be constructed using portable power tools. Build the cabinet from 3/4-in. maple-veneer plywood. Use less expensive lauan mahogany-veneer plywood for the drawer panels that hold the cups. Use solid maple for the drawer guides, drawer faces, cabinet trim and as edge band to conceal the plywood laminations. Note that the 2¼-in.-thick post (part **L** in Mate-

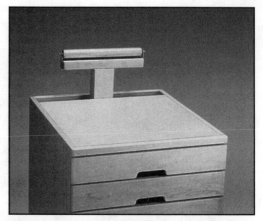

Cabinet features an adjustable-height outfeed roller that stores behind the drawers. Use roller to support long boards.

rials List) that supports the roller is made by gluing three pieces of 3/4-in. maple plywood.

Begin by cutting the cabinet's plywood panels to the dimensions given in the Materials List, using a portable circular saw. This includes the sides, back, partition and top and bottom.

Glue 1/8-in.-thick × 3/4-in.-wide maple edge band to the edges of the plywood panels, as indicated in the drawing. Only the partition (**D**) does not receive edge banding. An easy way to "clamp" the edge band in place until the glue dries is with masking tape. Before assembling the cabinet, bore a 1-in.-dia. access hole in the partition so you can take out the carriage bolt and remove the roller assembly, if necessary. Glue and nail two post guide strips (**K**) to the partition. Cut a 1/2-in.-wide × 12½-in.-long slot in the back panel to accommodate the carriage bolt. To do this, first bore two 1/2-in.-dia. holes to establish the top and bottom of the slot. Then, make two parallel plunge cuts with a circular saw to establish the slot width. Cut through the last bit of wood with a saber saw.

Assembly Procedures

Bore screw-shank clearance holes and 3/8-in.-dia. × 3/8-in.-deep wood-plug holes at each screw location. Glue and screw together the cabinet with 1½-in. No.8 screws. Conceal each screwhead with a 3/8-in.-dia. maple plug. Make the T-shaped post that supports the outfeed roller. Attach the roller to the cross support with two corner braces (**R**). Cut 3/4×3/4×18-in. drawer guides (**G**) from maple stock. Each drawer panel slides between two pairs of guides.

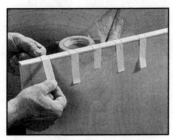

Use 1/8-in.-thick maple edge band to conceal the exposed plywood edges. Tape the edge band in place until glue dries.

To form the bolt slot in cabinet back, first bore two holes, then saw out the waste using a portable circular saw and saber saw.

Before attaching the partition to the cabinet, bore a 1-in.-dia. bolt access hole and attach two ply-wood post guide strips.

After partition is in place, install the cabinet top. Assemble the cab-inet parts with glue and 1½ in. No.8 wood screws.

This shows the outfeed roller as-sembly ready for installation. Note that carriage bolt is in place before the cabinet back is attached.

Wrap spacer block (arrow) with three thicknesses of tape to pro-vide clearance for the drawer pan-els to operate smoothly.

Cut cup holes with drill and hole-saw. Saw halfway through, turn over panel and continue sawing to remove the waste.

Clamp together all the drawer faces and use a 3/8-in. rounding-over bit to rout a radius on both ends of each drawer face.

The roll-around cabinet has four swiveling, locking casters and six drawers. Each drawer has 20 clear plastic cups for storage.

Bore three pilot holes in each guide to accept 3d finishing nails. Bore a 3/8-in.-dia. × 3/4-in. hole 1½ in. from the end in 12 of the guides.

The holes accept 1½-in.-long dowel rod sec-tions that act as drawer stops (J). Be sure to use these 12 parts as *lower* drawer guides.

When installing the guides, use spacer blocks to maintain uniform spacing. Use a 1 7/16-in.-wide spacer block to separate one pair of drawer guides from the next. Use a 3/4-in.-wide spacer between the upper guides and the lower guides. Wrap three thicknesses of masking tape around the 3/4-in. spacer to create clearance for the

panels to slide. Glue and nail the guides to the cabinet sides. Note that the uppermost guide on each side is 7/8 in. from the underside of the cabinet top. Finally, glue the dowel-rod stops into the holes bored in the lower guides.

Cut six drawer panels (I). There's no quick, easy way to cut out the 120 3-in.-dia. cup holes—20 per panel—but here's a method you can use. First, bore 1/4-in.-dia. holes at each hole center. Then, use a 3-in.-dia. holesaw in an electric drill and bore *halfway* through the panel. Turn over the panel to complete the cut. Sawing from both sides makes it easier to remove the

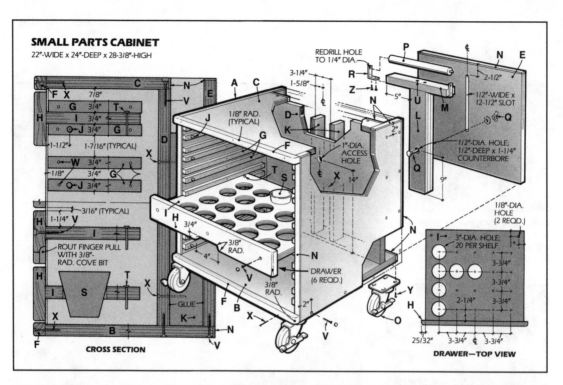

SMALL PARTS CABINET
22"-WIDE x 24"-DEEP x 28-3/8"-HIGH

CROSS SECTION

DRAWER—TOP VIEW

MATERIALS LIST
SMALL PARTS CABINET

Key	No.	Size and description (use)	Key	No.	Size and description (use)
A	2	¾×22¹⁵⁄₁₆×23⁷⁄₈″ maple plywood (cabinet side)	N		¹⁄₈×¾″-wide maple (edge band)
B	1	¾×20½×23¹⁄₁₆″ maple plywood (cabinet bottom)	O	4	caster with brake
C	1	¾×19¹⁵⁄₁₆×20½″ maple plywood (top)	P	1	1⅜″-dia. × 13″ steel roller
D	1	¾×20½×22½″ maple plywood (partition)	Q	1	½″-dia.×3½″ bolt, washer and wingnut
E	1	¾×20½×23⅛″ maple plywood (back)	R	2	2½″ corner brace
F	2	¹³⁄₁₆×⅞ ×22″ maple (trim)	S	120	9-oz. clear plastic cup
G	24	¾×¾×18″ maple (drawer guide)	T	12	6d common nail cut to 1½″ long (stop)
H	6	¹³⁄₁₆×3½×22″ maple (drawer face)	U	2	2″ No. 12 fh screw; ½″-dia. maple plug
I	6	¾×18×20⁷⁄₁₆″ lauan plywood (drawer)	V		1½″ No. 8 fh screw; ⅜″-dia. maple plug
J	12	⅜″-dia.×1½″ hardwood dowel (drawer stop)	W		3d finishing nail
K	2	¾×2⅜×20½″ maple plywood (post guide)	X		6d finishing nail
L*	1	2¼×3×20⅜″ maple plywood (post)	Y	16	1″ No. 12 panhead self-tapping screw
M	1	1¼×2¼×13″ maple (roller support)	Z	4	1″ No. 8 fh screw

Misc: Carpenter's glue; 100-, 120- and 220-grit sandpaper, satin-finish polyurethane varnish.
*Form post by laminating together three pieces of ¾×3-in.-wide maple plywood.

waste plug from the holesaw. Bore holes in the back corners of each panel to receive pins (**T**) made from 6d common nails. The pins, when inserted in the holes, will hit against the protruding dowel-rod stops when the drawer is fully opened. Lift the pins to remove the drawer from the cabinet.

Cut six drawer faces (**H**) from maple stock. Use a saber saw to cut a ¾×4-in. handgrip in each face. Rout a recessed finger pull—on the backside of each face—around the handgrip with a ⅜-in. cove bit. Rout a radius on both ends of each drawer face with a ⅜-in. rounding-over bit.

Clamp the faces together and rout them all at once. Glue and screw the faces to the drawer panels. Attach four locking casters to the cabinet's bottom. The *overall* height of the casters is 4⅜ inches.

Finish-sand the cabinet and apply one coat of polyurethane varnish thinned one part thinner to six parts varnish. Then, apply two full-strength varnish coats. Sand lightly between coats with 220-grit sandpaper. Install the steel-roller assembly and secure it with a carriage bolt and extralarge wingnut. Install the drawers and drop in the cups.

Ready for work, the power table is a self-contained work center with ample shelf space below for storage. In addition to the router and circular saw, you can mount a saber saw, drill and belt sander. The drill can be used vertically as a drum sander or horizontally for boring operations.

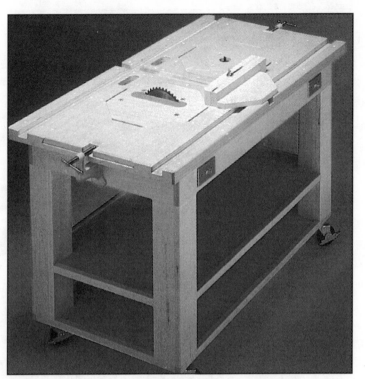

This power-tool table gives you stationary tool performance from your portable power tools.

Power tool table

This versatile stationary power-tool center will provide a workshop base for many of your power tools. You can build this table with the same portable power tools you'll use later to achieve stationary-tool performance.

BUILDING THE TABLE

The heart of this table consists of two octagonal tool-mounting plates. These self-aligning plates are easily removed for tool adjustment. Although the power table is shown with a circular saw and router, you can use it to mount virtually any portable power tool from a saber saw to a belt sander. A sturdy miter gauge lets you cut angles, and the table's ripping capacity, with fence, is over 24 inches. Best of all, you can have two tools mounted at once to speed multiple machining operations.

Construction Details

Start construction by cutting the maple stock to width and length for the legs. Bore ⅛-in. pilot holes, counterbored for plugs, and glue and nail the leg pieces together. Then prepare the apron pieces for assembly. As shown in the drawing, cut two notches in the center partition to allow for clamp access when securing the rip fence. Bore a ¾-in. hole for the wiring and cut the switch-box cutouts in the front apron. Then fasten the ledgers to the short-end aprons. Temporarily clamp the apron pieces together and counterbore screw pilot holes for 2-in. No.12 fh screws. Install the blocking at the end aprons.

The legs are secured to the frame with dowels. Transfer the dowel locations from the legs to the frame with metal dowel centers. Clamp two blocks of wood at the corner to guide the leg into position and tap with a mallet to mark the centers on the aprons. Bore the dowel holes in the frame corners and glue and clamp the legs.

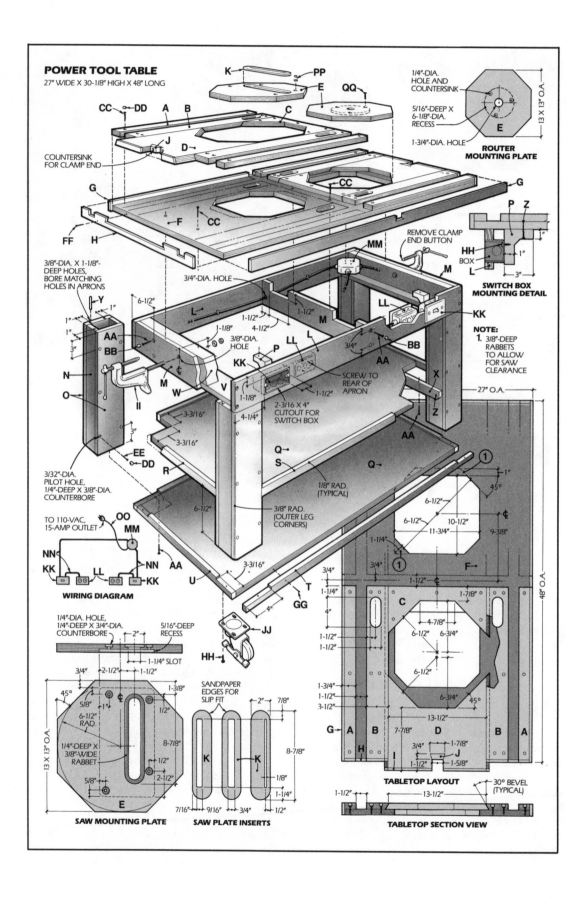

MATERIALS LIST—MITER GAUGE AND BRIDGE FENCE

Key	No.	Size and description (use)	Key	No.	Size and description (use)
A	1	3/4 × 1 1/2 × 18″ maple (guide)			
B	1	13/16 × 5 × 12″ maple (plate)	L	1	13/16 × 6 13/16 × 30 1/8″ maple (top)
C	1	13/16 × 2 × 12″ maple (fixed beam)	M	2	13/16 × 6 13/16 × 4 maple (side)
D	1	7/16 × 2 × 14″ maple (adjustable beam)	N	2	13/16 × 4 × 4″ maple (brace)
			O	1	13/16 × 6 1/2 × 20 3/8″ maple (pivotal plate)
E	1	7/16 × 2 × 4 1/2″ maple (adjustable beam)			
F	1	7/16 × 2 × 5 1/2″ maple (adjustable beam)	P	1	13/16 × 5 1/2 × 30 1/8″ maple (fence)
			Q	2	3/4 × 1 1/2 × 26″ maple (guide)
G	1	13/16 × 2 × 14″ maple (adjustable beam)	R	2	1/2 × 13/16 × 15″ maple (stop)
			S	2	2 × 3 1/16″ butt hinge
H	1	3/8-dia. × 3″ carriage bolt, washer, wing nut	T	2	3/8-dia. × 3″ hexhead bolt
			U	14	1 1/2″ No. 10 fh screw
I	2	1 1/2″ No. 10 fh screw	V	6	1 1/8″ No. 8 fh screw
J	2	1 1/4″ No. 8 fh screw	W	2	2 roller catch
K	1	2 × 3 1/16″ brass butt hinge	X		3/8″-dia. plug

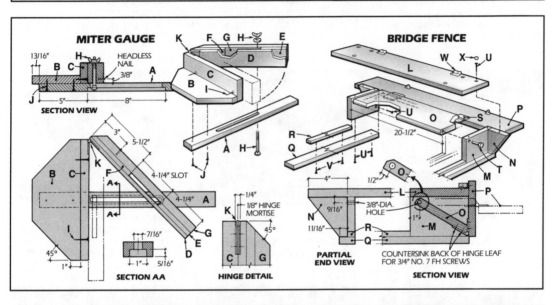

MITER GAUGE — 13/16″, HEADLESS NAIL, 3/8″, SECTION VIEW, 5″, 8″, 3″, 5-1/2″, 4-1/4″ SLOT, 4-1/4″, 45°, 1″, 7/16″, 1″, 5/16″, SECTION AA, 1/4″, 1/8″ HINGE MORTISE, 45°, HINGE DETAIL

BRIDGE FENCE — 20-1/2″, 4″, 1/2″, 9/16″, 3/8″-DIA. HOLE, 1″, 11/16″, PARTIAL END VIEW, COUNTERSINK BACK OF HINGE LEAF FOR 3/4″ NO. 7 FH SCREWS, SECTION VIEW

MATERIALS LIST—POWER-TOOL TABLE

Key	No.	Size and description (use)	Key	No.	Size and description (use)
A	4	3/4 × 1 3/8 × 22 7/8″ birch plywood (outer guide)	X	2	13/16 × 1 1/2 × 22″ maple (cleat)
			Y	12	3/8-dia. × 2″ dowel
B	4	3/4 × 3 1/2 × 22 7/8″ birch plywood (inner guide)	Z	6	1 1/2″ No. 10 fh screw
			AA		2″ No. 12 fh screw
C	2	3/4 × 6 5/8 × 14 3/8″ birch plywood (fixed plate)	BB		1/2″-dia. plug
			CC		1 1/4″ No. 8 fh screw
D	2	3/4 × 12 1/4 × 14 3/8″ birch plywood (sliding plate)	DD		3/8″-dia. plug
			EE		4d common nail
E	2	3/4 × 13 × 13″ birch plywood (mounting plate)	FF		2d finishing nail
			GG		4d finishing nail
F	1	3/4 × 25 1/4 × 47 1/4″ birch plywood (base)	HH		5/8″ self-tapping screw
			II	2	Holddown clamp (Jorgensen)
G	2	3/8 × 1 1/2 × 48″ maple (edge band)	JJ	4	Braking caster
H	2	3/8 × 1 1/2 × 25 1/4″ maple (edge band)	KK	2	Surface-mount electrical box
I	2	3/8 × 3/4 × 14 3/8″ maple (edge band)		2	ON/OFF switch
J	2	3/4 × 3/4 × 17 7/8″ maple (insert)		2	Switch cover plate
K	3	1/4 × 2 × 8 7/8″ hardboard/plywood (saw plate insert)		4	Cable connectors
					Wire nuts
L	2	13/16 × 4 × 43″ maple (long apron)	LL	2	Surface-mount electrical box
M	3	13/16 × 4 × 22 3/8″ maple (short apron/partition)		2	Duplex outlets with ground
				2	Duplex cover plate
N	8	13/16 × 2 3/8 × 19 1/2″ maple (leg)	MM	1	Octagonal junction box
O	8	13/16 × 4 × 19 1/2″ maple (leg)		1	Cover plate
P	2	13/16 × 3 × 3 1/2″ maple (box mounting bracket)		3	Cable connectors
					Wire nuts
Q	2	3/4 × 22 3/8 × 41 3/8″ birch plywood (shelf)	NN		No. 12/2 plastic sheathed cable with ground (Romex)
R	2	13/16 × 1 × 16″ maple (edge band)			
S	2	13/16 × 1 × 35″ maple (edge band)	OO	36″	No. 12/3 type J wire and plug with ground
T	2	13/16 × 1 × 43″ maple (edge band)			
U	2	13/16 × 2 3/8″ maple (edge band)	PP	4	1/4-20 × 1″ cap screw, flat washer, hexnut
V	2	13/16 × 3 3/16 × 22 3/8″ maple (ledger)			
W	2	1 1/2 × 3 3/16 × 22 3/8″ spruce/fir (blocking)	QQ	3	1″ 12-24 fh machine screw

Assemble the legs with nails and glue. Bore ⅛-in. pilot holes and counterbore for plugs. Finish driving with drift punch.

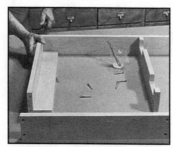

Screw the aprons together to make the frame. Cut two 1½×4½-in. notches in the partition for fence-clamp access.

Use dowel centers to transfer hole locations from the legs to the frame. Clamp two blocks at the corners to align the legs.

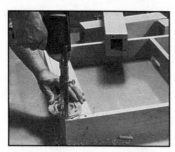

A drill guide ensures straight dowel holes. Bore 1⅛-in.-deep holes for 2-in. dowels to allow for excess glue.

Slide in the top shelf before attaching the support cleats. Screw and glue the cleats and screw the shelf in from below.

Trim the maple edge band flush on the lower shelf where the legs join. Screw the shelf in place with 2-in. No.12 fh screws.

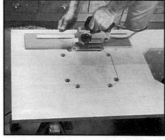

The cutouts in the base are started with 1-in.-dia. holes bored at the corners. Use a guide to make the cuts.

Rip the inner guides and the fixed and sliding plates. Be sure that the cuts are absolutely straight and parallel.

Install the fixed plates on, and square with, the centerline. Place sliding plates on centerline and install inner guides.

Making the Shelves

Cut the two plywood shelves to size. Notch the corners of the top shelf to fit around the legs. Prepare two shelf-support cleats as shown in the drawing. Slide the shelf in place and then screw and glue the support cleats in place. Screw the shelf to cleats from below. After it's secured, glue and nail the ⅜×1-in. maple edging.

Apply maple edging to the bottom shelf and trim it flush where the shelf will connect with the legs. After both shelves are in place, plug all holes, sand flush and use a ⅜-in.-rad. rounding-over bit to rout outer leg corners.

Cut the two electrical-box mounting brackets. Fasten the brackets and switch boxes and mount the outlet boxes inside the apron. Secure the octagonal box and bring it to the 12 gauge, 3 conductor type J wire for the power supply. Split the circuit into two lines, sending each through one switch and outlet to complete the wiring.

Bore pilot holes and counterbores for the guide mounting screws and plugs. Align outer guides with a 1½-in. spacer.

Cut the clamp access holes in the inner guides by first boring 1½-in. holes and cutting the waste with a saber saw.

Mount the switch and outlet boxes on the long apron. An octagon junction box splits the circuit to the two tools.

A ⅝₁₆-in. recess is routed in the saw-mounting plate to accept the circular saw base. Tailor the size and position to your saw.

The miter-gauge rail is recessed underneath for the carriage bolt head. Laminate maple stock for the adjustable beam.

Assemble the fence with the rails in the tracks. Use a piece of straight stock in the cross track to insure square.

Tabletop

Cut the tabletop base to size, lay out centerlines and mark the back for two octagonal cutouts. Bore a 1-in.-dia. hole at the corners of each octagon and use a saber saw to complete the cutouts. The circular saw shown required rabbets cut into the underside of the base to permit tilting the blade.

Tool-Mounting Guides

Prepare the inner guides and plates by setting your saw to 30° and ripping one inner guide to width. Then rip the stock for the sliding and fixed plates and mark the centerline. Set the saw to 90° and rip the other inner guide. Be careful to make these cuts straight and parallel. Then crosscut the guides to length.

Lay out the fixed and sliding plates and cut with a saber saw. Then, using a 1½-in. spacer between them, center the two fixed plates on the base to be square to the base centerline and screw in place. Temporarily clamp the two sliding plates in position so that their centerlines, and those of the fixed plates, are all on the same line. Lay the inner guides on both sides of the

plates and clamp. Check that the long edges of the inner guides are square with the gap between the fixed plates. Also make sure that and the sliding plates move freely but are not too loose. Then screw guides in place.

Cut four slotted holes in the inner guides to facilitate clamping the fence in position. Cut each hole by first boring two 1½-in.-dia. holes and then cutting away the waste with a saber saw. Screw the base to the aprons. Use 1½-in. spacers in the long track and cross track to position the outer guides.

Tool Mounting Plates

To cut the mounting plates, lay out a 13×13-in. square. Draw the diagonals and inscribe a circle. Where the circle intersects the diagonals draw a 45° line. Recess the saw-mounting plate to accept the base of your circular saw. Because each brand of saw is slightly different, you must adapt these dimensions to your saw. Drill holes for the mounting bolts in the saw base and corresponding ¼-in. holes and ⅝-in. counterbores in the mounting plate. You'll need to make a few throat plates to accommodate the most commonly used blade angles. Use ¼-in. hardboard for these inserts and recess the mounting plates to accept them. Also recess the router plate. Although the illustrations here show a circular recess, a square one will work just as well. Make sure the router is centered in the mounting plate.

Miter Gauge and Fence

Cut the miter gauge parts to the dimensions given. The miter guide rail must be trimmed to ¾ in. thickness so it lies flush with the table surface when in use. Assemble the slotted adjustable beam by laminating three layers as shown in the drawing. Cut the carriage bolt head recess by drilling successive blind holes with a 1-in. bit. Clean away the excess with a sharp chisel. Then rout the slot in the guide rail with a ⅜-in. straight bit. Take care to position the guide rail at 90° to the plate and clamp it in place before drilling the pilot holes.

The bridge fence is designed to be used in a closed position—when the tools are mounted in the table—or open position which allows stock to be passed underneath and a tool to be hand-operated from above. When assembling the fence, first place the two guide rails—complete with sides and braces attached—in the tracks of the table. Then place a straight piece of stock in the cross track of the table and align the fence guide rails against this. Secure the fence top with 1½-in. No.10 fh screws. Position the pivoting fence sections and insert the end pins. Two roller catches hold the pivoting fence in the upright position. When installing these, check to be sure that the fence is square with the table-top.

Use two holddown clamps to tighten the sliding plates on the mounting plates. Remove the button ends of the clamps by holding the buttons in a vise while backing off the screws. Bore clamp mounting holes through the short aprons and blocking. Countersink the maple inserts on the sliding plates to receive the ball ends and install the clamps.

Finishing the Table

Trim the power table edges (⅜-in.-thick maple) and apply three coats of urethane varnish, thinning the first for good penetration. Apply the first coat only to the inside of the tracks to seal the wood and permit easy sliding.

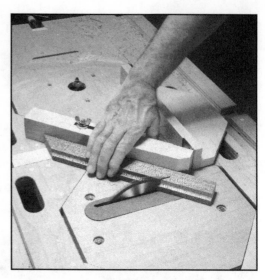

USING THE TABLE

Install tools by backing off the sliding-plate clamp screws and pulling back the sliding plate to insert the tool. The power tools that are natural first choices for installation are the circular saw and router. Installing these first lets you make other inserts and accessories.

As with all tools and machinery, keep safety foremost in your mind. Always unplug the tool before removing it from the table and making adjustments. Keep the table surface uncluttered and wear suitable eye protection.

Mounting Power Tools

In addition to the circular saw and router, the electric drill, saber saw and belt sander are ideal for use with the power table.

Mounting an Electric Drill. The drill mounting plate is designed to hold the drill in one of two positions—parallel to, and above the table, for use in horizontal boring, disc sanding or buffing, and below the table for use as a drum sander. A drill guide connects the drill.

Mounting a Saber Saw. The saber saw is perhaps the simplest to mount. When cutting the blade slot, make sure it's long enough to accommodate the full range of bevel angles and recess the saw base plate for maximum blade exposure.

Mounting a Belt Sander. The belt sander is used above the table and features a pivoting table for sanding bevels. Because different belt sanders vary considerably in their housing design, you'll have to adapt these drawings to suit your model. When designing your custom plate, avoid blocking the tool's air vents.

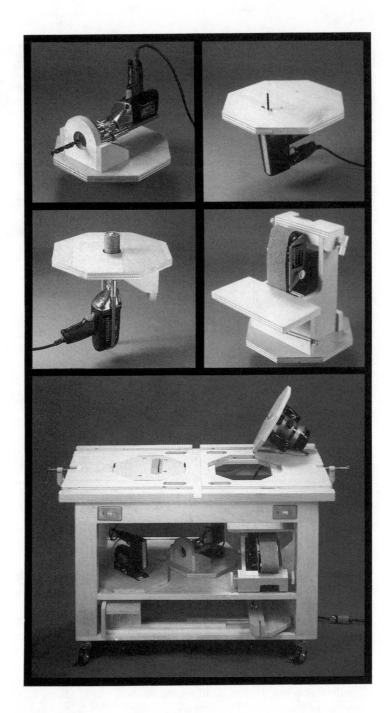

Ripping Stock

For ripping, slide the bridge fence in the tracks to the desired distance from the blade and clamp in place with two 6-in. bar clamps. Two clamp access holes are provided for positioning the fence near the center.

For normal ripping, keep the fold-down fence in the upright position. The extra width of this fence is an advantage when holding stock on edge. For ripping narrow strips, fold the fence down and gain extra room for holding the stock as you pass it by the blade. To cut bevels, unplug the tool and remove the plate to make adjustments to blade angle and cutting depth.

Because of the way the hand circular saws pivot, you'll need a selection of blade inserts for the most common bevels. After adjusting, simply reinsert the tool, adjust the fence and make your cut. Alignment is automatic.

To rip, clamp the fence at the desired position. Adjustable outfeed roller on a small-parts cabinet supports stock.

The extra-wide fence helps when passing the stock on edge. Tilt the saw blade for making these beveled panel edges.

Crosscuts on long unwieldly stock are easy with a handheld saw when the stock is held under the bridge fence.

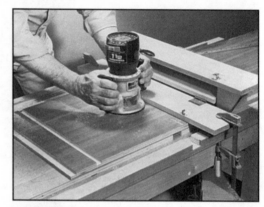

Use the bridge fence to guide your router when cutting dadoes square to the panel edge, as in shelf construction.

Using the Bridge Fence

You can use the fence with many other power tools, including the router. Here, you can cut grooves, rabbets and dadoes with consistent results. Of course, you can use the router without the fence by using router bits with pilots.

The fence is called a *bridge fence* because it provides an additional function. When folding down the fence, you'll notice it lifts up and down allowing stock to be passed underneath. Use this feature when crosscutting long stock with a handheld circular saw. Slide the wood under the fence and hold it firmly against the rail stop on the far side. Then let the fence edge guide your saw for square cuts every time. Make sure the fence is clamped in position so the blade runs in the center track. You can also rout straight, square-to-the-edge dadoes in boards of any length up to 20-in. wide.

Using the Miter Gauge

The miter gauge is adjusted by backing off the wingnut and pivoting the arm to the desired location. It's a good idea to mark the most commonly used angles on the miter gauge rail for quick setup. Sawing a miter is only the beginning. Now you can trim the cut at the exact angle and length by using the miter gauge to guide the work past the router and straight bit or drum sander. For mitering picture frames or molding corners, use the sliding-table miter jig. This permits cutting both sides of the miter joint without turning the stock upside down.

Because the power table has two long tracks as well as the center cross track, you can slide the miter gauge along the length of the table on either side. Set the circular saw in place so the blade is parallel to the length of the table. Use the miter gauge for crosscutting up to 20 inches.

Jointing Edges

The real time-saving feature of the power table is its ability to have two tools installed at once. Ripping stock to width and edge jointing are two operations that you can do efficiently with the circular saw and router with straight bit. Construct a jointer fence by truing one edge of a 1×4 and cutting a circular notch for bit clearance. Then, to achieve the appropriate offset between infeed and outfeed edges, add a strip of plastic laminate or other thin veneer to the outfeed edge, or remove a similar amount from the infeed side. Clamp the fence to the table so the bit-cutting edge lines up with the outfeed edge of the fence. Now you can joint a rough edge, rip to width and joint the freshly sawn edge quickly and accurately without changing machines.

Making Mortise and Tenon Joints

You can also make open mortise and tenon joints with these tools. First, cut the open mortises on the circular saw with the fence in the upright position. Then mill the tenons by using the miter gauge to guide the stock over a straight bit mounted in the router.

Cutting and Dressing Curved Profiles

The saber saw and drum sander combination is ideal for cutting and dressing curved profiles. You can also make straight, smooth rips. Use the fence to rip and set up an auxiliary guide strip next to the sander to dress the edge. For profiles with beveled edges, use the saber saw in conjunction with the belt sander.

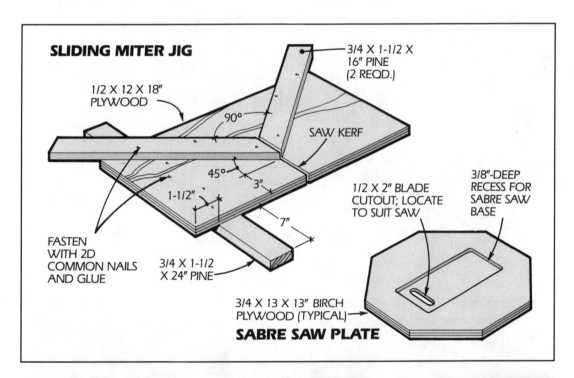

SLIDING MITER JIG

3/4 X 1-1/2 X 16" PINE (2 REQD.)

1/2 X 12 X 18" PLYWOOD

90°

SAW KERF

45°

3"

1-1/2"

1/2 X 2" BLADE CUTOUT; LOCATE TO SUIT SAW

3/8"-DEEP RECESS FOR SABRE SAW BASE

FASTEN WITH 2D COMMON NAILS AND GLUE

3/4 X 1-1/2 X 24" PINE

7"

3/4 X 13 X 13" BIRCH PLYWOOD (TYPICAL)

SABRE SAW PLATE

Clamp a stop block to the miter gauge for repetitive cutting. For longer pieces, clamp the block to the table surface.

Cut compound angles by adjusting the miter gauge and bevel the angle on the saw. Use backup stock to cut small pieces.

Picture frames require that stock be held molding side up for smooth cuts. Use this miter jig for accurate, clean corners.

Clamping

Although you might have thought your work-bench was the only place to clamp your work for sanding, handheld routing or carving, the two end clamps also permit this table to be used for holding stock up to 33 in. wide.

You'll need to construct special clamping plates as shown in the drawing. Each of these has a series of ¾-in.-dia. holes to insert clamping pins. The auxiliary clamping blocks are especially useful for holding irregular shapes, and two can be used with the split plate for holding thin stock.

Horizontal Boring

Horizontal boring machines are a luxury even in a well-equipped shop. Mount your drill horizontally in the drill mounting plate and use the stock-support jig with wood or cardboard shims to hold the workpiece at the proper height. The stock support is held in place by clamping plate and pins and the drill guide lets you advance the drill uniformly.

These are only a few of the many possibilities for using the power table. With a little experimentation, you'll discover other innovative ways to use this versatile tool.

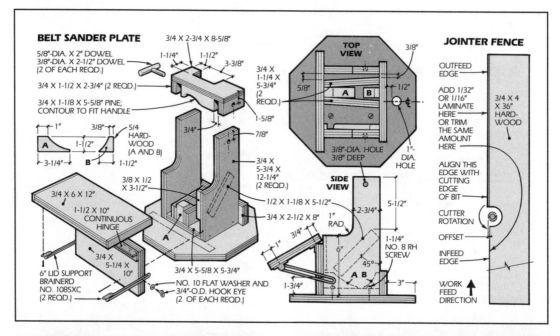

BELT SANDER PLATE

5/8"-DIA. X 2" DOWEL
3/8"-DIA. X 2-1/2" DOWEL
(2 OF EACH REQD.)

3/4 X 1-1/2 X 2-3/4" (2 REQD.)

3/4 X 1-1/8 X 5-5/8" PINE;
CONTOUR TO FIT HANDLE

5/4 HARD-WOOD (A AND B)

1"
3/8"
1-1/2"
3-1/4"
1-1/2"
A
B

3/4 X 6 X 12"

1-1/2 X 10" CONTINUOUS HINGE

3/4 X 5-1/4 X 10"

6" LID SUPPORT BRAINERD NO. 1085XC (2 REQD.)

NO. 10 FLAT WASHER AND 3/4"-O.D. HOOK EYE (2 OF EACH REQD.)

3/4 X 5-5/8 X 5-3/4"

3/4 X 2-3/4 X 8-5/8"

1-1/4" 1-1/2" 3-3/8"

3/4 X 1-1/4 X 5-3/4 (2 REQD.)

1-5/8"

3/4" 7/8"

3/4 X 5-3/4 X 12-1/4" (2 REQD.)

3/8 X 1/2 X 3-1/2"

A

1/2 X 1-1/8 X 5-1/2"

3/4 X 2-1/2 X 8"

1" RAD.

TOP VIEW

3/8"

5/8" A B 1/2"

3/8"-DIA. HOLE 3/8" DEEP 1"-DIA. HOLE

SIDE VIEW

1" 2-3/4" 5-1/2"

1-1/4" NO. 8 RH SCREW

6" 45°

1-3/4" A B 3"

JOINTER FENCE

OUTFEED EDGE

ADD 1/32" OR 1/16" LAMINATE HERE OR TRIM THE SAME AMOUNT HERE

3/4 X 4 X 36" HARD-WOOD

ALIGN THIS EDGE WITH CUTTING EDGE OF BIT

CUTTER ROTATION

OFFSET

INFEED EDGE

WORK FEED DIRECTION

Scrolling is easier when you move the work instead of the tool. Keep the drum sander mounted for dressing the edges.

After cutting the profile, move to the drum sander. It's powered by the drill mounted in a drill guide under the plate.

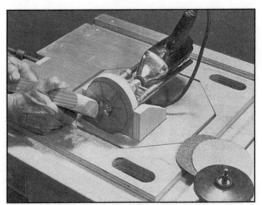

The top-mounted drill also powers a disc sander or disc rasp. Install a buffing wheel for polishing chores.

Flip over the drill-mounting plate and remount the drill and guide parallel to the table for horizontal boring operations.

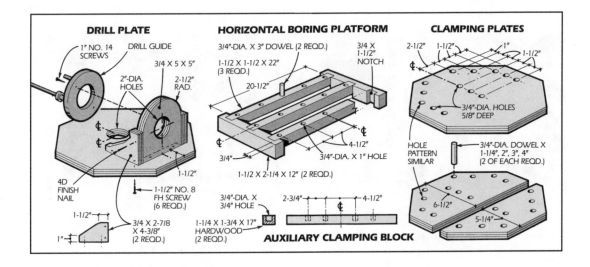

DRILL PLATE

1" NO. 14 SCREWS
DRILL GUIDE
3/4 X 5 X 5"
2"-DIA. HOLES
2-1/2" RAD.
4D FINISH NAIL
1-1/2" NO. 8 FH SCREW (6 REQD.)
1-1/2"
1"
3/4 X 2-7/8 X 4-3/8" (2 REQD.)
1-1/2"

HORIZONTAL BORING PLATFORM

3/4"-DIA. X 3" DOWEL (2 REQD.)
3/4 X 1-1/2" NOTCH
1-1/2 X 1-1/2 X 22" (3 REQD.)
20-1/2"
4-1/2"
3/4"
3/4"-DIA. X 1" HOLE
1-1/2 X 2-1/4 X 12" (2 REQD.)
3/4"-DIA. X 3/4" HOLE
1-1/4 X 1-3/4 X 17" HARDWOOD (2 REQD.)
AUXILIARY CLAMPING BLOCK

CLAMPING PLATES

2-1/2"
1-1/2"
1"
1-1/2"
3/4"-DIA. HOLES 5/8" DEEP
HOLE PATTERN SIMILAR
3/4"-DIA. DOWEL X 1-1/4", 2", 3", 4" (2 OF EACH REQD.)
6-1/2"
5-1/4"
2-3/4"
4-1/2"

Use the clamping plates to secure flat stock. Open the sliding plates, place the pins in position, then tighten clamps.

Auxiliary clamping blocks permit gripping work with small contact surfaces. Use them with a split clamping plate.

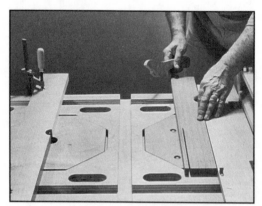

Install router and circular saw in tandem to speed jointing and ripping.

Line up the outfeed edge of the jointer fence with the straight-bit cutter edge.

Cut open mortises with the circular saw and move to the router to cut the tenons.

Guide the mortises with a jig to keep the workpiece square to the table when cutting.

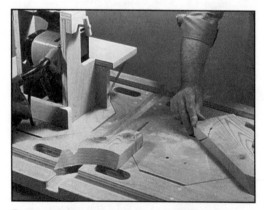

For smooth beveled profiles, mount saber saw alongside the belt sander.

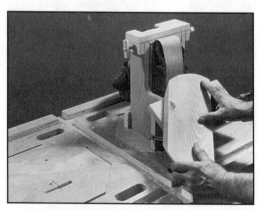

Unplug tools before adjusting the blade and tilt belt sander table to same angle.

The two major types of hardwood dowel pins available are spiral-grooved *(left)* and fluted *(right)*. Chamfered ends make pins easy to insert.

U sing dowel pins

Of the many joints used in woodworking, one of
the most popular is the dowel-reinforced joint.
Doweled joints are simply butt or miter joints
that are reinforced with hardwood dowel pins.

Dowel pins, usually made of maple or birch,
are commonly available in ¼-, ⅜- and ½-in.
diameters and in lengths of 1½, 2 and 2½
inches. Dowel pins have chamfered ends and
spiral grooves or flutes cut in their surface. The
grooves or flutes are necessary to let air and
excess glue escape as you apply clamping pressure. Hardwood dowel pins are sold at hardware
stores and through mail-order woodworking
catalogs.

You can also make your own dowel pins from
common dowel rods. Hardwood dowel rods,
sold in lumberyards and hardware stores, come
in various diameters and usually in 3-ft. lengths.

You must, however, cut the grooves or flutes in
the dowel rod yourself.

Spiral grooves are most easily cut on a band
saw, as shown. Tilt the saw's worktable about
15° and clamp the miter gauge in place so that
the blade cuts ¹⁄₁₆ in. deep into the rod. Start the
saw and slowly rotate the rod back toward you.
It will advance automatically up the worktable.
Cut the rod into pins of the desired length.

To cut flutes in a pin, make the fluting jig
shown. Bore a hole in a wood block equal to the
dowel pin diameter. Grind sharp points on two
8d common nails. Drive one nail into each side
of the block so that the nail points protrude into
the hole about ¹⁄₁₆ inch. Drive the dowel through
the hole with a hammer and drift pin. The
protruding nailpoints will cut flutes in the dowel.
Rotate the dowel slightly and drive it through
the hole again. Repeat until the pin is completely
fluted.

Cutaway of a typical dowel joint. Bore each hole slightly deeper, about ⅛ in., to prevent dowel pin from bottoming out.

Make spiral-grooved dowels on a band saw. Tilt table and clamp miter gauge in place. Rotate dowel rod backwards to cut spiral.

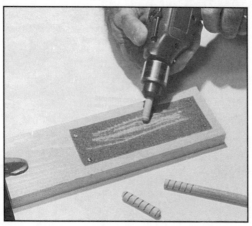

To chamfer ends of shopmade dowel pin, chuck pin in a drill and spin it on 80-grit sandpaper. Secure the sandpaper with tacks.

Make this jig to cut flutes in dowel. Drive in nails so points project into hole about 1/16 in., then hammer dowel through hole.

Slip-joint pliers can also be used to form flutes. Use curved, jagged-tooth portion of jaws to squeeze dowel pin and form flutes.

Using a shopmade jig, cut ¾ of the way through a dowel. Use these dowels to dry-assemble parts—they won't stick in holes.

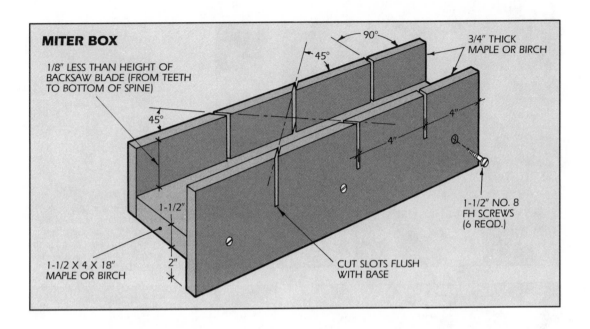

MITER BOX

1/8" LESS THAN HEIGHT OF
BACKSAW BLADE (FROM TEETH
TO BOTTOM OF SPINE)

90°

45°

3/4" THICK
MAPLE OR BIRCH

45°

4"

4"

4"

1-1/2"

1-1/2" NO. 8
FH SCREWS
(6 REQD.)

1-1/2 X 4 X 18"
MAPLE OR BIRCH

2"

CUT SLOTS FLUSH
WITH BASE

Making a miterbox

A miterbox and backsaw are essential for cutting trimwork, picture frames and other small-dimension stock accurately. A wide variety of store-bought miterboxes is available at hardware stores, home centers and through mail-order tool firms. You can, however, make your own miterbox; simply follow the plans shown here.

Make the box from three pieces of maple, birch or beech. Use ¾-in. stock for the sides and 4/4 for the bottom. Join the parts with glue and 1½-in. No.8 screws. The box shown lets you cut 90° square and 45° left and right. If desired, you can cut additional saw guide-slots for other angles such as 22½° and 30°. Also, the box dimensions can be altered, if desired, but note that the inside depth of the box must be ⅛ in. less than the saw blade height as measured from the teeth to the *bottom* edge of the saw's spine.

The accuracy of the miter box depends entirely on how accurately you cut the guide slots. Don't try to cut the slots freehand. Instead, clamp wood blocks to the box, as shown, to guide the saw and ensure perpendicular, accurate cuts.

When using the miterbox, clamp its overhanging bottom edge in a vise. Hold the work firmly in the box and start cutting by making a few light backstrokes. This will help to establish a starting kerf for the saw.

A miterbox guides a fine-tooth backsaw for cutting accurate 90° square and 45° miter cuts. The saw slides in guide slots cut in the box sides. Hold work securely to prevent shifting.

Glue and screw together the box. Then, use a combination square to mark cutting lines on the top edge of the sides. Mark 90° and 45° lines.

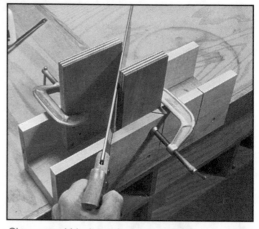

Clamp wood blocks to the box to guide the saw and hold it on the cutting lines. While sawing, the saw's spine should be against the blocks.

When cutting crown molding, insert a spacer strip to prop it up at the correct angle. Make a 45° cut to produce a compound-angle cut.

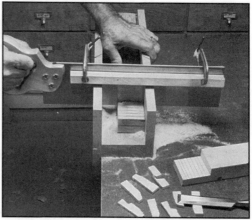

Clamp a wood strip to the saw blade to act as a depth stop. Here, it's used to cut halfway through the stock to produce a half-lap joint.

Sharpening cutlery

Kitchen knives are arguably the most used and abused tools in the home. Therefore, they become dull quickly. Household scissors fare no better in the struggle to stay sharp. A few properly executed strokes over a sharpening stone, however, will keep your knives and scissors on the cutting edge.

There are various sharpening stones available. One of the most popular is an aluminum-oxide stone that's coarse on one side, fine on the other.

Lubricant is important to help float away metal and abrasive particles. You can use special honing oil, but you also can get by with mineral oil or machine oil.

If a blade has lost its cutting edge completely, reform the edge on a coarse stone. Then, hone the cutting-edge bevels on a fine stone. Most knives, however, will just need honing. To start, apply oil to a fine stone and hold the blade flat on the surface. Tilt the blade until the cutting-edge bevel meets the stone. While holding this angle, slide the knife forward across the stone. Also slide it sideways to hone the entire blade length. Flip over the blade and draw it across the stone in the opposite direction. Continue alternate stroking until it's sharp.

Knife blades that are serrated on one edge can be sharpened as shown. Touch up the serrations with a needle file and then remove any burrs with the stone.

Push the knife across a well-oiled sharpening stone while holding the blade at the same angle as the original cutting-edge bevel.

Slide the blade, cutting edge first, simultaneously across the stone and sideways to hone the entire length of the blade.

Flip over the knife and repeat the stroke in the opposite direction. Be sure to maintain the same angle throughout the process.

To sharpen knives serrated on one side only, first touch up the serrations with a needle file. Hold the file at the proper angle.

Then, lay the blade flat on its back on the stone. Draw the blade lightly across the stone to remove any burrs made by filing.

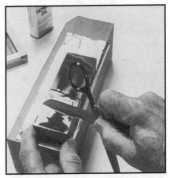

When sharpening scissors, hold the cutting edge flat on the stone and draw the scissors across at a slight angle. Repeat several times.

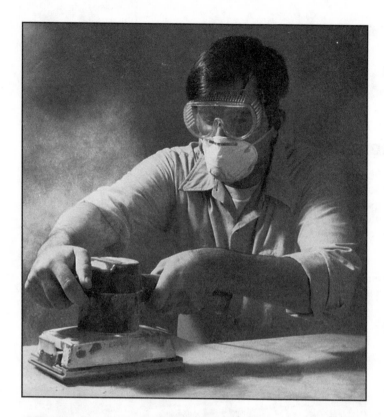

Sanding dust can irritate your eyes and respiratory system. Protect yourself by wearing eye goggles and a paper dust mask.

Preventative protection

Power tools, both portable and stationary, are indispensable in today's workshops. Using power tools, however, creates certain health hazards, primarily to your eyes, lungs and ears. Fortunately, protection from wood chip projectiles, sawdust clouds and screaming routers is easy and inexpensive. Visit any well-stocked hardware store to find all the protection you'll need.

Remember: Owning eye, lung and ear protection is not good enough. You must *use* them every time you're in the shop.

Eye Protection

For eye protection, there are goggles and face shields. Goggles have a pliable rubber frame, plastic lenses and an elastic strap that holds the goggles snugly over your eyes. The frames are perforated with ventilation holes to deter fogging. A face shield has a flip-down panel that is fitted to an adjustable head band. Face shields are comfortable to wear since no part touches your face, but goggles hug your face so they provide better protection.

Lung Protection

Nearly all woodworking power tools produce fine dust that can irritate your respiratory system. This dust can be filtered out with a dust mask. Essentially a paper filter, the dust mask hugs your face and covers your nose and mouth. Dust masks are available in various styles, including disposable types and those that accept replacement filters. Keep in mind that these masks are designed to handle wood dust only. They will *not* filter out harmful vapors or fumes. In such cases, you must wear a cartridge-type respirator.

Ear Protection

Ear protection is also important in the workshop. The two basic types are the earmuff style and soft-rubber ear plugs. Both styles are effective in reducing harmful noises, but the earmuff style is easier to slip on and off as necessary.

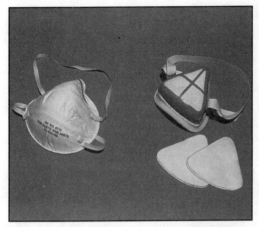

The two most common types of dust masks include the disposable kind *(left)* and the type that accepts replacement filters *(right)*.

Here are two types of disposable dust masks. On the left is a thin, cheap model. Thicker, better mask *(right)* has two head straps.

Eye protection, either goggles or face shield, is extremely important to block flying splinters and chips when using a table saw.

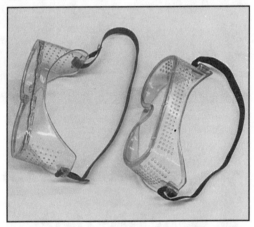

Two common types of eye goggles: Goggles on right have broader frame that offers more perforations for better ventilation.

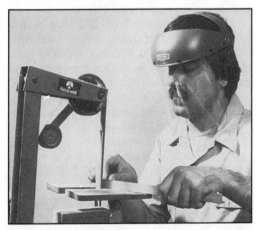

Face shield provides protection for eyes and entire face. Plastic shield flips up and down easily. Head band adjusts for exact fit.

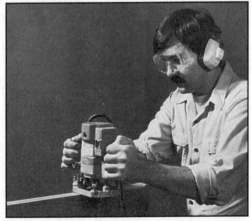

Comfortable earmuff-style protection quiets the piercing scream of a router. Note that eye goggles are also necessary.

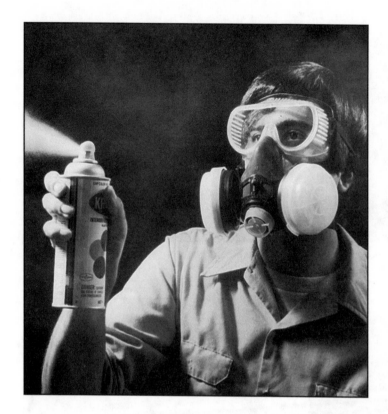

A dual-cartridge respirator offers valuable protection from airborne dust, mist and vapors. Keep the work area well-ventilated, too.

Respirators

You don't have to visit an industrial chemical plant to be concerned about inhaling toxic fumes and vapors. Most do-it-yourselfers need only to go into the workshop to face a contaminated atmosphere. Working with certain paints, finishes, solvents, acids, resins and pesticides can produce unsafe and, in some cases, deadly conditions.

To protect your respiratory system against harmful fumes and vapors, wear a cartridge-type respirator. The respirator consists of a rubber face mask fitted with two interchangeable cartridges and filters. A wide variety of cartridges is available and each one is designed to filter out specific contaminants.

It's very important to install the appropriate cartridges for a specific atmosphere. Remember, no one cartridge can filter all contaminants.

Here's a list of some of the contaminants that can be filtered out with a cartridge-type respirator: dust, organic vapors, pesticides, ammonia, chlorine, asbestos, hydrogen chloride, sulfur dioxide, paint, lacquer and enamel mist.

An obvious omission from this list is methylene chloride which is found in most paint strippers. No cartridge can filter out this highly toxic chemical. The best protection from methylene chloride is an air-supplied respirator.

When shopping for a respirator, be sure that it's NIOSH (National Institute for Occupational Safety and Health) approved. This indicates that it meets government standards.

For a respirator to offer optimum protection, it must fit tightly to your face. Adjust the headbands for a comfortable, snug fit. A beard or long sideburns will interfere with a proper fit. To verify a good fit, hold your palm over the valve cover, as shown, and exhale gently. No air should leak from around the respirator. If necessary, readjust the headbands.

Install the appropriate cartridges for a specific contaminant. Note that respirator houses a dust filter and an air-purifying cartridge.

Here the cartridges are removed and just the filters are installed. The filters provide protection from dust only, not harmful vapors.

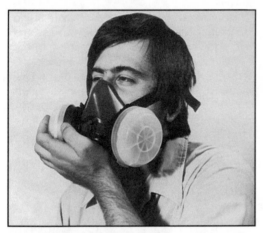

Make a positive pressure test to ensure a snug fit. Hold palm against valve and exhale. No air should leak from around respirator.

Check respirator fittings for dust buildup. Dust accumulation, shown around valve, allows contaminated air to enter face mask.

Inspect respirator periodically for signs of wear or damage. Any respirator that's dried out and cracked, as shown, should be discarded.

Store respirator in a tightly sealed plastic bag and keep it in a dry, cool place. Direct sunlight will promote rapid deterioration.

Apply a wax finish

Most factory-built furniture has a wax topcoat that adds a rich luster to the wood's surface while protecting the finish. It's important to maintain a protective wax finish on your furniture, including the shopbuilt pieces.

There are many liquid and spray-on furniture polishes available, but the one recommended by professional furniture finishers is old-fashioned paste wax. This is usually a blend of carnauba wax, beeswax and turpentine. When applied and buffed properly, paste wax forms a surprisingly hard, durable protective coating.

A waxed piece that has grown dull and flat can often be revived by simply buffing the surface with a soft, dry cloth. If this fails to restore the luster, it's necessary to rewax.

Apply paste wax with a soft, water-dampened cloth. Spread on a *thin*, even coat and let it dry about 20 minutes. Don't overapply the wax. A thick, heavy wax coat will be nearly impossible to buff out. Once the wax has dried, buff the surface by rubbing briskly—don't spare the elbow grease. Buff with a soft, *dry* cloth. You can also use an electric polisher with a lamb's wool bonnet.

Stop buffing when the surface acquires a uniform, highly polished sheen. A simple thumbprint test will determine if more buffing is necessary. Push your thumb on the surface. If a clearly visible thumbprint is left, continue buffing. Wait about one hour and then apply a second wax coat. Buff the second coat to a lustrous sheen.

If a furniture piece has several coats of old, dirty wax, it's best to clean off the wax and start from scratch. Use naphtha or mineral spirits on a soft cloth to remove built-up wax safely on pieces finished with varnish, shellac or paint. On lacquered surfaces, use mineral spirits; naphtha may dull a lacquer finish. Once the surface is clean, apply two coats of wax.

A highly polished surface is achieved by rubbing briskly with a soft cloth. Be sure to apply a thin coat. Don't overapply the wax.

An electric drill fitted with a polishing bonnet speeds the buffing process. A right-angle drive accessory converts drill into polisher.

If you can press a thumbprint into the wax coat, then more buffing is needed. The final wax coat should dry hard and reflective.

Use naphtha or mineral spirits to clean the surface before waxing. Rub gently with more solvent to entirely remove the old wax.

Apply paste wax with a soft, water-dampened cloth. Apply an even coat and let the wax dry for about 20 minutes before buffing.

Hand-rubbing will be more effective if you wrap the cloth around a firm rubber sanding block. The blocks are sold at paint stores.

Index

A

Air conditioner basics, 59
Aluminum house wiring hazards, 44
Analog recording: compared to digital, 129
Appliances: testing with ohmmeter, 50
Applying a wax finish, 174
Audio tape: digital, 127

B

Baking cart, 18
Ballast: fluorescent fixtures, 38
Ballcock replacement, 73
Band saw users guide, 131
Band saws
    accessories, 134
    basic cuts, 133
    blades, 132
Bathroom drain repairs, 67
Bathroom repairs
    drain cleaning, 76
    drain vents, 77
    faucets, 75
Bathroom ventilator installation, 46
Benchmark workbench, 145
Blades: band saw, 132
Book stand, 27
Bow window installation, 107
Briggs & Stratton engines
    overhauling, 118
    pull-rope replacement, 115
Butler's desk, 13

C

Cabinet: small parts, 150
Camcorders
    3-D, 126
    shutter advances, 126
Central air conditioners, 60
Chair and stepstool, 23
Circle jig: band saw, 135
Common bathroom repairs, 75
Cord and plugs: lamps, 42
Craft projects
    Baking cart, 18
    Book stand, 27
    Butler's desk, 13
    Custom designs, 4
    Dining table, 8
    Fine dining, 8
    Secret secretary, 13
    Stepstool and chair, 23
    Toboggan heirloom, 29
Custom designs, 4
Cutlery: sharpening, 169

D

Deadbolt lock installation, 82
Developing strategies, 92
Dialtone: telephone repair, 52
Digital audio tape, 127
Dining table, 8
Doorbell repairs, 56
Doors
    installing entry door, 110

lock installation, 82
repair, 80
Dowel pins, 165
Drain
    cleaning, 76
    repairs, 67
    vents, 77
Drawing plans, 4
Drop-type lawn spreaders, 113

E

Ear protection, 170
Electric water heater replacement, 66
Electrical
    Air conditioner basics, 59
    Aluminum house wiring hazards, 44
    Bathroom ventilator installation, 46
    Doorbell repairs, 56
    Fluorescent fixture repair, 37
    Incandescent lamp repair, 41
    Telephone repair, 52
    Testing appliances with ohmmeter, 50
Energy efficiency ratings, 61
Engines: overhaul, 118
Entry door installation, 110
Extension table: band saw, 134
Eye protection, 170

F

Fading memories, 91
Faucet repairs, 75
Fine dining, 8
Finishes: wax, 174
Fireworks: photographing, 87
Fix a problem door, 80
Floor tile installation, 98
Fluorescent fixture repair, 37
Flush valve replacement, 72
Focus on speed, 90
Folding stairway installation, 93
Fun with film, 85
Garage door repair, 78
Gas water heater replacement, 66
Glazing windows, 84
Grout: slate tile floors, 104
Guide to toilet repair, 68

H

Helical recording: digital audio tape, 128
Home additions
    Bow window installation, 107
    Entry door installation, 110
    Floor tile installation, 98
    Folding stairway installation, 93
    Slate tile installation, 103
Home electronics
    Digital audio tape, 127
    Home video, 123
Home Repairs
    Deadbolt lock installation, 82
    Fix a problem door, 80
    Overhead garage door, 78
    Reglazing windows, 84
House wiring hazards, 44

I

Incandescent lamp repair, 41
Infrared film, 86
Inner visions, 86
Installing slate tile floors, 103

J

Jamb Jacks: entry door, 110

K

Knives: sharpening, 169

L

Lab processing: photography, 92
Laminating: toboggan construction, 29
Lawn and garden
    Lawn spreader selection, 113
    Small engine overhaul, 118
    Starter pull-rope replacement, 115
Lawn mowers: pull-rope replacement, 115
Lawn spreader selection, 113
Lock installation, 82
Lunar photography, 89
Lung protection, 170

M

Making a miterbox, 167
Mastic: slate tile floors, 104
Miterbox, 167
Moon: photographing, 89

N

Night shots, 87

O

Ohmmeter use, 50
One on one, 88
Overhauling small engines, 118
Overhead garage door repair, 78

P

Photography
    Developing strategies, 92
    Fading memories, 91
    Focus on Speed, 90
    Fun with film, 85
    Inner visions, 86
    Night shots, 87
    One on one, 88
    Shoot the moon, 89
Plumbing
    Bathroom drain repairs, 67
    Common bathroom repairs, 75
    Guide to toilet repair, 68
    Water heater replacement, 62
Portrait photography, 88
Power tool table
    building, 153
    using, 158
Power tuneup: small engines, 118
Preventative protection, 170
Prints: restoring, 91

Processing film, 92
Pull-rope replacement: lawn mowers,
    115

────────── R ──────────

Race cars: photographing, 90
Recording digital audio tape, 130
Reglazing windows, 84
Repairs
    Deadbolt lock installation, 82
    Fix a problem door, 80
    Overhead garage door, 78
    Reglazing windows, 84
Respirators, 172
Restoring old prints, 91
Room air conditioners, 60
Rotary lawn spreaders, 113

────────── S ──────────

Saber saw users guide, 136
Saber saws
    basics, 138
    blades, 136
    guided saw cuts, 139
    table, 140
Saws
    band saw guide, 131
    saber saw guide, 136
Scissors: sharpening, 169
Secret secretary, 13
Sharpening cutlery, 169
Shoot the moon, 89
Shop projects
    Benchmark workbench, 145
    Power tool table, 153

Small-parts cabinet, 150
Shop tips
    Applying a wax finish, 174
    Making a miterbox, 167
    Preventative protection, 170
    Respirators, 172
    Sharpening cutlery, 169
    Using dowel pins, 165
Shop tools
    Band saw users guide, 131
    Saber saw users guide, 136
Shopbuilt saber saw table, 140
Shutter advances: camcorders, 126
Slate tile floors, 103
Small engine overhaul, 118
Small-parts cabinet, 150
Sockets
    fluorescent fixtures, 39
    incandescent lamps, 43
Speed: photography, 90
Spreaders: lawn, 113
Stairway: folding, 93
Starter pull-rope replacement, 115
Starters: fluorescent fixtures, 38
Stepstool and chair, 23
Super VHS
    picture quality, 123
    receiver compatibility, 125
    videotape, 124

────────── T ──────────

Table: power tools, 153
Tecumseh engines
    overhauling, 118
    pull-rope replacement, 116

Telephone repair, 52
Testing appliances with an ohmmeter,
    50
Three-dimensional camcorders, 126
Tile
    resilient floor tile, 98
    slate floor tile, 103
Toboggan heirloom, 29
Toilet repairs, 68
Troubleshooting
    fluorescent lamps, 37
    incandescent lamps, 41
    small engines, 118
    telephones, 52
    toilet repairs, 68
Tuneup: small engines, 118

────────── U ──────────

Using dowel pins, 165

────────── V ──────────

Ventilator: bathroom, 46
Video
    camcorder shutters, 126
    super VHS, 123
Videotape: Super VHS, 124

────────── W ──────────

Water heater replacement, 62
Wax finish application, 174
Windows
    glazing, 84
    installing bow window, 107
Wiring: hazards of aluminum, 44
Workbench, 145

METRIC CONVERSION

Conversion factors can be carried so far they become impractical. In cases below where an entry is exact it is followed by an asterisk (*). Where considerable rounding off has taken place, the entry is followed by a + or a – sign.

CUSTOMARY TO METRIC

Linear Measure

inches	millimeters
1/16	1.5875*
1/8	3.2
3/16	4.8
1/4	6.35*
5/16	7.9
3/8	9.5
7/16	11.1
1/2	12.7*
9/16	14.3
5/8	15.9
11/16	17.5
3/4	19.05*
13/16	20.6
7/8	22.2
15/16	23.8
1	25.4*

inches	centimeters
1	2.54*
2	5.1
3	7.6
4	10.2
5	12.7*
6	15.2
7	17.8
8	20.3
9	22.9
10	25.4*
11	27.9
12	30.5

feet	centimeters	meters
1	30.48*	.3048*
2	61	.61
3	91	.91
4	122	1.22
5	152	1.52
6	183	1.83
7	213	2.13
8	244	2.44
9	274	2.74
10	305	3.05
50	1524*	15.24*
100	3048*	30.48*

1 yard = .9144* meters

1 rod = 5.0292* meters

1 mile = 1.6 kilometers

1 nautical mile = 1.852* kilometers

Fluid Measure

(Milliliters [ml] and cubic centimeters [cc or cu cm] are equivalent, but it is customary to use milliliters for liquids.)

1 cu in = 16.39 ml
1 fl oz = 29.6 ml
1 cup = 237 ml
1 pint = 473 ml
1 quart = 946 ml
= .946 liters
1 gallon = 3785 ml
= 3.785 liters
Formula (exact):
fluid ounces × 29.573 529 562 5* = milliliters

Weights

ounces	grams
1	28.3
2	56.7
3	85
4	113
5	142
6	170
7	198
8	227
9	255
10	283
11	312
12	340
13	369
14	397
15	425
16	454

Formula (exact):
ounces × 28.349 523 125* = grams

pounds	kilograms
1	.45
2	.9
3	1.4
4	1.8
5	2.3
6	2.7
7	3.2
8	3.6
9	4.1
10	4.5

1 short ton (2000 lbs) = 907 kilograms (kg)
Formula (exact):
pounds × .453 592 37* = kilograms

Volume

1 cu in = 16.39 cubic centimeters (cc)
1 cu ft = 28 316.7 cc
1 bushel = 35 239.1 cc
1 peck = 8 809.8 cc

Area

1 sq in = 6.45 sq cm
1 sq ft = 929 sq cm
= .093 sq meters
1 sq yd = .84 sq meters
1 acre = 4 046.9 sq meters
= .404 7 hectares
1 sq mile = 2 589 988 sq meters
= 259 hectares
= 2.589 9 sq kilometers

Kitchen Measure

1 teaspoon = 4.93 milliliters (ml)
1 Tablespoon = 14.79 milliliters (ml)

Miscellaneous

1 British thermal unit (Btu) (mean) = 1 055.9 joules
1 calorie (mean) = 4.19 joules
1 horsepower = 745.7 watts
= .75 kilowatts
caliber (diameter of a firearm's bore in hundredths of an inch) = .254 millimeters (mm)
1 atmosphere pressure = 101 325* pascals (newtons per sq meter)
1 pound per square inch (psi) = 6 895 pascals
1 pound per square foot = 47.9 pascals
1 knot = 1.85 kilometers per hour
25 miles per hour = 40.2 kilometers per hour
50 miles per hour = 80.5 kilometers per hour
75 miles per hour = 120.7 kilometers per hour